# FOREST LIFE

## PRACTICAL MEDITATIONS on CANOEING, FISHING, HUNTING, and BUSHCRAFT

### THE CLASSIC WRITINGS OF
### GEORGE WASHINGTON SEARS,
### KNOWN AS NESSMUK

BLACK DOG
& LEVENTHAL
PUBLISHERS

Black Dog & Leventhal Publishers
Hachette Book Group
1290 Avenue of the Americas
New York, NY 10104

www.hachettebookgroup.com
www.blackdogandleventhal.com

*Woodcraft* originally published in 1884 by Forest and Stream Publishing in the United States.

First Edition: October 2018

Black Dog & Leventhal Publishers is an imprint of Running Press, a division of Hachette Book Group. The Black Dog & Leventhal Publishers name and logo are trademarks of Hachette Book Group, Inc.

The publisher is not responsible for websites (or their content) that are not owned by the publisher.

The Hachette Speakers Bureau provides a wide range of authors for speaking events. To find out more, go to www.HachetteSpeakersBureau.com or call (866) 376-6591.

Outside of some of the illustrations found in the Woodcraft section, none of the artwork is from the original publications but is from contemporary sources.

Print book interior design by Red Herring Design.

Library of Congress Cataloging-in-Publication Data

Names: Sears, George Washington, 1821–1890. author. | Sears, George Washington, 1821–1890.
Woodcraft. | Sears, George Washington, 1821–1890.
Forest runes. Selections.
Title: Forest life: practical meditations on canoeing, fishing, hunting, and bushcraft / the classic writings of George Washington Sears, known as Nessmuk.
Description: First edition. | New York, NY: Black Dog and Leventhal Publishers, 2018. |
Includes bibliographical references.
Identifiers: LCCN 2018012764| ISBN 9780762465538 (hardcover) | ISBN 9780762465545 (ebook)
Subjects: LCSH: Outdoor life.
Classification: LCC GV191.25 .S43 2018 | DDC 796.5—dc23

LC record available at https://lccn.loc.gov/2018012764

Printed in China

APS

10 9 8 7 6 5 4 3 2 1

# CONTENTS

Nessmuk.

# PREFACE

GEORGE WASHINGTON SEARS TRACED HIS passion for the outdoors back to his childhood mentor and teacher, a young Narragansett Indian man named Nessmuk. From him, Sears learned to not only hunt, fish, and travel in the wilderness but also to love forest life.

Sears was born in 1821 in Massachusetts. At age eight he was sent to work in a cotton mill, then trained under his father to work as a shoemaker. He later worked on a fishing boat off Cape Cod, on a whaling boat, then traveled all over the country doing various jobs. Largely self-educated, Sears considered himself unfit for an indoor working life and spent decades of his life camping in the woods, mostly alone. While he settled in Wellsboro, Pennsylvania, in 1848, set up a shop as a cobbler, married and had three children, he frequently escaped to the nearby Tioga State Forest.

In 1860, Sears began writing under Nessmuk for the outdoor magazine *Porter's Spirit of the Times*, among other publications. He also continued traveling, including spending months away trapping in Minnesota and traveling on the Amazon in Brazil. Outside of a column for a local paper, he didn't publish much until 1879, when he began a relationship with *Forest and Stream*, the nation's premier outdoor magazine.

During his lifetime, Sears would write more than ninety articles for *Forest and Stream*, a number of which appear in this collection. The stories of his adventures, his practical advice, and musing about nature helped popularize canoeing, camping, and conservation for a broad audience. Also included in *Forest Life* is his beloved camping guide *Woodcraft* (published in 1884) and selections from his book of poetry *Forest Runes* (published in 1887).

In the 1880s, Sears worked with boat builder J. Henry Rushton on a series of successively lighter canoes that went against the trends of the time. Sears's lightest canoe, the *Sairy Gamp*, weighed ten and a half pounds; even Rushton expressed doubt that surviving a paddle in such a canoe was possible. When sixty-one-year-old Sears took the *Sairy Gamp* to the Adirondacks, he was ill with tuberculosis and malaria, yet traveled 266 miles in one month. In his account of the journey, published in *Forest and Stream*, he praised the lightweight canoe for its sturdiness and reliability and encouraged readers to travel lightweight as well. The *Sairy Gamp* was acquired by the Smithsonian Institution and is displayed at the Adirondack Experience.

In 1886, Sears chronicled his final trip, one along the Florida coast, for the readers of *Forest and Stream*. Overcome by illness that had plagued him in the later part of his life, Sears died on May 1, 1890. *Forest and Stream* published the following announcement:

> *The sad intelligence, which came to us last Saturday, announcing the death of "Nessmuk," was not altogether unexpected. For several months past it had been known to his friends that Mr. Sears was in a very feeble condition…Last summer, too weak to make a camping excursion to the woods, yet powerless to withstand the longing for a taste of the old life, he pitched his tent beneath the hemlocks of his home yard and there, with his grandson, "played" at an outing. After the long and weary confinement of the winter just past, he craved outdoor life: and on the last day of April, supported by loving arms, he went out for a while under the same trees. The next morning at 2 o'clock, May 1, he passed away. Last Saturday, in the spot he had selected beneath those same hemlocks, they laid him to rest.*

Both a mountain and a lake near Sears's Wellsboro home bear the Nessmuk name, a physical reminder of his enduring legacy. In 1915, *Forest and Stream* published a tribute to Sears:

> *Nessmuk loved Nature as few men ever did. He knew her secrets, while shy almost to the degree of self-effacement, his character was as strong as his integrity was upright. How well he loved the waters and the woods and the light of day filtering through the leaves.*

# INTRODUCTION

**ADAPTED FROM THE INTRODUCTION TO *FOREST RUNES***

T IS A SAD NECESSITY THAT COMPELS A MAN TO speak often or much of himself. Most writers come to loathe the first-person singular and to look upon the capital *I* as a pronominal[1] calamity. And yet, how can a man tell aught[2] of himself without the "eternal ego"?

I am led to these remarks by a request of my publishers that I furnish some account of myself. Readers who take an interest in the book will, as a rule, wish to know something of the author's antecedents,[3] they think. It might also be thought that the man who has spent a large share of the summer and autumn months in the deep forests, and mostly alone for fifty years, ought to have a large stock of anecdote and adventure to draw on.

It is not so certain, this view of it. The average person is slow to understand how utterly monotonous and lonely is a life in the depths of a primal forest, even to the most incorrigible hunter. Few city sportsmen will believe, without practical observation, that a man may hunt faithfully in an unbroken forest for

---

1  Pronoun-related
2  Anything
3  Past history

an entire week without getting a single shot, and one wet week, especially if it be cold and stormy, is usually enough to disgust him who has traveled hundreds of miles for an outing at much outlay of time and money.

And yet, this is a common experience of the most ardent still hunter.[4] In the gloomy depths of an unbroken forest there is seldom a songbird to be heard. The absence of small game is remarkable, and the larger animals—deer, bears, and panthers—are scarce and shy. In such a forest I have myself hunted faithfully from Monday morning till Saturday night, from daylight until dark each day, and at the end of the last day brought the old double-barreled muzzle loader into camp with the same bullets in the gun that I drove home on the first morning. And I crept stealthily through the thickets in still-hunting moccasins on the evening of the last day with as much courage and enjoyment as on the first morning. For I knew that, sooner or later, the supreme moment would come, when the black, satiny coat of a bear, or the game-looking "short-blue"[5] coat of a buck would, for an instant, offer fair for the deadly bead.

And once, in a dry, noisy, Indian summertime, I am ashamed to say, I still-hunted seventeen days without getting one shot at a deer. It was the worst luck I'd ever had, but I enjoyed the weather and the solitary camp-life. At last there came a soft November rain, the rustling leaves became like a wet rug, and the nights were pitch dark. Then the deer came forth from swamps and laurel brakes, the walking was almost noiseless, and I could kill all I could take care of.

---

4  One who moves stealthily and quietly through the woods to track an animal
5  The color of a deer's coat in the fall, which turns gray before being shed in early summer

It is only the born woods crank who can enjoy going to the depths of a lonely forest with a heavy rifle and stinted rations, season after season, to camp alone for weeks at a stretch, in a region as dreary and desolate as Broadway on a summer afternoon in May.

It is only the descendants of Ananias[6] who are always meeting with hair-breadth escapes and startling adventures on their hunting trips. To the practical, skilled woodsman, their wonderful stories bear the plain imprint of lies. He knows that the deep forest is more safe than the most orderly town and that there is more danger in meeting one "bridge gang" than there would be in meeting all the wild animals in New York or Pennsylvania.

These facts will explain why I have so little to relate in the way of adventure, though my aggregate of camp-life, most of it alone, will foot up at least twelve years.

I can scarcely recall a dozen adventures from as many years' outings, culled from the cream of fifty seasons. Incidents of woods life, and interesting ones, are of almost daily occurrence, and these, to the ardent lover of nature, form the attraction of forest life in a far greater degree than does the brutal love of slaughter for the mere pleasure of killing something just because it is alive.

Just here my literary mentor and stentor,[7] who has been coolly going through my manuscript, remarks sententiously, "Better throw this stuff into the stove and start off with your biography. That is what the Editor wants."

I answer vaguely, "Story? Lord bless you; I have none to tell, sir. Alas there is so little in an ordinary, humdrum life that is worth the telling. And there is such a wilderness of biographies and autobiographies that no one cares to read."

"Well, you've agreed to do it, you know, and no one is obliged to read it. It will

---

6  A man in the Bible who was struck dead for lying

7  Someone with a loud voice, after a herald in Greek mythology who had a voice as loud as the voices of fifty men

make filling any how; and probably that's all the Editor wants." Which is complimentary and encouraging.

"I must say it's the toughest job of penwork I ever tackled: I don't know how to begin."

"Pooh! Begin in the usual way. Say you were born in the town of—"

"There's where you're out. I wasn't born in any town whatever, but in what New Englanders call a gore—a triangular strip of land that gets left out somehow when the towns are surveyed. They reckon it in, however, when it comes to taxes, but it rather gets left on schools."

"Ah, I can believe it. Well, fix it up to suit yourself. I suppose the Editor keeps a 'Balaam box.'"[8]

Taking his leave and a handful of my Lone Jack,[9] C. saunters off to the village, and I am left to myself. Perhaps his advice is good. Let's see how it will work on a send-off. For instance, I was born in a sterile part of sterile Massachusetts, on the border of Douglas Woods, within half a mile of Nipmuc Pond and within three miles of Junkamaug Lake. This startling event happened in the "South Gore," about sixty-four years ago. I did not have a fair average start in life at first. A snuffy old nurse who was present at my birth was fond of telling me in after years a legend like this: "Ga-a-rge, you on'y weighed fo' pounds when you wuz born, 'n' we put ye inter a quart mug 'n' turned a sasser over ye."

I could have killed her, but I didn't. Though I was glad when she died, and assisted at her funeral with immense satisfaction.

Junkamaug Lake is six miles long, with many bays, points, and islands, with dense thickets along its shores at the time of which I speak, and a plentiful stock of pickerel, perch, and other fish. It was just the sort of country to delight the Indian mind, and here it was that a remnant of the Nipmuc Indians had a reservation, while they also had a camp on the shores of Nipmuc Pond, where they spent much time, loafing, fishing, making baskets, and setting snares for rabbits and grouse.

---

8  A place to put rejected writings
9  A brand of cigarettes

The word *Nipmuc*, or, as it is sometimes spelled, Nipmuck, means wood-duck. This, in the obsolete lingo of the once-powerful Narragansetts. The best Indian of the band was "Injun Levi," as the whites called him. He was known among his tribe as "Nessmuk," and I think he exerted a stronger influence on my future than any other man. As a fine physical specimen of the animal man I have seldom seen his equal. As

a woodsman and a trusty friend, he was good as gold. I will add that Junkamaug is only a corruption of the Indian name, and the other names I give as I had them from the Indians themselves:

>  And I remain yours sincerely, Nessmuk, which means in the Narragansett tongue, or did mean, as long as there were any Narragansetts to give tongue. Wood-duck, or rather Wooddrake.
>
>  Also, it was the name of the athletic young brave, who was wont to steal me away from home before I was five years old, and carry me around Nepmug and Junkamaug lakes, day after day, until I imbibed much of his woodcraft, all his love for forest life, and alas, much of his good-natured shiftlessness.
>
>  Even now my blood flows faster as I think of the rides I had on his well-formed shoulders, a little leg on either side of his neck, and a death-grip on his strong, black mane; or rode, "belly-bumps"[10] on his back across old Junkamaug, hugging him tightly around the neck, like a selfish little egotist that I was. He tire? He drown? I would as soon have thought to tire a wolf or drown a whale. At first, these excursions were not fairly concluded without a final settlement at home—said settlement consisting of a head-raking with a fine-toothed comb that left my scalp raw, and a subsequent interview, of a private nature, with Pa, behind the barn, at which a yearling apple tree sprout was always a leading factor. (My blood tingles a little at that recollection too.)

---

10  A term that usually referred to jumping on one's stomach onto a sled in the snow

*Gradually they came to understand that I was incorrigible, or, as a maiden aunt of the old school put it, given over; and, so that I did not run away from school, I was allowed to "run with them dirty Injuns," as the aunt aforesaid expressed it.*

*But I did run away from school, and books of the dry sort, to study the great book of nature. Did I lose by it? I cannot tell, even now. As the world goes, perhaps yes. No man can transcend his possibilities.*

*I am no believer in the supernatural: mesmerism, spiritualism, and a dozen other 'isms are, to me, but as fetish. But, I sometimes ask myself, did the strong, healthy, magnetic nature of that Indian pass into my boyish life, as I rode on his powerful shoulders, or slept in his strong arms beneath the soft whispering pines of Douglas Woods?*

*Poor Nessmuk! Poor Lo! Fifty years ago the remnant of that tribe numbered thirty-six, housed, fed and clothed by the state. The same number of Dutchmen, under the same conditions, would have over-run the state ere this.*

*The Indians have passed away forever; and, when I tried to find the resting place of my old friend, with the view of putting a plain stone above his grave, no one could point out the spot.*

*And this is how I happen to write over the name by which he was known among his people, and the reason why a favorite dog or canoe is quite likely to be called Nessmuk.*

The foregoing will partly explain how it came that, ignoring the weary, devious roads by which men attain to wealth and position, I became a devotee of nature in her wildest and roughest aspects—a lover of field sports—a hunter, angler, trapper, and canoeist—an uneducated man, withal, save the education that comes of long and close communion with nature, and a perusal of the best English authors.

Endowed by nature with an instinctive love of poetry, I early dropped into the habit of rhyming. Not with any thought or ambition to become a poet but because at times a train of ideas would keep waltzing through my head in rhyme and rhythm like a musical nightmare, until I got rid of measure and meter by transferring them to paper, or, as more than once happened, to white birch bark, when paper was not to be had.

I never yet sat down with malice prepense[11] to rack and wrench my light mental machinery for the evolution of a poem through a rabid desire for literary laurel. On the contrary, much of the best verse I have ever written has gone to loss through being penciled on damp, whitey-brown paper or birch bark, in woodland camps or on canoeing cruises, and then rammed loosely into a wet pocket or knapsack, to turn up illegible or missing when wanted. When

> *I looked in unlikely places*
> *Where lost things are sure to be found*[12]

and found them not, I said, all the better for my readers, if I ever have any. Let them go with the thistle down, far a-lee.

(The rhymes, not the readers.)

I trust that the sparrow hawks of criticism, who delight equally in eulogizing laureates and scalping linnets,[13] will deal gently with an illiterate backwoodsman who ventures to plant his moccasins in the realms of rhyme. Maybe they will pass me by altogether, as "a literary tomtit, the chickadee of song."

There must be a few graybeards left who remember Nessmuk through the medium of *Porter's Spirit of the Times*,[14] in the long-ago fifties, and many more who have come to regard him kindly as a contributor to *Forest and Stream*.[15] If it happens that a thousand or so of these have a curiosity to see what sort of score an old woodsman can make as an off-hand, short-range poet, it will be a complimentary feather in the cap of the author.

*Wellsboro, Pennsylvania, October 9, 1886. Geo. W. Sears.*

---

11 Premediated
12 From William Morris's poem "The Lost Rune"
13 A common small finch
14 A weekly newspaper for sportsmen
15 A magazine devoted to outdoor activities and wildlife conservation

# FOREST AND STREAM

## AND

# FOREST RUNES

# NEW YEAR'S EVE IN CAMP

## Mercury Lo'* Below Zero, Northwest Gale.

The winds are out in force to-night, the clouds, in light brigades,
Are charging from the mountain tops across the everglades.
There is a fierceness in the air—a dull, unearthly light—
The Frost-king in his whitest crown rides on the storm to-night.
Far down the gorge of Otter Run I hear the sullen roar
Of rifted snows and pattering sleet, among the branches hoar.
The giant hemlocks wag their heads against the midnight sky,
The melancholy pine trees moan, the cedars make reply.
The oaks and sugar maples toss their frozen arms in air,
The elms and beeches bow their heads, and shriek as in despair.
Scant shield to-night for flesh and blood is feather, hair, or fur:
From north to south, for many a mile, there is no life astir.
The gaudy jay with painted crest has stowed his plumes away,
The sneaking wolf forbears[16] to howl, the mountain cat to prey.
The deer has sought the laurel brake, her form the timid hare,
The shaggy bear is in his den, the panther in his lair.

*From east to west, from north to south, for twenty miles around,*

*To-night no track shall dint[17] the shroud that wraps the frozen ground.*

*I sit and listen to the storm that roars and swells aloof,*

*Watching the fitful shadows play against the rustic roof,*

*And as I blow an idle cloud to while the hours away,*

*I croon an old-time ditty, in the minor key of A.*

*And from the embers beams a face most exquisitely fair—*

*The maiden face of one I knew—no matter when or where,*

*A face inscrutable and calm, with dark, reproachful eyes.*

*That gaze on me from limpid depths, or gusty autumn skies.*

*And there may be a reason why I shun the blatant street.*

*To seek a distant mountain glen where three bright waters meet*

*But why I shun the doors of men, their rooms a-light and warm.*

*To camp in forest depths alone, or face a winter storm,*

*Or why the heart that gnaws itself will find relief in rhyme,*

*I cannot tell: I but abide the footing up of Time.*

---

17  Mark

# ROUGH NOTES FROM THE WOODS, 1880

## Moose River, July 21
### FOREST AND STREAM, AUGUST 12, 1880

S HE'S ALL MY FANCY PAINTED HER, SHE'S LOVELY, she is light. She waltzes on the waves by day and rests with me at night. But I had nothing to do with her painting. The man who built her did that. And I commence with the canoe because that is about the first thing you need on entering the Northern Wilderness. From the Forge House, at the foot of the Fulton Chain, on the west to Paul Smith's and Lower St. Regis Lake on the east is ninety-two miles. About five miles of this distance is covered by carries; the longest carry on this route is about one mile; the shortest, a few rods.[18] If you hire a guide, he will furnish a boat and carry it himself. His boat will weigh from sixty to one hundred pounds and will carry two heavy men with all the dunnage[19] you need. He will "take care" of you, as they express it here, and will work faithfully to forward your desires, whether you

---

18  A rod is a unit of length equal to 16.5 feet.

19  Baggage

be artist, tourist, angler, or hunter. His charges are $2.50 per day and found.[20] The tired, overworked man of business who gets away from the hot, dusty city for a few days or weeks cannot do better than come to this land of lake, river, and mountain and hire a guide.

What the mule or mustang is to the plainsman the boat or canoe is to guide, hunter, or tourist who proposes a sojourn in the Adirondacks. And this is why I propose to mention at some length this matter of canoeing and boating. Being a lightweight and a good canoeman, having the summer before me, designing to haunt the nameless lakes and streams not down on the maps, and not caring to hire a guide, it stands to reason that my canoe should be of the lightest, and she is. Perhaps she is the lightest cedar-built canoe in the United States, or anywhere else.

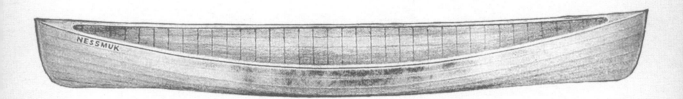

Her stems and keel are oak, her ribs red elm, her gunwale spruce, and six pairs of strips, three-sixteenths of an inch thick, with copper fastenings from stem to stem, leave her weight, when sandpapered ready for the paint, fifteen pounds, nine and one-half ounces. The paint adds about two pounds. She is ten feet long, with a twenty-six-inch beam and eight-inch rise at center, and, propelled by a light double paddle, with a one-fool power in the middle, she gets over the water like a scared loon. I propose to take her on a rather extended trip before snow flies, if she does not drown me. I reckon her carrying capacity, in ordinary weather, at one hundred fifty pounds. If she proves reasonably safe on the larger lakes of the wilderness, she is an achievement in the boat-building line.

She was built by J. H. Rushton of Canton, New York, and is by several pounds the lightest canoe ever made by him. I will only add that she is too light and frail. I would recommend ten and a half feet in length, with a thirty-inch beam, and ribs two inches apart instead of three. Such a canoe would be staunch and safe for one and need not weigh more than twenty-two pounds. She can easily be carried on the head in an inverted position, first placing a blanket or old coat on the head by way of cushion.

When I reached here just one week ago, tired with a twelve-mile ride on the corner of a trunk, while I hugged that frail boat like a faithful lover, I only

meant to stop until I could get my traps carried through to the Fulton Chain, which, in the case of the canoe, was not so easy. I was in no hurry—the hotel here is neat, well kept and prices very reasonable. While waiting for the man to turn up who wanted to carry the little craft on his head to the Forge House, it dawned on me that I was well enough where I was for a few days. Parties were constantly coming and going, and all stop at Moose River, which is the halfway house between Boonville and the lakes.

For interviewing guides and taking notes of the region to the east, there could be no better point than this, and I needed practice with the canoe before taking her over the larger lakes. Moreover, I came here for a superior quality of water, air, and angling, with a little hunting thrown in at the proper season.

What if these things were at my hand, right here, and parties hurrying through posthaste to the Browns Tract or the Raquette waters were running away from what they sought? Those coming out of the woods do not, as a rule, claim notable success with the trout. Many of them would eat salt pork oftener than broiled trout were it not for the guides, and one of the latter told me that "trouting" was poor on and around Big Moose, while he thought Little Moose and Panther Lakes not worth a visit. "I could catch all the trout I wanted right around here," he added.

So I overhauled my fishing gear and went in for brook trout and, as I supposed, found all I wanted and found that I could, by angling just enough for recreation, catch more speckled trout by far than I need, while there is very pretty fly-fishing at the spring holes in the river. Many gentlemen who go far into the wilderness, at much expense of guides, and so on, would be well content with just such fishing as I am enjoying at Moose River. Then there are, within an easy walk of the hotel, several small lakes where deer "water" nightly and may be "floated" for[21] with a fair prospect of success.

But this is not camping out—not a genuine woods life. We seek the forest for adventure and a free, open-air hunter's life, for a time at least. Well, it may be a little tame, but it is very pleasant and healthful, all the same. As for camping for the benefit of open air, bright fires, and beds of browse, fresh picked from hemlock and balsam, we have that right here.

Just under my eyes as I write, there is an island in the river some twelve rods long by six wide. It is well timbered with spruce, balsam, hemlock, cedar, pine, birch, and maple. It is one of the pleasant spots that nature makes and man

21 Hunted by boat

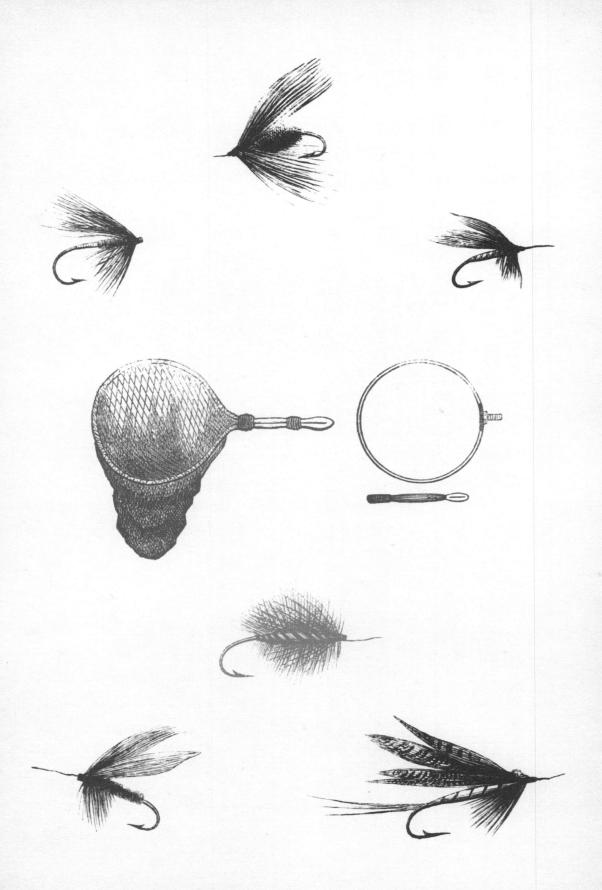

neglects. The island lies high, with roaring, rushing rapids on the left and a broad rock dam on the right, which at low water becomes a cool, clean promenade one hundred feet long by forty feet broad. Near the center of this rock is a natural depression, forming a basin into which the water slowly filters from the river. In this little dock I let the canoe rest at night; against the largest spruce on the island my light tent of oiled factory is erected, and there I rest o' nights—for a few days only, and then for broader waters and deeper woods; perhaps to go farther and fare worse.

# Rough Notes from the Woods, 5

**_FOREST AND STREAM_, NOVEMBER 18, 1880**

Yes. Let us leave the hot pavements, the baking, blistering walls, and sweltering sleeping, or sleepless, rooms. Let us, i' God's name, take to the cool waters and calm shades of the forest.

> _For brick and mortar breed filth and crime,_
> _And a pulse of evil that throbs and beats;_
> _And men are withered before their prime_
> _By the curse paved in with the lanes and streets._
> _And lungs are smothered, and shoulders bowed,_
> _In the poisonous reek of mill and mine,_
> _And death stalks in on the struggling crowd,_
> _But he shuns the shadow of fir and pine._

It was on the morning of the last seventh of August when I started from Third Lake to fish for salmon, as lake trout are invariably called here. The weather could not have been fairer. I was well organized to fish a buoy of my own, with an informal permit to fish others, and I had not the slightest intention of doing anything else. And just here comes in the fascination of this happy-go-lucky, care-free sort of forest life. You never know, or care, one day what you are going to do the next.

After a delightful paddle through First and Second Lakes, I passed the Eagle's Nest and entered the Third. Then it occurred to me that I had a blanket-roll at Sam Dunakin's camp, consisting of gum coat,[22] blanket, pocket hatchet, and revolver. It was a good time to get the traps. Fourth Lake is at times rough. Now it was smooth. Sam is one of the oldest guides in the wilderness, and of course we had a chatty sort of visit, which made me a little late in paddling out for the Third Lake.

Now, a short mile below Dunakin's camp is the cold-spring, or Snyder camp, which I had a standing invitation to visit. As I was passing, Mr. M., the head man of the camp, hailed me with a cordial invitation to land. I did. Found the cold-spring camp rather a high-toned affair for a forest residence. There was an icehouse, a good boathouse, and a log house that would be a palace to an early settler. They had a guide who, like most guides, was an excellent cook, and of course I was not to be let off until after dinner. I wish to record the fact that the best lake trout I have eaten in the wilderness was at that camp. They were also capable of a glass of good wine, and people of culture, withal.[23] What wonder if it was 4:00 p.m. when I said good-bye and paddled out into the Fourth?

22 Made of material treated with gum to make it waterproof
23 Besides

Then it struck me that I had a seven-mile start toward Blue Mountain Lake, with such weather as I might not get again for a month. True, I had no supplies, but they could be had at Arnold's, some two miles above, and I struck across and up the lake for Arnold's place. Got some lunch, arranged my duffel for a trip, and paddled out for a log camp I knew of at the foot of Fifth Lake. It was getting dusk when I struck the inlet, and by the time I reached the camp it was nearly dark, but I found the camp in good condition. There was fresh browse[24] and plenty of dry birch wood, with a roof invulnerable to rain.

I had no tea or coffee, or any sort of dish, but I foraged an old tomato can and made a pot of hemlock tea, had a glorious fire, and a night just such as a woodsman loves. There was not a soul within miles of me, and the shriek of the steam whistle was afar off, beyond the keenest earshot. The owls were plentier than usual, and in exceptionally good voice, while a loon, just above in the Fifth, kept up his strange wild cries at intervals through the night.

At daylight I repeated the dose of hemlock tea, finished the little lunch I had left, and paddled up the Fifth Lake, which is only a frog pond of some ten acres.

24  Boughs to use as bedding

From Fifth to Sixth Lake there is a carry of three-quarters of a mile, which rather turned my hair, for it was a warm morning. But from Sixth to Seventh it is clear paddling. From Seventh to Eighth is a stiff carry of one mile and twenty rods, according to the best-informed guides, and before I got over this I was pretty well winded.

At the landing on the Eighth I met a young man, one of a party of two engaged on the Adirondack Survey, who very considerately invited me to his camp for dinner. It was well. Like Falstaff when he took a foot command, I was "heinously unprovided," and I felt too weak and tired to make the tedious carry from Eighth Lake to Browns Tract Inlet without food and rest.

I found the two young men encamped in a shanty-tent on the south side of a point that makes out from the mainland, and their landing so hidden that they were not likely to be bored with visitors. Stayed with them two hours and got partially rested; I also feasted on pork and beans, and paddled around the point to the carry, not feeling very well competent to make it. To a strong, well man it might have been a trifle. To me it was most exhausting. I arrived at the landing on the inlet so tired and beaten that I lay down on the leaves for more than an hour before launching out. I found the Inlet to be modeled after the letter *S*, with an occasional oxbow thrown in for variety, and a dull, sluggish stream, deep and dark, fringed with aquatic plants, shrubs, and dank cold grass, with not a place in its course of four miles where I would like to venture a landing.

At last the broad Raquette lay before me, dotted with green islands, and with its quaint bays, points, headlands, and islands so mixed and mingled to the eye that although my directions had been lucid I was puzzled just which way to steer. My destination was Ed Bennett's, and I was to turn a green island that lay to the left, when I was assured I would see his landing with a flagstaff and flag, which on the larger lakes is the usual sign of a forest hostelrie.[25]

---

25 Hotel

I saw no flag, but afar off what looked to be a new building and from thence came a sound as of one who drives nails into resonant boards. As I live, it turned out to be a new church in the course of erection on an island. Just where the congregation is to come from I cannot say, but preachers are plenty enough here in the summer, and perhaps it is well that they should have a regular house of worship somewhere in the woods in order to keep their hands in while doing the wilderness.

At length, after much desultory paddling, I sighted Bennett's flag and made my best time for the landing. It was time; the wind was rising, and Raquette

Lake can get too rough for a ten-foot canoe very easily. I was surprised to find Bennett's as well furnished and more neatly kept than many a first-class hotel in larger towns on the direct line of railroad travel. Table, beds, and rooms were furnished forth in a manner that left little to be desired, and when it is remembered that all supplies must be brought by a long and expensive route from the eastern side of the wilderness, his terms seem very reasonable. Two dollars per day, or ten to twelve dollars per week, are Ed's figures, and having been a guide for years he knows just what the tourist requires better than a greenhorn.

But alas! For the romance of paddling through the forest alone in an eighteen-pound canoe.

Before I was half rested, my ears were pained, my soul was sick with the shriek of a steam whistle, and a small steamer rounded to and made a landing after the manner of small steamers outside the Adirondacks.

The little canoe serves as a letter of introduction all through the woods, and I soon struck up an acquaintance with the pilot of the steamer—she wasn't large enough to sport a captain—who said, "You don't want to paddle that cockle-shell over this lake. Put her on deck and come with us." And I did. I was very tired and far from strong. It seemed silly to do so much hard work needlessly, and I went the rounds of the little steamer with the unpronounceable name. Across the lake we made another landing—Kenwell's—and found another hotel, new, neat, well found, and moderate in price. Kenwell's terms are $1.50 per day, $7 to $8 per week, and his place is very pleasantly located. From Kenwell's to the Forked Lake House landing, and here I struck tourists and guides in force. Leavitt's was full to overflowing. I could find a place to sleep after some managing, and the table was excellent, but people were becoming too numerous, and I had a suspicion that I had left the wilder part of the wilderness behind me when I left the Eighth Lake.

Game and fish were by no means plenty. The Forked Lake House had a corps of guides employed, but they could not keep the house in fish or venison. I did not take either after leaving the Fulton Chain. All the same, every tourist had his breech-loading battery, and a full supply of rods, reels, and lines, which is a great comfort to the average tourist and does small damage to trout or deer.

From Forked Lake I went by steamer mostly to the carry on the Marion, made the carry, and found another little steamer to make connections on the upriver side. Went on board of her and became resigned to steam and a teeming civilization that increased nearly every hour.

Passed up the Marion through Utowana and Eagle Lakes and saw an old settled farm and an ordinary farmhouse on the northern shore of the latter, which being the only imitation of a farm on the trip usually induces inquiry. You will be told that long before the grand rush of tourists and the advent of costly hotels this place was cleared and occupied by "Ned Buntline."[26] Here he secluded himself during a part at least of every year for many seasons; here he did his literary work, and the place is, and probably always will be, known as the "Ned Buntline Farm."

A very clear and beautiful sheet of water is Blue Mountain Lake. It has often been called the gem of the wilderness. But its days of natural wildness are gone forever. There are three large hotels on its banks filled to overflowing with guests. Lines of stages[27] leave daily for different points to the east. All luxuries of the season are to be found at the hotels, and billiards, croquet, boating, lounging through the groves, singing, and piano-playing give the shores of the lake quite a Long Branchy air. Besides the hotels, there are private boardinghouses, while many families have private residences on the prettiest sites on the lake, which they are pleased to call camps.

The Blue Mountain Lake House, kept by a genial, thorough landlord, once a guide, had 150 guests, and, more coming in, the house was overcrowded. John Holland is not the man to turn anybody out of doors, and he worked hard until nearly midnight to stow the whole party away for a comfortable sleep.

---

26  Popular American West writer Edward Zane Carroll Judson Sr., who used the pseudonym Ned Buntline
27  Stagecoaches

Chairs, sofas, lounges, and finally the dining room floor were utilized, and at last the ultimate citizen was quieted. I succeeded in getting a short lounge with a back-breaking bend in nearly the middle of it but could not get so much as a cotton sheet in the way of bedding.

I went down to the canoe, got my tent cloth and gum coat, wet with the heavy dew, put the dry sides next me, and turned in; soon got warm and slept soundly.

Of the other hotels, the American, just across the bay, had up eleven wall tents, all of which were full, and the house overrun with guests. The Blue Mountain House (Merwin's) was also full, as well as every boardinghouse, and some of the guides at 11:00 p.m. took their blankets and went out to seek a spot to camp in for the night. And little more than eight years ago there stood a bark shanty just above, the only sign of human habitation on Blue Mountain Lake. Speaking of this rush to the Northern Wilderness in '79, Colvin[28] says, "Where one came last year, ten come this, a hundred the next." He is just well right. You meet them everywhere. They permeate every accessible lake and stream, and it is hard to say what lakes and streams are not accessible. You meet them in the most out-of-the way places, just where you expected to be alone, and always the breech-loader and fly rod that they hang to like grim death.

28 Verplanck Colvin was the superintendent of the Adirondack Survey and a force behind the creation of the Adirondack Forest Preserve.

Said an old guide to me, "If they averaged one deer to three guns there wouldn't be a deer left in the wilderness at the end of three years." Said another guide, one of the oldest and best, "What few deer are killed here had better be killed by parties who employ us; it encourages them to come again." And P. Jones, guide to the Stickney camp and one of the most intelligent, spoke thus: "We don't care to kill many deer ourselves, or to catch many trout. Just enough for use. When we hunt for market we go to Michigan, on the Au Sable. Killed twenty-five there last fall, and am going again when the guiding season is over. The deer in these woods are worth more to us guides alive than dead. They are worth fifty dollars a head as they run." That is about the view taken of fishing and hunting by the average guide in the North Woods.

As I had come to do the lake and the mountain, I concluded to go through. Climbed Blue Mountain on a hot August morning and on arriving at the verge found Colvin's lookout ladder, made by nailing cross strips to the trunks of two spruce trees. It was rather an old affair and looked shaky, but I went up and took in the view, which was really extensive and fine, and then I followed the trail that leads to the signal on the highest point of the mountain, climbed the signal, and tried to make out the twenty-eight lakes I had been told I should see, but could only make out about half of them. As to mountain peaks, the number was rather confusing than satisfying. They ran together and over and by each other in a manner to throw an ordinary mind into a state of temporary imbecility.

I could dimly discern Marcy, and I thought I identified Mounts

Haystack and Skylight. But they rose in such innumerable and unknowable billows, peaks, points, and ridges that the mind—at least my mind—can retain only a confused recollection of them. It had been hot work making the ascent. It was cold and windy on the summit of the mountain, and the immediate surroundings were cheerless and desolate. One entire summit had been slashed in 1873 to give an outlook for the signals of the survey, and the dead, decaying trees, lying just as they fell, were not pleasant to look upon.

There was an excellent bark shanty between the spruce ladder and the signal, and in a swampy depression near the summit under the edge of a boulder, I found a pool of cold spring water that rendered the bottle of water I had brought from the hotel quite superfluous.

I had done the mountain, and it seemed the proper thing to do the lake. I did it. I paddled in and around among the islands, landed up and launched out again, greatly to the delight of the youngsters, who were there in force with parents or chaperones and who were exceedingly taken with the little boat, and then I ignobly placed her on the deck of the round-sterned little packet[29]

---

29  A boat that ferries passengers, mail, or cargo

and paddled by steam to Ed Bennett's landing on the Raquette. And then it came down to the double blade again.

After a night's rest and an excellent breakfast, I started out to cross the lake, and rather got down on my muscle, for the wind was ahead and rising. By the time I got into smooth water at the mouth of Browns Tract Inlet, it was getting rough, and I was glad to be in the tortuous but safe inlet once more. A tedious paddle of four miles, a weary carry of one and a half, brought me to the Eighth Lake. Wind ahead and hard traveling. Another tiresome carry of a mile and over and I was on the Seventh, with the wind strong and the second largest lake of the chain to cross. I was a long time making it, and was almost too tired to make the next carry from Sixth to Fifth, but I finally shouldered the canoe and made the distance slowly and wearily to the Fifth, which at least ended carrying for that day. It was well that the wind went down with the sun or I could not have made the rough and stormy Fourth, which often drives the best guide boats to land. As it was, the canoe pitched and danced about quite lively, and it was nearly dark when I landed at Ed Arnold's, on the south shore of the Fourth.

The Fourth, by the way, is the largest lake of the chain and is famed for its lake trout. Arnold's is a central point for catching them, and he is an experienced guide. His terms are low, $1 per day, or even less by the week. He has buoys at the best points near the house, at which you can fish as much as you please, and you are supposed to bring your fish to the house. A night's rest at Arnold's, a pleasant canoe ride down the Fourth, through the placid Third, by the Eagle's Nest into the Second, by the Stickney camp into the First, with its dead timber and long marshy outlet, and at 9:00 a.m. I hauled in at the Forge House landing, well pleased with my Blue Mountain trip, but with no idea of repeating it this season. I can do better.

# THAT
# TROUT

I've watched that trout for days and days,
I've tried him with all sorts of tackle;
With flies got up in various ways,
Red, blue, green, gray, and silver-hackle.
I've tempted him with angle-dogs.[30]
And grubs, that must have been quite trying,
Thrown deftly in betwixt[31] old logs.
Where, probably, he might be lying.
Sometimes I've had a vicious bite.
And as the silk was tautly running.
Have been convinced I had him, quite:
But 'twasn't him: he was too cunning.
I've tried him, when the silver moon
Shone on my dew-bespangled trousers.
With dartfish; but he was "too soon"—
Though, sooth[32] to say, I caught some rousers;

---

30 Earthworms
31 Between
32 True

And sadly viewed the ones I caught,
They loomed so small and seemed so poor,
'Twas finding pebbles where one sought
A gem of price—a Kohinoor.[33]
I've often weighed him (with my eyes),
As he with most prodigious flounces
Rose to the surface after flies.
(He weighs four pounds and seven ounces.)
I tried him—Heaven absolve my soul—
With some outlandish, heathenish gearing—
A pronged machine stuck on a pole—
A process that the boys call spearing.
I jabbed it at his dorsal fin
Six feet beneath the crystal water—
'Twas all too short. I tumbled in,
And got half drowned—just as I aughta.[34]
Adieu, O trout of marvelous size.
Thou piscatorial speckled wonder.
Bright be the waters where you rise,
And green the banks you cuddle under.

---

33 The Koh-i-Noor, one of Britain's crown jewels, is a very large diamond from India.
34 Ought to

# CRUISE OF THE *NIPPER*

**FOREST AND STREAM, DECEMBER 8, 1881**

SHE MET ME BY APPOINTMENT AT BOONVILLE. With praiseworthy punctuality—considering her sex—she had arrived several hours before me. The express agent assured me that her conduct had been most exemplary.

The tourists, male and female, were just then thronging into the wilderness from either side. Everything on the northern road brought its quota of seekers for pleasure, recreation, or health. The *Nipper* was interviewed remorselessly. Well-dressed ladies, neat young girls, and even children approached her irreverently. They examined her graceful lines. They made comments on her unknown owner, and invariably ended with lifting her gently by the nose, with exclamations quite irrelevant. No gentleman tourist passed her by without critical examination and comments. As they raised her carefully, they said if they were worldlings[35]—"Holy Moses! who's going to paddle *that* eggshell?" Clergymen said: "I do declare! Is that intended to go on the lakes?" The ladies remarked, "Oh, my!" "Did you ever?" "Dear me!" "What a beauty!" etc.

---

35 Someone who is absorbed by worldly or material concerns

None noticed the little gray-haired fellow who, dressed in coarse blue flannels, smoking a clay pipe, dangling his short legs off the platform, and reading the last number of *Forest and Stream* was quietly taking in the thing until the agent pointed him out as the skipper of the light craft they were admiring. He was immediately interviewed, and questions were frequent and fast.

"Do you expect to live in her on Raquette Lake?"

"Can you stand rough water?"

"Can you throw a line from her, and handle a good-sized fish?"

"Isn't she too frail?"

"And what is that little green canoe in the corner? She looks still smaller."

The skipper answered the last question first. The little green canoe is the *Nessmuk* that was paddled last summer over 550 miles, came out tight and staunch, was taken 230 miles to northern Pennsylvania by rail, paddled on the rocky affluents[36] of the upper Susquehanna, and is going back to the wilderness, still tight and seaworthy. The second question. Yes, she is frail. She is intended, both by her owner and builder, to be the lightest canoe of her dimensions ever built of oak, elm, and cedar, with light spruce gunwale. (Here the skipper showed a letter from her maker, Rushton, expressing doubts as to her strength, and giving pen and ink diagrams of the way she might be strengthened by bracing, thwarts,[37] etc.)

"But," said the skipper, growing enthusiastic, "she don't need strengthening. The two pairs of strips nearest the keel are of full thickness—three-sixteenths of an inch. The third pair taper a little toward the gunwale, and the three upper pairs run light, very light. Her weight is sixteen pounds; length, ten feet, six inches; beam, twenty-eight inches; rise at center, eight inches; at stem,

---

36  Tributary streams
37  Seats for rowers

thirteen inches; ribs, forty-five inches. Gentlemen, if any of you are canoeists, you know that you have no business to put weight on the upper strips or the gunwale. All weight in a light canoe must come on the keelson,[38] and the first two, possibly three, pairs of strips. The *Nipper* is strong enough for me. As to throwing a line from her, she is the very best possible craft for fly-fishing. You can make a ten-ounce trout tow you in any direction you please until he floats helpless. I have done it in the *Nessmuk*.

"As to rough waters and squalls, I expect to stay as long as the average guide boat of the Adirondacks and ride more steadily in a short, sharp sea."

With expressions of sympathy and hopes that they might see the light canoe and her skipper on the lakes, the tourists went off on the inevitable buckboards, and the skipper began to organize for a cruise. It was necessary to make the first twelve miles of it overland, and the route was not pleasant. Hills, hollows, sand up to the hub, boulders, and six miles of corduroy road.[39] Such was the first twelve miles—as every man knows who has made the route from Boonville to Moose River.

The trip was made in and on a lumber wagon, with the canoes packed in straw and guyed with heavy twine, the skipper kneeling on the port side and keeping a death grip on the gunwale of the *Nipper*, unmindful of the hemlock leeboard[40] that was steadily abrading his spinal column. The charge for the tow was four dollars, with a stipulation that the horses should walk all the way. When the latter clause of the contract was enforced by the skipper, the disgusted driver relieved his feelings by a twelve-mile string of oaths that would have struck a Missouri bullwhacker[41] with paralysis.

It is a weary trip, that road from Boonville to the "Tannery." But it has an end, and both driver and canoeist felt better when the two canoes made a landing

---

38  A crosswise beam attached to the keel, used to add strength
39  A road of logs constructed over a swampy area
40  A board that can be dropped into the water to lessen a boat's sideways drift
41  A freight wagon driver

on Tom Nightingale's porch without crack or scratch. A double nip of whiskey quieted the driver, while the hearty greeting of Jolly Tom, Si Holliday, Charley Phelps, Colonel Claskin, and a dozen others made the skipper feel as though he had got home.

Moose River is not by any means a bad place to stop at. The hotel is well kept, family very pleasant, and charges reasonable, let alone that pretty fair trout fishing may be had in several spring brooks easily reached in an hour's walk. It took four days to work these brooks and a few spring holes in the river, the result being a reasonable supply of fine brook trout, saving none under six inches.

The road from the "Tannery" to the foot of the Fulton Chain is so rough that no prudent tourist will send a light canoe in by the buckboards, and boats are usually sent in from the west side, via Jones's camp, on the shoulders of guides. And even in this way they do not always get through safe. There was a fine new boat sent in that way last July in which the guide contrived to knock an ugly hole. So the skipper decided to send his duffel by buckboard to the Forge House, make the nine-mile carry through the woods to Jones's, and paddle the twelve-mile still water to the lakes, which he did.

In fact, he overdid it by taking the right-hand trail when within three miles of Jones's and carrying the *Nipper* over to Little Cull Lake. This lengthened the carry to twelve miles, but the visit to this lonely, beautiful lake almost compensated for the extra labor. It was late in the afternoon when Jones's camp was finally reached and the skipper learned that the camp was bare of trout. Pork, potatoes, and tea were indulged in to a moderate extent, and the night's rest that followed was of the soundest.

The next day was spent in a faithful but vain attempt to inveigle a mess of speckled trout from their old haunts in the Moose, and it was remembered with regret that these same haunts gave a daily supply of trout on the previous season. Everywhere, so far, trout had been found less plenty than in the summer of '80.

A second night of sound sleep at Jones's camp, and the *Nipper* was put afloat for the first time, her owner boarding her rather cautiously for a canoeist who has faith in himself and his craft. She proved marvelously steady, however, and a paddle upstream of three and a half miles in one hour brought her to the carry around the flood-raft and gave the skipper confidence in her steadiness. The Forge House landing was easily made inside of four hours, and, once in the boathouse at Barrett's, the cruise of the Fulton Chain was fairly commenced.

And here let us drop the third-person singular and pick up the Eternal Ego, which I am as sadly weary of as my readers possibly can be.

At the Forge, I met very many whom I knew last season; also, many who were visiting Browns Tract for the first time. Among the latter were invalids of the lung disorder type, who did not seem very favorably affected by the damp, chilly weather that prevailed during July and well into August of the past summer. As to the brigade of consumptives who came to the Northern Wilderness last summer in search of health, which they were destined not to find, I shall have something to say further on. Many were induced to come through reading a magazine article entitled "Camp Lou,"[42] and the disappointment felt by most of them was sad and bitter.

It was 4:00 p.m. on the 16th of July when I paddled out from the Forge House for a rather extended cruise through the Fulton Chain, Raquette Lake, Forked and Long Lakes, the Raquette River, Tupper Lake, and, by a circuitous route, back to the Fulton Chain. It was a very pretty program, destined to be carried out only in part.

The afternoon was gusty and stormy. Black, wind-laden clouds went whirling across the sky with ominous speed, and I heard a guide remark, "Uncle Nessmuk ain't anxious to take this in." So I made my gum coat into a cushion and struck out. For a mile and a half up the channel, the canoe flew along smoothly with the wind dead aft. Then came the open water of First Lake, white and spumy,

---

42 An article that appeared in *Harper's Magazine* in 1881 and recounted how the author, Marc Cook, recovered from a lung disease while in the Adirondacks

with short, sharp seas, that I must take fairly abeam to the inlet, where I could see the waves dashing white over the large boulder at its mouth. I hesitated for a minute about trying for the inlet. But it was the trial trip of the *Nipper*. If she would swamp in a blow, better do it on one of the smaller lakes, and I pulled out. When fairly out of the roughest water, her behavior surprised and delighted me exceedingly. She rose and settled on an even keel with a steadiness I should have scarcely looked for in a boat of twice her size and threw off the steep, sharp seas like a duck. I thought then, and still think, that for a light, comfortable cruising canoe, under paddle, her model cannot be improved.

When about halfway across the lake, a low, ugly-looking black cloud came up from the southwest, and when just over the lake let go a torrent of water that drenched me to the skin in three minutes. It was no time nor place for struggling into a gum coat, and I wanted both hands on the paddle, so I took it as philosophically as possible. It ceased as I rounded the rock at the inlet, and I went flying up Second Lake with the wind astern, only dipping the paddle for steerage way, and again there came a thunder gust with a downpour of rain. But, as I could be no wetter, I rather enjoyed it.

Rounding the Eagle's Nest, I ran under the lee of the forest-crowned point and sponged out the canoe, for she was getting logy[43] with the water that had fallen into her, and then paddled across to Third Lake camp. Perrie, with several old acquaintances, met me at the landing and gave me a woodland welcome, besides lending me dry clothes that I greatly needed.

I found the camp enlarged to thrice its former capacity and filled to overflowing with boarders and tourists. Four of the inmates were suffering with pulmonary troubles and did not seem to be getting much benefit from "balsamic breezes" or "ozone."[44] Each one had his or her peculiar cough; the season had been wet and cold, and the bright, open-air fire that should be inseparable from a camp in the wilderness was, for the most part, lacking.

---

43 Sluggish

44 In this sense, referring to fresh air

On the night of my arrival, the wind shifted to northeast with a cold drizzling rain, and in less than forty-eight hours after landing, I had joined the little band of coughers, coughing oftener and louder than any of them. As I had made the trip to the woods for health mainly, this was most provoking. I thought it was only a surface cough, so to speak, but it was constant, hard and irritating. There were plenty of cough remedies in the house, and I tried them all, with little or no effect until I resorted to balsam, taken directly from the little blisters on the balsam fir, soaked into sugar, and allowed to percolate slowly down the throat. This gave relief, and I mention it for the benefit of any future tourists who may get landed upon a cruise by a cough and cold.

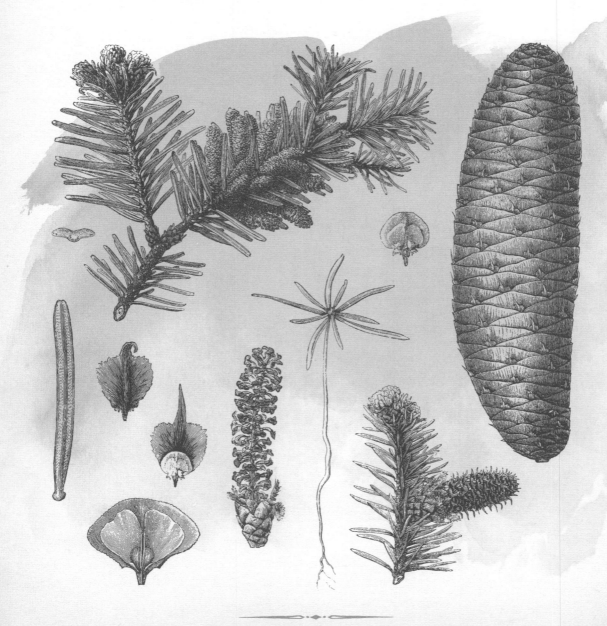

By the 22nd, I was sufficiently recovered to assist at a dinner given at Dunakin's camp, on Fourth Lake, by Messrs. F. J. Nott, S. F. Fish, and M. M. Crowell. The dinner was entrusted to Sam Dunakin as cook and purveyor, and it was a neat affair. The guests, estimated at six, turned out thirteen strong at the table, State Game constable Dodge being one of the number, and I thought he looked a little glum as he tasted the "mutton," which had a rather gamy flavor, as though it "had lain in the roses, and fed on the lilies of life" (or of the lakes). Whatever he thought, he said nothing, and the dinner was one of the pleasant episodes one never forgets. Our hosts were capable of good red wine, with a bottle of Martell at the finish. The trout were excellent and well cooked, and all three of our hosts sang glees[45] in capital voice and good taste, aided by the game constable, who, by the way, struck me as being the right man in the right place. Just at dark, I paddled leisurely down to Third Lake with the impression that the 22nd of July, 1881, would be a good day to mark with a white stone.

Next day I tried salmon trout at the buoys and brook trout at all the spring holes, with no success. In fact, the fishing on Third Lake after the first of July was not worth the trouble of putting a rod together or wetting a buoy-line.

---

45  A type of song, English in origin, for three or more parts

# Cruise of the *Nipper*, 2

## *FOREST AND STREAM*, DECEMBER 15, 1881

The *Nipper* was up for a rather extended cruise, to start July 3. I quote a brief entry from my journal under date of July 23: "Slept later than usual and on rising found my knapsack missing. The loss is irreparable. Spent the day paddling around the lakes trying to trace it. It has gone to Blue Mountain in the duffel of Mr. Durant and his guide Moody taken by mistake." The guides assured me it would come back by the first boat coming from Blue Mountain, or, perhaps, the Raquette. The mistake was a most natural one. The knapsack was of oiled ducking,[46] black, not heavy, and easily taken as a part of the oilcloth goods that hung on the same large nail. I was fain[47] to wait with what patience I could.

Days passed, and the knapsack did not come back. I put the time in by climbing the hills—Bald Mountain, especially; paddling, botanizing, digging blisters off the fir trees for the few drops of balsam contained in them, and fishing for lake and brook trout—with little success. I interviewed guides and tourists, studied maps of the wilderness, and strove—in vain—to keep dry. To give an idea of just what the weather was like at this time, I will give a few brief quotations from a journal kept faithfully on the spot:

July 16th. Gale with heavy rain. Frequent showers; wind mainly from the north.

17th. Heavy wind and cold rain from the north, everyone shivering with cold. Five people in the house with hard, chronic coughs. Bark, bark, all night.

---

46  A type of sturdy fabric, typically cotton
47  Obliged

18th. Rain, rain; blow, blow, from the north, as usual. Cough, cough. Five of us keep it up. Two will most likely never be better.

19th. Like the 18th, cold and rainy. Rained all night.

20th. Put on a gum coat, took my little hatchet, and went for the woods. Made a fire that would roast an ox, and got nearly dry—for once. Still raining. Rains nearly all the time. 'Tisn't the most favorable weather for lung diseases; not the healthiest region, I should say. Parties who come for health are every day going out, disgusted and sick. Still the camp is full.

21st. John D. Fraser visited us. He has been taking views of the scenery in Browns Tract, and taking them well. But what American pays for American sketches? Let him go to Switzerland or the Rhine. He painted, artistically, a name on my canoe; for I hurried her maker so that he did not have time to do it, and I would as soon have a wife or daughter without a name as an unnamed canoe. Still it rains and still we miserables cough night and day. Is it cheery? Do we feel exhilarated? "Like the Crank Turk?" as Mr. Quilp remarks. Not to any great extent, I should say.

22nd. Weather a little better. Better myself. Dinner at Sam Dunakin's. Warmer. Wind SW, and showers during the night.

23rd. Already noted.

24th. Paddled to Forge House. Wet again. Am wet all the time. The whole wilderness water-soaked.

25th. Just a repetition of 24th for rain and wind. Tried the spring holes just before and after sundown—with the usual luck. Guides, boats, and parties coming and going all the time.

26th. More parties and more rain. Many going out disgusted. Tried fly-fishing again—with no luck.

27th. Weather better. Am making up a blanket roll and getting ready for a good start tomorrow, if it is fair.

28th. Rained in the fore part of the day, but cleared off in the afternoon and I started for a cruise at 6:00 p.m.—rather late, as I found; for, what with stopping at Ed Arnold's for a visit and loitering on the way, night overtook me long before I reached the head of Fourth Lake. Here I found a roaring torrent coming down the inlet from Fifth Lake, which after an hour of hard work, I was unable to stem, and so drifted back into Fourth Lake, where I paddled around until midnight, finally landing on an island where Fred Hess has a good house and camp. Here he lives with his family, but happening to be absent just then, could not welcome me, so I made myself welcome to his open camp, found a lamp and a good bed, lighted the one and took possession of the other, managing to put in a few hours of solid sleep before sunrise.

Started early and tried the inlet by daylight, but the current was too stiff, and I was forced to back down and take the carry to Fifth Lake. Found the fishing camp at the foot of the lake partially submerged and untenable. Last year it was a fine camp to stop at, but the state has seen fit to back up the water in Sixth and Seventh Lakes with a dam ten feet high; the gate had just been raised "by order," and the pent-up waters were rushing downward to the Black River, to turn mill wheels and swell the profits of some manufacturer or corporation having influence at Albany.

Making the three-quarter-mile carry from Fifth to Sixth, I landed at the dam and rested for a time to take in the desolate scene.

The water at and above the dam was clogged with rotting vegetation, slimy treetops, and decayed, half-sunken logs. The shoreline of trees stood dead and dying, while the smell of decaying vegetable matter was sickening. Last season Sixth Lake, though small (fifty-three acres), was a wild, gamy place, and the best of the chain for floating. Its glory has departed. None care to stop there longer than is necessary. Seventh Lake, containing 1,609 acres, is the second largest lake of the chain and lies but a trifle higher than Sixth. There is no rapid water and no carry between the two, and a dam that raises the water eight or nine feet in the Sixth will raise it almost as high in the Seventh. The channel up to Seventh was as plain as a highway last year, and pleasant withal. The present season finds the channel wiped out, the forest of balsam, spruce, and hemlock converted into a dismal swamp of dying trees; foul, discolored waters; and fouler smells, while the channel has puzzled more than one guide who had been used to the route for years.

However, by the help of a few blazed trees and fallen timber, with short sections cut out of the trunks for the passage of boats, I contrived to keep the channel and debouched[48] into the once-pleasant Seventh, only to find it a scene of desolation and decay. All along the shores, the timber was dead or dying, and the odor of rotting vegetation was not suggestive of "ozone" or balsam-laden breezes.

As you enter the Seventh by the outlet, turn to port, follow the shore for one hundred rods, and you will find an open, free-for-all bark camp. It has been there for many years, and many are the names and dates carved on the square logs of which the sides are built. I expected to find Sam Dunakin, with Dr. Nott and party here, but they had left, though their fire was still burning. So I stopped for a rest and dinner. Across the lake, looking by the high rocky point, you could see, last season, a white, long strip of clean sand beach. Just back of the beach was a hedge-like row of green shrubbery, some fifty yards long, and just here came in the stream of Eighth Lake—the inlet of Seventh.

This, too, is all changed. Beach, hedge, and inlet are all drowned out, and the dense forest, for a long distance, is underwater on either side. This is bad, for the open spaces among the trees are easily mistaken for the inlet by a stranger, while the tortuous channel is hard to follow and the landing still more difficult to find. And thereby I came to grief; for, taking an after-dinner nap, I must have slept too long. The afternoon was cloudy, and my watch, that very useful companion of the lone tourist, had got wet, and, though keeping up a feeble semblance of life, had become utterly reckless as to any proper division of hours and minutes. The hands pointed to half-past two. The hands lied.

Probably it was nearer half-past five when I paddled leisurely across Seventh Lake and, after losing half an hour looking for the inlet, started up the channel all right. I ought to have found the landing in less than one and a half miles, but I went on and on until the roar of the rapids admonished that I had gone too far upstream. Also, I had lost the marked trees that the guides had blazed to indicate the route. So I turned and paddled back, looking carefully for some sign of the landing. None was to be seen.

---

48 Emerged

I skirted along the north shore, as near it as I could get, and got into a fearful mess of dead logs, submerged treetops, and sunken brush, but no landing. All at once darkness shut down on this miserable, dismal forest like a wet blanket. A heavy black cloud showed in the southwest, and thunder began to growl ominously. And now for the open channel; for any place where dry ground may be found, with a chance to put up the shelter tent. Too late. One end of the canoe was fast on a floating log, and the first attempt to back off resulted in sticking the other end in a scraggy treetop, while the log stuck tighter than a brother.

It began to look like an uncomfortable scrape. The canoe was hung up, stem and stern, and the furious gust that usually precedes a thunderstorm was roaring through the forest, tipping a balsam or spruce over here and there, making one feel uneasy as they plashed into the muddy water, their loosened roots making them an easy prey to the wind. On the heel of the wind came the rain, and how it did pour; while the lightning was almost incessant, and the thunder was highly creditable for a country with so few advantages.

I unjointed the paddle, and, using the single blade, got free of that execrable[49] log. Then I worked free of the old treetop, and, aided by the flashes that lighted the whole forest momentarily, got out into clear water, but quite idiotic as to the points of the compass. So, as there seemed nothing better to do, I sat still and watched the strange, wild scenery, as shown in different colors by electricity. There were white flashes that appeared to dash all over the forest in a broad, white glare of light, with no distinctive point of stroke. Pale-blue, zigzag chains that gave a peculiar ghastly light among trunks and limbs, and orange-colored bolts that seemed to my eye like round globes of fire. These last struck twice within a short distance of the canoe—once, a tree that stood in the water, and once on dry land. I could tell by the sound of the shattered tops, as they plashed into the water or clattered to the ground. Comfortless as the situation was, it was a grand display, also—a little unearthly and a trifle scary. It was some satisfaction to reflect that I was insured in two companies, and a random bolt or a tumbling tree might be worth three thousand dollars to the widow.

---

49 Detestable

The storm lasted an unconscionable time but was followed by a bright, clear night, and when I had made out the north star, I slowly worked down the channel, got into the lake, and made the camp again just as the eastern sky began to show streaks of light. There was plenty of dry kindling wood in the camp, and a roaring fire was in order, with a pint of strong, hot tea, broiled pork, bread, and potatoes. Thanks to the waterproof shelter-tent, I was capable of a dry blanket, shirt, and drawers, so, hanging my wet clothes to dry by the fire, I swathed myself snugly in blanket and tent, lay down on fragrant browse, and slept the sleep of the just man.

It is not to be supposed that a man far on the wrong side of fifty years can take an all-night soaking in a wicked storm, seated in a sixteen-pound canoe, where to rise, or even turn around, may mean drowning—can turn out, after needed sleep, with a general disposition to throw handsprings, or perform feats of muscular agility. I awoke at about 10:00 a.m. on the morning of July 30, lame and sore, unwound myself from blanket and oiled shelter-tent, took a wash, built a huge fire, made some strong coffee, and tried my best to make a cheery thing of it.

It wouldn't do. The miserable dead line of timber was about the only cheerful outlook; it was a long distance either way to human habitation or to human sympathy, and—I was just mad. I limped down to the soddened beach, sat down on a soaked log, and "nursed my wrath to keep it warm."[50] I cursed the weak, selfish policy (if it deserves the name) that is turning the finest sylvan region on the face of the earth into a disgusting, malarial nuisance. I cursed the miserable, illogical hoodlums, who, from high positions, sing the praises of the Adirondacks as a finer, more

---

50  From Robert Burns's poem "Tam O'Shanter"

romantic land than the Swiss Alps; begging that it be kept as a "state park"—"an inheritance for our children's children,"[51] while, from the other corners of their mouths, they explain how the waters that, by nature, seek the St. Lawrence, may be dammed, backed up and turned, to flow into the Hudson. (See Verplanck Colvin Reports, which I have before me.) Now, let any man, with as much brains as a hen-turkey, look over the Colvin Reports and say what the result will be if his suggestions are ever practically carried to their consummation.

But enough for the present. "An' if the beast an' branks[52] be spared"[53] I will ventilate this subject by another year, quite to the satisfaction of all those who advocate the damming of lakes and rivers, regardless of health, recreation, and the preservation of a region the like of which does not exist on the surface of this globed earth. More anon.

---

51  From Proverbs 13:22
52  Bridle
53  From Robert Burns's poem "To J. Lapraik: Third Epistle"

# Cruise of the *Nipper*, 3

*FOREST AND STREAM*, DECEMBER 29, 1881

The 30th of last July was a bright day along the Fulton Chain, clear and cloudless. The shelter tent and blanket were made into a snug roll, the canoe lay hidden from the heat in the shade of a thicket, and everything was ready for a trip over to Raquette Lake, when two sharp-stemmed Long-Lakers darted from the outlet into the placid Seventh, and I recognized "Slim Jim" and Fred Rivett, with parties, bound to the eastern side. Seeing me on the shore, they came to a halt, and Jim sang out, "Come on, Uncle Nessmuk, go through with us to Raquette."

"You'll outrow me. I'll get left."

"No, we'll keep company; come along," said Jim.

"Can you wait five minutes?" I asked.

"Yes, fifteen of them," answered Fred.

"These gentlemen would like to see your canoe work; come on," said Jim.

It struck me that the guides had got the idea. They had been at it all the season and knew just where to strike the landing that had eluded me the evening before. So I launched out and soon laid them alongside. The gentleman who headed the party was much interested and pleased with the canoe. He asked many questions and was a little skeptical about her weight, and the three youngsters who composed the balance of the party were enthusiastic. Their questions "little meaning, little relevancy bore,"[54] but the guides made some

---

54  From Edgar Allan Poe's poem "The Raven"

queries with meaning in them. For instance, Fred asked, as he leisurely picked up his oars, "Did the storm keep you awake last night?" And I, remembering that my little hatchet had gone on to the Raquette, answered stoutly, "Not a bit; never slept better in my life."

As the guides took up the easy, effective stroke that sends the Long-Lakers through the water so speedily, I crept under Fred's counter, took the draw of his wake, and made the inlet without parting company. Then I said, "Boys, your boats can and ought to beat any paddle on open water, but when you come to these crooked channels, outlets, and inlets in the form of the letter 'S,' where you have to look over your shoulders right and left to see the course and pull first to starboard, then to port, why you see the paddle—the double blade—has rather got the bulge on you." We had stopped under a huge cedar for a modest nip, for which the leader of that party has my thanks, and, as Jim and Fred very quietly resumed their oars, a meaning glance passed between them. They said nothing, but I thought it as well to lay aside extra clothing, spit on my hands, and settle down to work.

For the first half mile, the odds were rather in my favor. The water was deep, the channel crooked, and the chances for cutting off bends and "going as you look" rather made an easy thing of it. Then the course grew straighter and less distinct. The swift Long-Lakers drew rapidly away, and I saw them turn a bend forty rods ahead. I tried to cut off the bend and ran onto a sunken log. Backed off, took the channel, and put on all the steam I had at command, but in vain. I was left. I paddled up the stream until I lost the blazed trees that marked the course, stopped, listened a moment, and then used my spare wind in a loud, long la-whoop. An answer came from the swampy forest far to the left, where I found the party landed up on a shaky sort of corduroy platform, which is the landing now. They were waiting for me, they said. And Fred remarked, "A double blade does take the skates on these crooked channels. Notice how he cut the corners and went the way he looked?" Boys, I hope that wasn't "sarcasm." I have faith to think you wouldn't make fun of grayhairs!

I like to see
the guides organize for a
"carry," and I watched
Jim and Fred as they
prepared for the trip over
to Eighth Lake. First, the
"party" was loaded up with
fishing rods, guns, packbaskets,
gum blankets, and the usual
impedimenta[55] of the average
tourist and started over the carry
looking like a crew of pack-
peddlers. When they were out of
sight, Jim remarked coolly, "We
can take it easy; they ain't going to hurry." Then he and Fred tied in oars,
seats, etc., snugly and neatly, made the neck-yokes fast at the balancing point,
and then, inverting the lightest boat, Jim held the stern high in the air while
Fred crept under and adjusted the neck-yoke nicely to his muscular shoulders,
saying, "All right; let go," which Jim did, and the inevitable blue boat, with a
pair of sturdy legs beneath, disappeared rapidly up the trail.

---

55 Baggage or accessories that impede progress

Jim raised his own boat and said, "Think you can hold her up?" I thought I could and did, though balancing on a point at the stern, and weighing over ninety pounds, she was a lift. And then Jim quietly seized my blanket roll and hung it on his broad shoulders without comment before shouldering his boat. It was a kindly thing to do and like his generous nature, but I was ashamed and raised a feeble remonstrance; he went away with a long, quick stride, paying no heed, and I thought of honest old Jack Falstaff, that Prince of Deadbeats— "Hal, an thou seest me down in the fight and bestride me, why so; 'tis an act of friendship." Was I a beat?

I organized my own canoe for the carry and tried to overtake the party, but the guides walk fast. I found them on the clean, sandy landing, and it was a relief to see the fresh green shores, wholesome waters, and healthy trees of Eighth Lake, after an experience of Fifth, Sixth, and Seventh. At the Eighth, the leader of the party began to feel hurried. He wished to reach Bennett's Landing on Raquette in time for the little steamer to Blue Mountain, and guides always follow the wishes of employers so far as they can. I saw I was likely to get left, but, meaning to keep up as far as possible, I paddled out with the party and rather got down on the double blade. The guides went in for an ash breeze.[56] The distance is less than one and one-half miles, and they led me to the landing just about one hundred rods. Yes, the Long-Lakers are fast—but cranky and uncomfortable to ride in.

As you strike the landing at the head of Eighth Lake, there is a path, leading along the shore to the right, which leads you to a cool spring. Here the guides, having seen the party off, stopped a few minutes for a lunch. Let me commend that spring, with its bright, cold water and restful surroundings, to any lone canoeist who may happen to strike the landing at the head of Eighth Lake. Again the boats and canoe were shouldered, Jim, as before, toting my blanket roll. Again the guides beat me over the carry, though they stopped for a rest and I did not—and when I arrived at Browns Tract Inlet, guides and boats had disappeared. I was in no hurry. The carries were all made, and six and a

---

56  Rowed; the expression originates from the fact that oars were made of ash.

half miles of paddling lay between me and Ed Bennett's. The day was fine. The wind just brisk enough to be lively, and I reached Bennett's about three-quarters of an hour behind the guides.

Going down the inlet, I was interested by the movements of the fish that lay basking near the surface among the lily pads and darted off with a plash and swirl as the canoe neared them. A man with oars would hardly have seen this. But paddling silently downstream, looking the way I went, I probably started more than a score of good-sized fish, without being able to decide on the species. I intended to return and try them, both with fly and bait, but failed to do so, though I certainly shall if I find myself there in the summer of '82. I thought they might be pickerel, but the guides assured me there were no pickerel in Raquette Lake.

I found Bennett's hotel crowded with tourists and sportsmen and was unable to get a room, or even a bed. But the bark-roofed guide camp, "For guides only," had a bright fire in front, with balsam browse for bedding, and was preferable to a close room. I took up my quarters there while on the Raquette and had no cause to regret it. As to the fare, whoever has stayed with Ed Bennett knows that his table would rank as first-class anywhere. And there is no pleasanter lake than Raquette in the North Woods. It is the largest; the water is clear, and the shores, while being well wooded, are mainly rocky. Large as the lake is, I should not know where to paddle to get more than a mile from the nearest land. The numberless bays, capes, indentations, and islands make it difficult to describe on paper, and even the best maps fail to give just the correct idea of it.

I do not know a better place to investigate the now popular bass question. In the summer of '80 the smallmouth had got a pretty strong fin-hold and was evidently making his way. A few were being taken with spoon and bait. His increase for the next twelve months was to me marvelous. Starting from Bennett's landing with an hour's sun and paddling to the mouth of the Marion, I could get all the sport I wanted and more fish than I needed before dark. I used an eight-ounce rod and the scarlet ibis fly with silver body, as the best. But a brown hackle was also killing. And the gold-bodied ibis is about as good. The three, taken as a cast, and no others are needed.

Father Gavan, an intelligent young Catholic priest, was an enthusiastic bass fisherman and used a powerful rod with minnow or spoon. His favorite ground was the mouth of South Inlet and adjacent shores. He was nearly always successful. I liked the mouth of the Marion and the rocky shores below, with the islands in front of the hotel. There was not much to choose. His fish averaged about twice the size of mine, and I could take about two to his one. On the whole, I should say that the bait-fisherman had the best of it. The guides' complaint, that the bass has destroyed all the lake trout, would have more point had there been any lake trout worth mention to destroy.

I took a lively interest in the tourists, or boarders, who had worked their way into the wilderness for health and not for sport. There were many of them on

the waters of the Raquette and more on the Saranac. News travels fast in the woods. Every day that I was on these waters I saw guides and tourists from almost every route you can mention. I heard that more than a dozen consumptives had already died on the Saranac waters. Others were dying, and many more had crept away, beaten and exhausted, to die at home among friends and relatives.

Paul Smith had said he would, by five hundred dollars, rather the article entitled "Camp Lou" had never been written. I saw for myself that parties who had sought the Adirondacks for health were sick, disgusted, and only anxious to get away anywhere that dryness, warmth, and rest were easily attainable. I was interviewed and questioned time and again as to the healthfulness of the mountainous regions about the headwaters of the Susquehanna, and truth compelled me to say that all my observation and experience led to the conclusion that the high lands about the headwaters of

the Delaware and Susquehanna afforded more hope of healing to the sufferer from pulmonary disease than the damp, cold high lands of the Northern Wilderness. That some unexpected and surprising cures have happened in both regions is certainly true.

And it is equally true that the Northern Wilderness is unrivaled for boating and canoeing facilities and hardly to be excelled for scenery. All this is most attractive, and it is not to be wondered at that the average tourist much prefers a wild region, where, by making short carries, he can travel hundreds of miles by water.

But, as regards the single question of health, I can name half a dozen localities, easily reached in one day from New York, where I would rather take my chances as a consumptive patient than in the Adirondack region.

At Raquette Lake I met Mr. Durant, in whose boat my knapsack had gone off. I accosted him, and before I could make any inquiries he smiled and said, "I guess I know what you are going to say. Your knapsack is over at my camp. You can get it in two minutes." I found the camp a well-furnished summer residence, and the genial proprietor quite capable of keeping not only guides and boats, but also a neat little steam yacht. Money is a good thing—when one knows how to use it. I found the knapsack all right, to the last fishhook, and was more than glad to get it. When I had it well packed with blanket, shelter tent, hatchet, tinware, etc., I felt at home again and went over to Leavitt's on Forked Lake, bound down the Raquette River, and—just where the notion might take me.

At Leavitt's I found some guides whom I knew the previous season and got some useful notes and points on routes, carries, etc. Also met the justice of the peace who issued the warrant for Charles Parker,[57] the man who caused such a scandal in the Long Lake region last summer. I gave a summary of that unhappy affair in *Forest and Stream* last August, and it is pretty well understood now that it throws no stigma on the "guide class."

---

57  Charles Parker, a guide, allegedly attacked a female client in July of 1881. He was captured, then escaped, and was shot during his recapture; he died soon after of his wounds.

Forked Lake is one of the most beautiful sheets of water in the wilderness, and a healthy, delightful region for a summer camp, of which there are several on eligible points—well-furnished summer residences owned by men of taste, wealth, and leisure, who have the good sense to take their families to the forest for three months or more, rather than to such resorts as Long Branch, Newport, etc. It is possibly quite as expensive, but, I should say, worth the cost.

It was a most delightful morning in August. I got an early breakfast and launched out for Long Lake, intending to stop awhile with Mitchell Sabattis and investigate the fish question, of which I had heard a good deal in connection with this fine sheet of water. It is said that two guides who had been prosecuted for crusting deer stocked the lake with pickerel out of revenge and that the pickerel have exterminated the salmon trout. And now there are black bass in the lake, which, in turn, are demolishing the pickerel. Such is the tale as it was told to me.

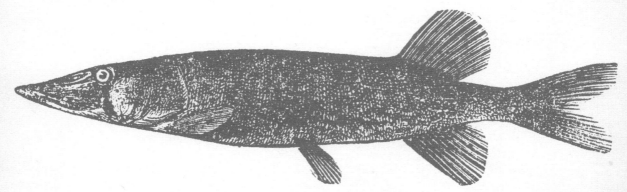

I doubt it. I do not believe that any freshwater fish can exterminate the agile, sharp-nosed pickerel. Though it is fair to add the testimony of Mr. E. Rose, who has a fine summer resort on Silver Lake, Susquehanna County, Pennsylvania, and is a lifelong sportsman. Pickerel were certainly plenty in that lake twelve years ago. The lake was stocked with smallmouth bass, and now he assures me the pickerel are gone. The bass have cleaned them out. Maybe. I dunno; I dunno. I cannot believe that the smallmouth whips the pickerel in fight. But he may starve him out.

From Leavitt's to the outlet of Forked Lake are four miles of as pretty water and scenery as a tourist could ask. If you are a canoeist, don't swing over to port for the sake of an open channel. Keep near the right shore, and when you open the course to the outlet, you may have a mile or so of heavy paddling among the lily pads, but you will cut off considerable distance, and the double blade works in lily pads, while oars tangle up. You will be interested, too, in seeing at every open space fair-sized fish drop away from the canoe, leaving a funnel-shaped swirl on the surface, and you will be puzzled, as I was, to name the fish. I am sorry I did not put the rod together and try them with the fly, but I promised myself to do that when I came back.

When you reach the landing at the outlet, take the double blade apart, turn the stems to the ends of the canoe, tie them fast, organize your duffel for the carry, and then spend an hour following along the bank and taking in the rapids, with the scenery on either side. If you have an eye for nature, the time will not be lost. The carry is one and a half miles, and a man who lives there will drag your canoe across for a dollar and a half. As you can carry it in thirty minutes more safely, you had better trust your own shoulders.

As you reach the foot of the carry, you launch again for an east trip of one and a half miles; another and a shorter carry, then a half mile by water, then a carry of one hundred rods, and you strike the head of Long Lake. It is four miles to the landing at Kellogg's and a little less to Mitchell Sabattis's landing. To make the latter, you turn to the right on sighting the bridge at Kellogg's and steer to the right end of the sandy beach before you. Take the steep path that leads up from the landing, and Auntie Sabattis will take care of you. She has been doing that sort of thing for a good many years. What the famous Indian guide, Mitchell Sabattis, is in the woods, his wife can supplement him as camp-keeper.

I found no tourists at the Sabattis house, but it was not lonely. Two married daughters, a son and his wife, with eight grandchildren pretty nearly of one size, made it quite lively for Grandma Sabattis. She managed the household well and kept the unruly youngsters in order to a degree that won my admiration. I was glad to meet the son, Ike Sabattis, whose acquaintance I had made in the summer of '80 and was sorry that Mitchell was away guiding.

I should have been pleased to meet Ike's suggestion that we go down Long Lake floating, but, alas, we were both on the sick list. Ike was suffering from a severe attack of cholera morbus, and I had been growing weaker every day since leaving the Forge House. I coughed almost incessantly and had sweating spells every night. I lost appetite. My knees jackknifed going over the shortest carries, and I began to realize that I might get laid by the heels in the middle of the wilderness, hundreds of miles away from home. I have little feeling for myself or any other man, as a sick patient. But no man can transcend possibilities, and, as it happens, sickness does come to us all, soon or late.

The muscular young guide, Ike Sabattis, was on his back. Two other young guides, Hall and Staunton, were far gone with consumption, the latter in a dying condition at the Long Lake settlement. All the same, I was ashamed of the physical weakness that steadily headed me off from day to day and did my best to beat it, but in vain. I kept my feet, however; fished, excursed in the woods, paddled down to Kellogg's every day and picked up all the information possible.

Not a day passed that I did not hear of a death in the Saranac region from consumption. Landlords and guides looked serious at these reports but did not dispute them. They said, "These people were past help when they came in. They should have stayed at home." Perhaps, but it does not go to prove that a residence in the North Woods is a cure for lung diseases.

It was on the sand beach in front of Kellogg's that I met a young invalid of the feminine persuasion who interested me more deeply than any human being had ever done on so short an acquaintance.

It was a perfect morning. The lake was like a mirror. I had paddled down without particular aim or object and was drawing the canoe up the beach when I noticed a little girl walking with cat-like tread up and down the shore and humming an opera catch[58] softly to herself.

---

58 Fragment

Suddenly she stepped up to the canoe, raised it by the stem, turned it to port and starboard, read the name, and said sharply, "Humph! 'Susan Nipper.' Dickens. 'Master Dombey is a permanency; Miss Edith is temporary.' Why don't you name her Miss Edith? She looks sufficiently temporary."

She was about the first one who had recognized the name, and I looked her over with more interest. Why, she was a woman! Hair and eyes like an Indian princess—weight and size like a girl of ten years. A thin, attenuated form, a bright glow in either cheek, and a sharp, intellectual expression, with the worn, womanly outlines, told the story. She pushed the canoe afloat, drew it back and forth, hauled it up on the beach, and said in a low, sad voice, "Oh, I should *so* like a ride in it—would you dare let me?"

"Dare? My dear young lady, can you trust yourself?"

"I am used to boats and water; we have a guide and a good boat," she answered, "but I would like to ride in this."

So I took the old handkerchief with its stuffing of hemlock browse and ferns that serves me for a seat, placed it well forward, made the shelter-tent and blanket into a comfortable lean-back in the bow, and seated her as I would an infant. Got in carefully myself, with the old grass coat between the keelson and the terminus of my spinal column and paddled cautiously up and down the shore in three feet of water to test her seagoing qualities. She was steady and immovable as a sandbag.

Then she said: "You see I am safe? Now cross the lake and land me in the woods."

I did. When we were more than halfway across, there came a loud *"halloo"* from the landing. She opened her large black eyes, waved her sailor hat, and settled back, saying, "It's my father. He will understand."

I landed her on the beach just where the firs and spruce were thickest, spread tent and blanket on a dry sunny spot, and left her to herself. For an hour she reclined on the improvised couch or gathered the trifling ferns and lichens of which young ladies are so fond, and then she said, quite as though I had been her guide, "Now take me back to my father. I am tired—so tired." So I landed her on the clean, white beach where *pater familias* was impatiently poking the sand with his gold-headed cane, and resigned my position as amateur guide. She held out her thin little hand at parting, saying, "I trust you will understand me? I am a dying girl. They let me do as I please now. I have left conventional fetters and forms behind, with a good deal more that I valued once—but no matter. Good-bye." Was there a little romance connected with her case, I wonder?

As the old gentleman seemed nervous, I thought it a good time to leave, and went up to the village to call on Ike Sabattis. Found him much better and disposed to go down the lake floating. Thought he could "put me on to a deer." But the man who is liable to a hard coughing spell at a minute's notice is more likely to scare three deer than to get a shot at one, so I declined and paddled around the point to the grove near Sabattis's landing, where I spent hours sitting on a log—a style of amusement in which I was fast becoming an adept—bidding fair[59] to rival "Old Phelps."[60] Indeed, it was getting to be my "best hold."

And here while listlessly watching the calm, clear water, I witnessed one of the little incidents that the lone tourist who knows the value of silence may often pick up. It was only a couple of little fish; a bullhead four or five inches long and a bass much smaller. The former was working his way laboriously along the beach, his nose at the surface and his rudder gone, while the bass was spitefully nipping him at the counter. It was evidently a hopeless case for the bullhead, and such a piece of uncalled for cussedness[61] on the part of the bass that, unthinkingly, I seized a stick of flood-trash and made a vicious clip at him. As often happens in this world, the innocent suffered while the guilty rascal "lit out" for deep water. May he grow to a four-pounder, to be worried and tormented along that same beach, with a sharp hook in his gills.

---

59  Seeming probable

60  A popular Adirondacks guide

61  Obstinacy or perversity

(The continuation of Nessmuk's narrative, detailing the further incidents of his story at Mitchell Sabattis's, forms a stirring story of Adirondack life. It is given below. —Editor, *Forest and Stream*)

# A Night Race Against Death

After dark, as I was smoking by Auntie Sabattis's gate, two brisk-stepping young guides came hurriedly by through the yard and made for the landing below the hill. They carried a sharp-stemmed Long-Laker and a lantern. They were bound on a night trip to Raquette Lake and return, to be back before sunrise, for young Staunton, the sick guide, lay dying, and his one wish was to see and know a favorite brother before crossing the Dark Carry. And the doctor had said that, if the brothers were to know each other again on earth, the meeting must take place before another sunrise.

It was rather a manly, plucky thing to make a night cruise of between thirty and forty miles, mostly in a fog, and with four carries, two stretches of rocky, tortuous current, and two lakes, all to be "doubled" in the darkness. The lantern would only be available on the carries. On water the course is better seen without it. I followed the guides to the landing and watched them with interest as, bending to oar and paddle, they disappeared swiftly into the darkness.

Then I went up to the house, consumed the time cutting up plug and smoking it, tried to feel at ease, but the dying guide and absent brother somehow got in on my nerves. I mentioned that I would like to know just how the sick man was getting on, if he was likely to pull through the night.

"You'll know," said Auntie Sabattis, "when anyone dies here, the bell is tolled as soon as anyone can get to it, night or day."

I went to my room. The night was very warm, and I was unwell and weak. I am not nervous. I have no sympathy or pity for nerves—my own or others'. But how the dread of that bell did worry me. I pictured to myself the guides racing over the course in the foggy summer night, going quickly over the slippery carries, one carrying the boat, the other lighting the path with glimmering lantern, rowing swiftly across long stretches of water by the shimmer and glitter of starlight, reaching the camp on an island in Raquette Lake, only to find George Staunton gone off, floating with his "party."

I thought of the "ride from Ghent to Aix,"[62] but that race was on horseback. The strain of muscle came heaviest on "Roland."[63] Here, the Roland was a cranky, narrow Long-Laker, and the muscle was of men. Would they win? I walked the room, smoked and listened. A stroke of that bell would have made me stagger like a drunken man. But it came not.

At midnight I turned in for a few hours of drowsy, feverish unrest, and at 3:00 a.m. I dressed and walked down to the landing, where I made a fire against the rock used as a washing station by the House of Sabattis, lighted a pipe, and resumed my favorite exercise of sitting on a log. The fog still hung over the lake, thick and dark.

Then came faint, dull streaks of light, gray and brown, from the east. It grew lighter; gray and brown turned to dull yellow. "Owl's Head" began to be

---

62  Referencing Robert Browning's poem "How They Brought the Good News from Ghent to Aix"
63  In Browning's poem, Roland is the horse that carries the narrator on the ride.

visible. The fog grew denser, brighter, and began to rise in well-defined lines from off the water, like the lifting of a blanket, and from under the blanket darted a sharp-stemmed regulation Long-Laker, the same oars and paddle playing with unabated vim, but with three men instead of two.

She came to the landing with a swift, silent rush, and before she was fairly still, an athletic young man sprang to the beach and took his way through the grove toward the settlement at a seven-knot gait. I had no need to ask if it were George Staunton. It was less than a half mile from the landing to where his brother lay dying.

Now, suppose, just as he came in sight of the house where his brother lay that the bell should give his nerves a trial with its first, fearful, death-announcing clang! Would he stagger some? Would he sort o' swerve off to port and sit down on a log, faint, and white and sick? It might be. It was painful. I took out my watch as he disappeared in the grove. I said, "He will be there in five minutes." The minutes passed. One guide said, "How long?" "Six minutes," I answered. "Six minutes is enough to get there," he said. I still held the watch. Ten minutes passed. "He is there," I said. "Has been there five minutes." Then the guides tied in oars, paddle, and seats, took up lantern and boat, and started for the little hamlet, called on the maps "Long Lake P.O."

I never did and never shall like the Long-Lakers. They are swift but frail, weak, cranky, and tiresome to ride in. Nevertheless, as the fagged[64] guides brushed past me, I instinctively raised my old felt hat to the craft that had run an all-night race against death—and won.

---

64 Exhausted

# Cruise of the *Nipper*, 4

## FOREST AND STREAM, APRIL 13, 1882

Whoever makes a lone cruise in a light canoe through the Adirondacks will be nearly certain to take in Long Lake. He can hardly avoid it. He will do well to give to it as much time and attention as he can afford. No one tourist can even approximately go over what I may call the Long Lake region in a three months' cruise. There are more than fifty snug nooks and camping spots on the shores of the lake proper. There are twelve small lakes and ponds easily reached by easy carries from the main lake. The quiet, shady, peaceful, lonely retreats that may be picked up and occupied by the way-wise tourist are beyond computation. It is true there is a settlement, a hotel, and a post office on the west shore of the lake. Also, a road. But an hour's paddling takes you quite away from civilization. You can choose your ground where to camp and be utterly alone for a month, or an entire season, if you choose.

Paddling across the lake from Kellogg's, one half mile brings you to the inlet of Clear Pond. About the mouth is grand fishing for pickerel. A little more than a half mile below is the mouth of Big Brook, also an excellent fishing ground for pickerel, and you may take the much despised but toothsome bullhead, or catty, in plenty. You may go up either of these streams, with a few carries, to Little Tupper Lake, going through Mud Pond, Little Slim and Slim Ponds, with Stoney Pond at last. And all the way you may select camping grounds that ought to more than satisfy any man who is seeking healthful rest and sylvan life.

I had formed an adverse opinion of Long Lake. I had thought it too civilized. Too many guides. Too much landlordism. Too much cost for the accommodations. Every day that I was on Long Lake, the hotel detailed employees to go around the village with guests, to quarter them in private houses. Why so few of them found quarters at the old and time-honored house of Sabattis was because the house of Sabattis was too prolific of young half-breeds. There were nine of them when I was there. One little blue-eyed fiend, as white as a Saxon, ran altogether to fight. He would pitch into his half brother—a fine, pleasant, bright-eyed half-breed—with teeth, nails, and fists, without a sign of provocation. I got tired of seeing it. I said to the strong, muscular, dusky, dark-eyed descendant of the house of Sabattis, "Cuff him up to a peak and knock the peak off." And he did it. Auntie Sabattis came around and I explained. She gathered a yearling plum sprout, and I hope the lacing that vicious little imp got then and there will last him awhile.

It was on a bright August morning that I paddled across the lake from Kellogg's, with a notion of going to Little Tupper, via Clear Pond, etc. I had heard all the guides' stories about the introduction of pickerel to Long Lake. How Lysander Hall and a guide by the name of Shaw had been prosecuted for crusting deer,[65] and in revenge, had brought pickerel from the "eastern side." If so—and I think it is—they "builded better than they knew." At that time the lake trout were almost a myth. Today I can take more pickerel and other toothsome fish than a camp of six hearty men can eat from day to day.

Now, my sporting friends, will you heed a little logic from the standpoint of fifty years' experience? You work eleven months in the twelve at desk or bench. All through the year you are looking to an outing; a chance to get away for one, two, or three weeks' vacation. You know, and I know, and we all know, that you need it and deserve it. But why in the name of all sense and reason should you boast of "bags" and "baskets"? About how much, on an average, do you require as animal food? Say, in twenty-four hours? If you kill more,

---

65  Immobilizing a deer by getting it to fall through the thin crust of ice that forms on top of deep snow after a rain, then using clubs to kill it

why and wherefore? The man who brags to me of "bags" and "baskets" just tempts me to "shoot him on the spot."

With my hand on my mouth, and my mouth in the dust,[66] I admit that I shot thirty-six deer in a season. I deserved to be hung for it. Again, in Eaton County, Michigan, I killed seventeen deer. With these exceptions, I have never killed more than ten or twelve yearly. And yet my conscience squirms. Why should I ever have killed a deer that I did not need for immediate use? Why, in the name of heaven, was I looking for market prices and quotations? Well, I was young. I knew no better. Today, the mother doe or the spotted fawn can pass me on a runway as safely as my own mother.

Last summer, among the duffie that I took into the North Woods, was my favorite single-barreled, hair-triggered rifle. With it I have driven the nail five times in succession at the distance of one hundred feet. At one hundred yards the deer would be lucky that got away from me with a standing shot. Now, when the season opened, I could have had an open standing shot any morning when I chose to seek it.

I took in just twelve bullets.

I brought the entire twelve home again. I did not load the rifle once last summer. There was no occasion. At Mr. Lamberton's camp, at Ed Arnold's, at the Pratt camp, at Sam Dunakin's, and other places, I could get a piece of venison when I needed it. What earthly excuse had I for sending a bullet crashing through the bones and quivering flesh of a bright-eyed, graceful denizen of the woods? And so the old rifle rests by the ingle-lug,[67] and I only take it out once a month to keep my shooting up in offhand practice, which is, after all, the only rifle practice worth talking about.

And just here and now I want to put in my oar on offhand shooting. Offhand

---

66  This phrase is likely a colloquial misquotation of two verses in the Bible, Job 40:4 and Lamentations 3:29.
67  Fireside

shooting is not done by sticking a hickory wiping rod in your left pocket, extending the other end, and gripping rod and barrel together to steady the hand. It is not done by twisting your body out of all grace and comeliness to get a "hiprest." It is done by taking a firm, free stand on both feet, drawing the rifle to a graceful and natural position, with both elbows free of the body, getting the best bead you can, and cutting loose at the right instant. That is offhand shooting. As for all rests, they are well enough in sighting a gun, but once sure that your sights are plumb center, take no more resting shots. It may be good civil engineering but is unworthy the notice of American riflemen. This is by way of digression.

At the mouth of Big Brook, I tried the pickerel, with light tackle and an eight-ounce rod. With a two-oared skiff and strong tackle I would have lain just inside the lily pads and cast outside into clear water. With a sixteen-pound canoe and a light trout rig, I thought it wiser to lie off about forty feet in clear water and cast toward the thick mass of lily pads, hoping to stop any fellow I might hook before he could get into a bad tangle among the lily stems. It worked very well at the start. A lively, bright-sided little fellow of a pound and a half took the lure handsomely, almost at the first cast, and got the canoe to the fringe of lily leaves that covered the water like a carpet before I could get him in. I laid off again and soon had the mate[68] to him. The sport was fine. I began to wake up. Paddling up a few rods, off the deepest part of the inlet, I began to cast with a bigger bait and deeper trolling.

And then and there I saw a huge pickerel driving straight at the lure and in the morning light showing distinctly as though lying on the beach. I might easily have jerked the hooks away and saved my rod, but I was in the humor for a racket, so let him snap his huge, sharky jaws over hooks, bait, and more than half the strong wire snell,[69] which he did, and turned with a heavy swirl for his mysterious cavern among the lily roots. I gave him the butt (I think that is the correct term), and the brave old rod took the form of a loop for a few seconds; then the top

---

68 Checkmate
69 The short line that connects the fishhook with the fishing line

joint broke down to a right angle, the canoe commenced a lively waltz into the lily pads, and the next minute I was sitting in the canoe holding a line in my hand that ran to the bottom—straight up and down—the broken rod dragging overboard, and a wrathy angler trying to raise a big pickerel by the hand-line dodge. It didn't work well. Somehow he seemed to have collateral security on the heavy toad-lily roots at the bottom. First he would creep slowly away with a yard or two of line; then I would as slowly get it back inch by inch. I gathered loose line, got a long bight, and passed it under a rib of the canoe, hauled taut and making all fast. Took in the old rod, filled a pipe, and made a "dead set" at patience.

Once, under similar conditions, I saved a twenty-two pound muskellunge in Highbank Lake, Michigan. I thought I might tire out this fellow, but he was not to be had. I spoke of light tackle. The rod was light, made by Heyling of Rochester. It was a beauty in '60; in '82 it may have been a little dull and dead. The line was the taper, waterproof, in common use at present. The wire snell and hooks had been tested at forty-four pounds. For two mortal hours I sat in that eggshell, trying all sorts of dodges to start my customer. Then my patience went by the board. I seized the line and got down on muscle. Something gave way. It was the line. What would he weigh? Perhaps twelve pounds, certainly more than eight. He weighed enough to wreck my tackle and rod.

I gathered and stowed the wreck of rod and line. I was not so very sorry. It was quite an experience and a partial excuse for backing down from a trip I was physically unfit for. I paddled across the placid lake to Kellogg's and asked for mail. There was none. I was glad of it. No news is good news. I had a set of tin dishes that I think can hardly be beaten. They were made without handles, or wire in the rims, nesting together, and filling all requirements of boiling, frying, and baking. The old shanty-tent, that had often sheltered me and a couple of friends through a rainy night, and only weighed four and one-quarter pounds, that could be put up in an emergency as quickly as I could cut a twelve-foot pole—this and these I gave away, reserving a single dish in which to make coffee.

Once, I would not have believed that I could pass "Owls Head" without ascending it to the uttermost peak. Now, I said, the view of a mountaintop from the bosom of a placid lake is much finer than a view of many lakes from the top of a cold, windy, cheerless mountain.

I was getting weak—demoralized, maybe. I paddled up Long Lake, took the carries slowly and wearily, and brought up at Leavitt's late in the afternoon of a model August day. Even as I went over the carries, Charles Parker, with his wife and boat, was lurking near the trail, and his nemesis, in the person of Warren Cole, was also on his very heels. When Parker launched his boat at the second carry, Cole was there and ordered a halt. Parker dodged behind his wife and tried to get off. Cole shot him. The public knows the rest.

Going up the carries, I was passed by two guides with their boats and parties. One of them carried a boat that struck me as being the best guide boat of the Long Lake model I had seen in the North Woods. It would carry three persons with baggage, was finished in oil and varnish, and weighed forty-eight pounds. Had it been put together with white cedar strips instead of pine, and oval, red elm ribs one and a half inches apart, instead of clumsy spruce knees six or seven inches apart, it would have been nearly perfection as a guide boat.

There was a crowd at Leavitt's, on Forked Lake, and, crossing Raquette Lake to Ed Bennett's, I found the hotel full to overflowing, the overflow finding sleeping quarters in open bark camps. It suited me. The table was excellent, as I have always found it. And an open camp with a fire in front is breezier, freer, healthier than any indoor arrangement for sleeping.

I preempted a corner of the "guides' camp," mended the old rod, and spent days paddling around the rocky shores of mainland and island, fly-fishing for bass. They nearly always rose to a red ibis or brown hackle, though here, in Pennsylvania, we can hardly coax the smallmouth to notice a fly. With us, he runs entirely to crayfish and dobsons.[70] I shall come to understand his various ways in various waters—about as soon as I solve the grouse problem.

---

70 Dobsonfly larva

It was on a bright morning in August that I let go and started for Third Lake, leaving my dunnage, save a light knapsack, to be taken charge of by "Slim Jim," who had gone across to the Saranac. The morning, the lake, the scenery, all would justify a younger man in a little enthusiastic description, and it was not altogether lost on me. Bass were jumping all along the rocky shores, a brace of hounds—although it was out of season—were sending the deer along the high ridge to the southward at a killing pace, and I met two guide boats with parties who had been out all night, floating. Each party had a deer, and I was pleased to see that they were both bucks. I reached Browns Tract Inlet before the west wind commences to blow—as it does about every fair day— and, going up that very crooked stream, again saw the disappearing fish among the lily pads, the same that had puzzled me before. But I was too weak and listless to try them without bait or fly.

Halfway up the inlet, I came near getting cut down by a seventeen-foot Long-Laker. She was coming down at a rapid rate, and just as I was rounding one of the numerous short bends, her sharp iron prow came in sight at steamboat speed, pointed directly at my midships. The old whaling instincts came to the surface at once. I yelled "starn-all," dropped the paddle, seized the cutwater[71] of the threatening boat, and held her off with all my strength. The guide behaved finely. At the first sound of my voice, he dipped his oars deep and backed for all the ash was worth. But she was a large boat, coming downstream under strong headway, with three men and baggage, and not to be stopped instantly. But her headway was deadened. She came on until her stem pressed heavily on the side of the frail canoe, bending it inward. I was pressed and crowded as a hare among marsh grass and bushy tangles of muddy vegetation; then she stopped, receded; the guide dipped his oars and dashed away. I was faint, but the canoe was safe. No word was spoken. But that guide has impressed me as a cool, capable fellow. Getting your canoe crushed in a lonely forest is quite as bad as being "put afoot" on the Western plains, through losing your bronco.

Though my entire load—canoe and knapsack—was less than twenty-six pounds, the carry from the inlet to Eighth Lake was trying, in my weak state.

Alvah Dunning had loaned me the key of his camp on the Eighth, and I rested there a couple of hours, taking a lunch from his stores and leaving the key hidden at the root of a stump as agreed on. The Eighth was a beauty on that bright, warm day. There was not a human being save myself about the lake. The water, lying as nature made it, was ruffled into breezy waves, capped with white. But for the quavering cry of a solitary loon and the gentle lapping of the water on the island shore, there was no sound, and the next relay would take me to Seventh and Sixth, with backwater and dead timber lines, decaying vegetation, nauseous smells, and all the curses that come of destroying forest lakes and streams for man's selfish greed. (N.B.[72] Does it ever occur to the average guide that he has a better moral right to explode a can

---

71 The point of the bow
72 *Nota bene*, Latin for "mark well"

of dynamite under one of these dams than a selfish monopolist has to poison the air that men, women, and helpless children are forced to breathe and drink?) To say nothing of the destruction of fish, the converting of a beautiful sheet of water into a scene of desolation that will last long after the porcine instigator has rotted in his grave, and his ill-gotten gains are scattered by his pampered worthless offspring. "The evil that men do lives after them."[73] As it ought.

Let me pass quickly over the desolate Seventh and Sixth. They were of course worse than when I cruised up the "Chain." The air at the foot of Sixth was sickening. One year before the Sixth would have been a pleasant location for an all-summer camp. At the foot of Sixth the gate was up, and a broad sheet of white, foamy water was rushing like an arrow toward the Fifth. Of course, this affected the five lower lakes.

I found the camp at the foot of Fifth lowered by the rush of water, for which I was sorry, for there was heavy thunder in an ominous-looking cloud in the southwest. But the distance is short between Fifth and the "Stormy Fourth," as Colvin calls it. And the outlet was rushing like a mill-tail. I jumped the canoe, and the only use I had for the paddle was in holding back and dodging dangerous obstructions.

In less than five minutes I was on Fourth Lake, and as I saw the black, whirling cloud and listened to the heavy, stunning peals, I thought it as well to put on a little extra muscle for the Pratt camp, half a mile below. As I rounded the point on which the camp is located, I saw Tom Jones and another gentleman— stranger to me—with Dick Cragoe, their guide, sitting on the porch watching the coming storm. Dick, in accordance with North Woods etiquette, came down to "land" me, and it struck him as a good idea to also house his own boat. And hardly had we made all snug when the tornado swooped down on the lake. It was sublime.

---

73  From William Shakespeare's play *Julius Caesar*

I have been in a white squall in the tropics, in a pampero off the Argentine coast, and have seen the terrific electric storms of the West. But I never saw so heavy a sea kicked up on an inland lake at such short notice. In two minutes the water was dashing up the sloping landing to the door of the boathouse; sharp, steep, white-crested waves were chasing each other like racehorses; the gale tore their spumy tops off and sent them whirling to leeward in a white mist of blinding spray; tall trees a century old were seized by the hair of the head and dashed to earth, while the zigzagging of lightning and the heavy bellowing of thunder were just the adjuncts to make the scene perfect. When the storm was at its fiercest, Dick Cragoe had his hands full to free, with mop and broom, the sitting room from water that drove in under the door.

In twenty minutes the storm had howled and whirled itself away to the northeast, the sun came out warm and mellow, the air was a delight, and the lake subsided to a placid, sleepy roll as quickly as it had risen.

It was a model evening for a cruise, and the Pratt camp organized for a thirteen-mile row down to the Forge House (foot of First Lake). I paddled out for Third Lake and was soon passed by the strong pull of Dick with his party. Fred Hess, another guide, came out from the Fifth, where in a thicket he had been dodging the storm. Two other guides, "Slim Jim" and Fred Rivett, overhauled me soon after. They, too, had been dodging under their boats in the wood between Fifth and Fourth Lakes. It was nearly dark when I halted at Ed Arnold's. His hostelry was crowded to its utmost, and his grounds were jubilant with lively parties and well-paid guides. It was pitch dark when I arrived at Perrie's on Third Lake. The camp was overrun with boarders, parties, and guides. There was not spare sleeping room for a cat. He assured me that he had been sleeping for a week on tables, chairs, trunks, any place where he could get a few hours' nightly rest. A. C. Buell, who owns the Third Lake House, had a newly made fragrant bark camp, and was alone. He invited me to stay with him during my sojourn on the lake and divide any sport or work that might turn up. As I like cooking and he detests it, we managed to make the arrangement very satisfactory.

For a few days I fished, frogged, cooked, picked berries, climbed hill, paddled, and doctored. All in vain. I grew weaker day by day. I was getting to the point where the grasshopper becomes a burden. I had sought the wilderness for health. I had lost instead of gaining. I had found many others with a similar record, and also many who claimed to have been decidedly benefited.

I had planned a cruise of 1,000 miles. The log showed 206, besides many short trips not noted. I was listless, easily tired, and slow to rest. I lacked strength and spirit for a respectable cruise. It was time to go home, and so on a bright August morning I paddled down to the Forge House, hung the canoe up in Barrett's boathouse, and the cruise of the *Nipper* was ended, for one season at least.

Perhaps at some time in the near future, I will have a word to say regarding the cost, healthfulness, and pleasure of a trip to the North Woods, as compared to [one] among the mountains of the Upper Susquehanna.

# OUR CAMPING GROUND

There is a spot where plumy pines
Overhang the sylvan banks of Otter,
Where pigeons feed among the vines
That hang above the limpid water.
There wood-ducks build in hollow trees,
And herns[74] among the matted sedges,
While, drifting on the summer breeze,
Float satin clouds with silver edges
'Tis there the blue jay hides her nest
In thickest shade of drooping beeches.
The fish-hawk, statue-like in rest,
Stands guard o'er glassy pools and reaches.
The trout beneath the grassy brink
Looks out for shipwrecked flies and midges.
The red deer comes in search of drink.
From laurel brake[75] and woodland ridges.
And on the stream a birch canoe
Floats like a freshly fallen feather—
A fairy thing, that will not do
For broader seas or stormy weather.
The sides no thicker than the shell
Of Ole Bull's Cremona fiddle[76]—
The man who rides it will do well

To part his scalplock[77] in the middle.
Beneath a hemlock grim and dark,
Where shrub and vine are intertwining,
Our shanty stands, well roofed with bark,
On which the cheerful blaze is shining.
The smoke ascends in spiral wreath.
With upward curve the sparks are trending,
The coffee kettle sings beneath
Where smoke and sparks and leaves
  are blending.
Upon the whole this life is well:
Our lines are cast in pleasant places.
And it is better not to dwell
On missing forms and vanished faces.
They have their rest beyond our bourn,[78]—
We miss the old familiar voices.
We will remember—will not mourn:
The heart is poor that ne'er rejoices.
We had our day of youth and May,
We may have grown a trifle sober;
But life may reach a wintry day.
And we are only in October.

---

74 Herons

75 A place overgrown with one type of plant

76 Sears is referring to a Stradivari violin named for its Norwegian owner, Ole Bull, and made in Cremona, Italy.

77 A lock of hair on an otherwise shaved head, a style practiced by warriors of some Native American tribes

78 Boundary

# CRUISE OF THE
# SAIRY GAMP

**FOREST AND STREAM, JUNE 28, 1883**

O H, THE BEAUTIES AND DELIGHTS OF RURAL surroundings. The cheerful awakening from sound, healthful slumber. For instance, the time is about 4:00 a.m., or a little before. Dick, the gamecock, having gone to roost at sundown, suddenly awakens to a sense of his responsibility as boss of the entire premises and sends out a clarion note that may be heard one mile away. Nine female geese and one old gander at once respond, with outstretched necks and voices shrill and deep. Three guinea hens, with their Brigham, take up the cry. The old peacock gets on his wings, sails up to the peak of the barn, and lets go to the bottom of his lungs. A flock of ducks starts up suddenly and waddles off to the creek with much noisy quacking. Four mild-eyed, deer-faced Alderney cows commence a musical bellowing from the paddock on the flat by the creek; four fawn-like calves answer with responsive bleatings from the calf-pasture above.

It is not yet 5:00 a.m., and the thrush, the robin, the song sparrow, the phoebe bird, the catbird, the peewee, the chewink, the blue jay, and the vireo are making the whole business very musical.

How about the awakening of a summer morning in New York? I am not so certain. I have tried both sides. I prefer the donkey engine to the guinea hen; the steam whistle to the peacock. The rattle and roar of the wakening city is hardly more disturbing to nerves than the racket of a farmyard. I know something better.

> *I know a spot where plumy pines*
> *O'erhang the verdant banks of Otter,*
> *Where wood-ducks build among the vines,*
> *That bend above the crystal water.*
> *'Tis there the bluejay makes her nest,*
> *In thickest shade of water beeches;*
> *The fish-hawk, statuesque in rest,*
> *Keeps guard o'er glassy pools and reaches.*

Well, I am "going through the wilderness." The *Sairy Gamp* meets me at Boonville the first week in July. The *Sairy* weighs ten and one-half pounds. I noticed since I commenced writing about light canoes in *Forest and Stream*, several makers have discovered that a ten-pound canoe will carry a light canoeist and his duffel. Have they ever seen it done? Have they placed a few ten-pound canoes in the hands of skilled canoeists for lone, independent cruises in the North Woods and other glorious lake-dotted forests? Am I to meet one of them here and there, go into camp with him, divide the last ounce of provisions, and then paddle in company with him over the blessed clear waters, and over the inlets, outlets, etc.? I guess not. There is no ten, eleven, or twelve-pound cedar canoe afloat this season with a live man in her.

I think a sixteen-pound canoe would be safer and more comfortable. All the same, she is bound to go through. Maybe she will do better than her maker thinks. Possibly he has built better than he knew. There is a possibility that I may turn out to be an old gray-headed expert in light canoeing. Maybe I have been there. Perhaps I have paddled a kayak, the most ticklish boat that ever floated a man. And I may get drowned. I shall certainly take in some ducklings.

August 8, 1883

Dear *Forest and Stream*:

I am here at the First Lake of the Fulton Chain (July 20), however
I came.

Have paddled the *Sairy Gamp* on the four first lakes until my arms
are lame. Sitting in her this afternoon I took in six fine trout. She
yields to the rush of a thirteen-inch speckle like a split bamboo.
For a 10 ½ pound canoe she is a marvel of steadiness. I ride her
in pretty rough water without a wiggle. I shall try no lighter one,
however. She makes a good sideshow wherever she appears, but
a larger canoe would be more comfortable; say eighteen pound.
However, she carries me well.

I cannot be with you on the occasion of the tenth anniversary of
*Forest and Stream*. Not in the flesh, but in the spirit, I will be there.
Most likely when that little event comes off I shall be under the
hemlocks, or on (perhaps under) a forest lake. I shall be sorry to
miss seeing you. I shall be glad to miss the blistering, seething city.

You meet my views handsomely. Since the days of *Porter's Spirit of
the Times*, I have not written for any paper or magazine with which
I seemed to be so fairly en rapport as with *Forest and Stream*. You
strike the men at home that I strike on lake, river, carry, outlet,
and inlet; that I meet in the deep woods, under the hemlocks,
on the loneliest routes, in forest camps. Occasionally I meet a

man like Capt. Beardslce ("Piseco") who hails me as a "*Forest and Stream* man." Then we sit up and hold street converse until the "wee short hour ayont the twal."[79]

It is wonderful, how the average outer can spend so much money for such meager returns in sport and recreation. The heavy loads of useless *impedimente* with which he fatigues himself, are past understanding. I always sympathize with him. He is liberal, genial, and always willing to pay two prices for what he requires, and he is mostly swindled. He pays his money but has no choice.

The mosquitoes, black flies, and punkies deplete his arterial circulation; landlords, guides, and buckboarders deplete his pockets. He only asks a good time for his brief outing. He is more than willing to pay for it. He is safe to pay. The good time is not so certain as it should be. But I'll write more when I have more time. Am driven just now with fishing.

---

79  From Robert Burns's poem "Death and Doctor Hornbook"; *ayont the twal* translates as "beyond the twelve."

## Raquette Lake, July 27

Thus far the *Sairy Gamp* has brought me in safety, and without wetting me once. The *Sairy*, I may remark, is a Rushton canoe, weighing just ten and one-half pounds.

And it is not that I may boast of cruising the lightest canoe ever built of cedar, that I paddle such an eggshell by river and lake through the Northern Wilderness. Not for the cheap notoriety that leads a man to tempt the ocean in a dory. But I have been testing light canoes for years, and my experiences may be of some value to the future canoeist who contemplates a lone cruise with the double blade.

We, the "outers," who go to the blessed woods for rest and recreation, are prone to handicap our pleasures in the matter of overweight; guns, rods, duffel, boats, etc. We take a deal of stuff to the woods, only to wish we had left it at home, and end our trips by leaving dead loads of impedimenta in deserted camps.

I should be glad to see this amended. I hope at no distant day to meet independent canoeists, with canoes weighing twenty pounds or less, at every turn in the wilderness, and with no more duffel than is absolutely necessary.

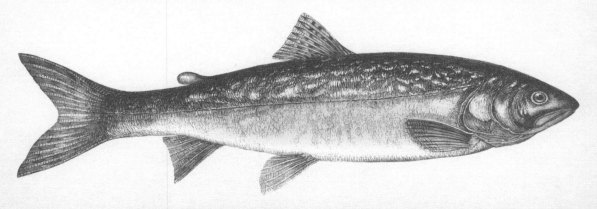

I met the *Sairy* at Boonville; also my old friend, Si Holliday, who contracted to land her at Moose River without a scratch, and he did it, though he came within an ace of capsizing. At Moose River I stayed several days, fishing for brook trout, testing and practicing canoe and paddle, likewise trying to brace up weak muscle, which sadly needed it.

I found the canoe much stauncher and steadier than I had been led to expect. Her maker had warned me that he would not warrant her for an hour. "She may go to pieces like an eggshell," he said. He had tested her with his own weight (110 pounds), and she closed in at gunwales an inch or more. He advised bracing her, and he thought with me and my duffel aboard she would only be two or two and a half inches out of water at center. "He builded better than he knew." She does not close in perceptibly at gunwales, and she has full five inches rise above water when on a cruise, with her skipper and light cargo properly stowed.

The only part of the cruise to be dreaded was the thirteen and one-half miles of muddy rock trail between Moose River and the Forge House, called the "Browns Tract Road." I dared not trust her on the buckboards, and I hardly felt like making such a carry at the start, but I did it. I started before 5:00 a.m. and made the first three miles bravely. Began to weaken a little. Got some breakfast and went on. At the "six-mile tree" felt beaten. Buckboard came along with party. Party got out to lift and admire canoe. Driver said if I would leave my knapsack at the tree he would fetch it in on his return. Left it gladly.

Went on and got caught in drenching thunderstorm. Crept under canoe until it passed over. Road a muddy ditch. At the "eight-mile tree" caught another and harder storm. Kept sulkily on, too mad and demoralized to dodge under canoe. Arrived at "ten-mile tree" pretty much tired and stopped (4:00 p.m.) to get some tea and lunch. Felt it to be the hardest carry I had ever made and wished I had gone in by Jones's camp and the Stillwater of Moose River, as I had always done on previous trips.

Just then along came Ned Ball, a muscular young guide, and though he had four hounds in charge, he volunteered to hoist the canoe on his head and carry it in. "It don't weigh more'n a stovepipe hat," he said.

The last three and one-half miles of road were much better, and at 8:00 p.m. I arrived at the Forge House wet, bruised, and looking like an ill-used tramp. Some dry woolens, much too large, with a bright fire in front of the hotel, a night's rest, and a good breakfast brought me around and "paradise, reached through purgatory," was attained. Paradise meaning Browns Tract, and purgatory, the twenty-five and one-half miles of wretched road between Boonville and the Forge House. That is how the admirers of Browns Tract put it.

And the *Sairy* was safe on the lakes at last, without check or scratch. I paddled her about the first four lakes of the chain. Practiced getting into and out of her in difficult places and best of all, caught all the speckled trout I wanted, sitting in her at the spring holes. This mode of fishing I pronounce the culmination of piscatorial sport. With a one-pound trout on the hook, it was not necessary to yield more than a yard or two of line at the start, and then play the fish to a standstill by the easy movement of the canoe, reeling up to about ten feet of line, leading the fish about as one pleased, and let him tow the canoe until he turned on his side utterly exhausted, and refusing to raise a pectoral in defense of his life. Then gaff him by sticking a thumb in his open mouth and taking him in.

I had a very fair amount of this kind of sport and came to have a deal of confidence in the *Sairy* as I learned her light but reliable ways. I visited the camps, picked up old acquaintances, was fed daily on trout, got up better muscle, and, best of all, gained health with every day's exercise and sport. I found new camps on all the lakes, while the old camps were enlarged or improved, and fishing, I am pleased to say, much better than when I was here two years ago. This may be owing to restocking the lakes and streams. At any rate, I have seen thrice as many trout during a little more than two weeks' stay in the woods as I saw in twice the time two years ago.

In spite of the exceptionally cold, wet summer, sportsmen and healthseekers are enjoying the woods most satisfactorily. With at least five out of every six

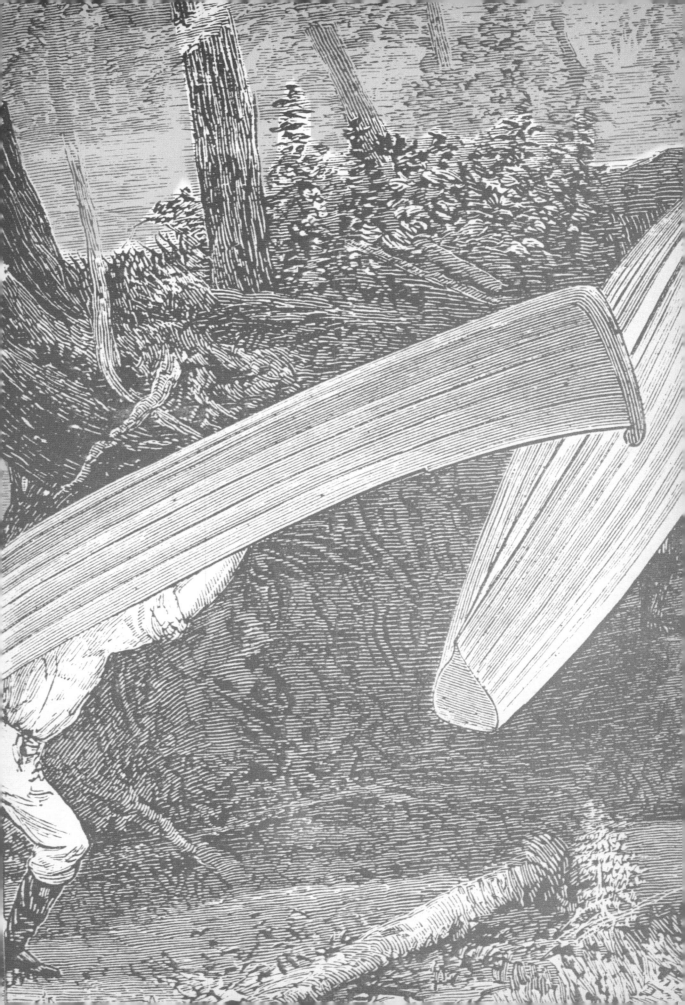

who come to this region for health, the improvement is decided and speedy. I have personal knowledge of some cases that seem almost marvelous, but there is a case here and there, mostly asthmatic, with which the cool, damp air does not agree. I know of two such cases. But I have conversed with a score who have gained in health to an extent that exceeded their most sanguine expectations.

There is some complaint about the winged things that bite and sting. Black flies were bad early in the season, and mosquitoes, as well as punkies, were never hungrier or plentier. To the man who prepares himself for the North Woods by getting up a pelt like a cellar-grown potato sprout and then runs a clipper over his head to give the insects a fair chance, no doubt they are a constant torment, especially if he is too aesthetic to use his fly medicine copiously, or so cleanly as to wash it off every day.

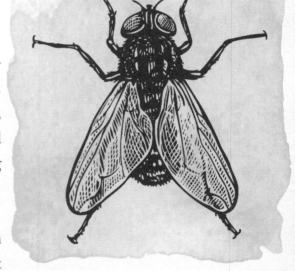

As for myself—even on Browns Inlet— they pass me by as if I were a hot griddle. On starting in, I established a good, substantial glaze, which I am not fool enough to destroy by any weak leaning to soap and towels.

I once published the recipe for insects in *Forest and Stream* but will close by giving it once more. It is as follows: three ounces pure tar, two ounces castor oil, one ounce oil pennyroyal.[80] Simmer together thoroughly, apply copiously, and don't fool with soap and water till you are out of the woods.

---

80  A type of mint

# Cruise of the *Sairy Gamp*, 3

*FOREST AND STREAM*, AUGUST 16, 1883

Having loafed about Moose River for a week and spent another week loitering, fishing, and paddling about the Fulton Chain, it struck me that, if the little canoe was to carry me on a cruise to the other side, it was time she was about it. I had several excuses for such utter laziness. I said the weather was too stormy, too "catching" for a start through the woods in a boat where a man can carry no change of clothes save an extra blue shirt and a pair of socks.

Moreover, I had met with an accident on the Browns Tract Road that made my port deadlight look as though I had been in a "fight mit table legs" at "Hans Breitman's Barty";[81] looking like a tramp with a black eye, I disliked to introduce the *Sairy* among strangers. Again, there was good fishing, good fare, and plenty of deer about the Fulton Chain. True, we might not shoot the deer just yet. But it looked wholesome and woodsy to see them come down in broad daylight and feed fearlessly within sixty rods of the hotel, while the ladies waved their handkerchiefs, and the party chatted in tones that must have been very audible to sharp, cervine ears. I shall not soon forget one brave old fellow who came down to the water's edge, raised his antlered front boldly, calmly surveyed the party at the hotel, and then resumed his feed among the lilies. "The old rascal knows it's close time," remarked a guide. "He won't be quite so tame after the first of August."

But there came a bright, clear afternoon, with good promise of one clear day, and the next morning the *Sairy* was making good time up the inlet of Fourth Lake.

The little Fifth, containing only nine acres, but good for floating and frogging, was run over in a few minutes, and then came the first carry, only three-

---

81  Referring to Charles Godfrey Leland's poem "Hans Breitmann's Barty"

quarters of a mile, but a muddy landing, and, like all carries, including "taking out" and "tieing in."

The Sixth Lake is made a desolation by the dam at its foot. The large, desolate rock on the left as you paddle up looks the more dreary for the dead timber at its base, and the inlet that leads to Seventh is a dismal swamp.

The trees around the once bright shores of the Seventh were dying when I was there two years ago. They are dead enough now. But the open camp, fifty rods to the left, is still there, and I turned to it for rest and a lunch. And as my newly made fire sent up its smoke, there came a succession of rifle shots from the opposite side of the lake, a mile away, as of those who go through the wilderness wasting cartridges with poor aim and no object.

Then a boat pulled out and came swiftly to my camp. I had met the two occupants before. They reported that "Slim Jim" (James P. Fifield) was on the opposite side with a bark camp and a "party." He would like to see me. Now, Jim had been very friendly to me on previous visits to the woods, and I could not go by. So I paddled over for a handshake and an hour's chat. The time passed too quickly, and by the time I got back, made some tea, and got packed up, it was nearly 3:00 p.m.

There were two carries (one of a mile, the other a mile and a half) with nine miles of water between me and my destination on the Raquette, and it was time to move. Over the desolate Seventh, up the drowned-out inlet, tie in, and over the carry to the Eighth and last lake of the chain. Here is a lake to admire and camp. No dam has backed up the water here. The bright green shores are as nature made them. Dunning's lone island is still a sylvan, restful emerald set in peaceful waters, and, by the way, Dunning was not at home, and as I couldn't burgle into his camp, I thought it as well to play the paddle, for there is no landing on Browns Tract Inlet, and if, at the mouth, it should happen to get backed in by rough water on Raquette, it would be most unpleasant.

So I hurried over the lake, took a short rest by the spring on the right, tied in, and went for the inlet on time. In thirty minutes I was afloat, and in an hour and ten minutes more was at the mouth. Luckily there was little wind—just the rolling swell a canoeist loves—and I turned down the shore of South Bay for a leisurely two-mile pull to the new camp of Joe Whitney, longtime guide, trapper, and hunter, though being crippled in his best arm.

When he saw the tiny canoe and found I was cruising through the wilderness alone, I think his old hunter's heart went out to me. He welcomed me like a brother and got me up a supper consisting mainly of crisp trout, with fresh bread and butter, and powerful tea. If there was anything more, I did not need it and have forgotten. There is a sort of freemasonry among woodsmen that only woodsmen know. Joe and I had heard something of each other—not much; it took us about five minutes to get acquainted. In two hours we were thick as thieves.

While he was caring for the supper duffel, I was building a rousing fire before the camp. Both understood by instinct that no lamps or indoor arrangements were in order, and we squatted around the fire until "deep on the night," swapping forest yarns and hunting adventures. Then Joe showed me a bed, springy, fresh and clean, whereon I slept sweetly, but awoke in time to take in a glorious sunrise on scenery that I shall not disgrace by attempting to describe. It was all the more welcome in that sunrises during the summer of 1883 have been mostly inferential. I half felt that on such a morning I ought to strike out and make Long Lake before night. But the day and the scenery were so delightful, the camp was so quiet, so restful, and the air so dry, so redolent of balsam and pine, that I let the hours go by, and the day wane in utter rest and indolence. What though? May there not come one glorious day in the weary year when we may cast aside every grief and every separate care and invite the soul to a day of rest? And in the future, when the days of trouble come, as they will come, I shall remember that grand day of rest, and the abundance of trout and bass wherewith I was comforted.

A finer, brighter morning never dawned on the clear waters of Raquette Lake than the one on which I paddled out from the fragrant, balsam-breathing camp of honest Joe Whitney for a new-made private camp on a point near Ed Bennett's, where I laid off while an enthusiastic young photographer took the *Sairy* in different positions, with and without her crew.

Then, by invitation, I went over the camp as amateur inspector, and although I have inspected dozens of these woodland residences called camps—all of them inviting and redolent of balsam and pine—I have seen none in more perfect sylvan taste than Camp Dick. I never feel the lack of wealth so sadly as when visiting these private camps, where, with a camp costing several thousand dollars, all in the way of food and drink that one can ask, two or three guides at $3 each per day, good fishing and hunting, the best of air and sweet sleep by night, one may dream away the hot summer solstice without ache, pain, or care.

"And it is not so very costly," said one of the fortunate ones, "not so expensive as the watering places. I bring my family here during the summer months and

get out of it for about $3,000 the season." Yes, it is cheap—for a millionaire. But it would break some of us to run such a camp for a single week. Fortunately, the woods are free, and we can make our own camps.

I stopped at Ed Bennett's Under the Hemlocks and then paddled slowly over to the Raquette House, kept by Ike Kenwell, and well kept, too. The selection of this hotel site was judicious. It stands—the hotel—on a dry breezy point of land jutting out into the lake, and it is always cool in the hottest weather. The house is well furnished, the table good, and the open bark camp with its fragrant bed of browse and rousing fire in front at night is a delightful woodland affair that should always be a part of the wilderness hotel. The best bass fishing on the lake is in easy reach of the landing.

Just at night I went down to the Forked Lake landing and carried over to the Forked Lake House, where I had a good supper and watched a couple of guides organize their boat and jack for floating,[82] though the close season had

---

82  Hunting deer

not expired. They were out nearly all night, and if they got a deer they kept their own. On the next night, however, a couple of guides went out and got a yearling buck. "It was so near the open season," they said, "what odds did it make if the deer were killed on Monday instead of Wednesday? The boarders were wild for venison." I think they were not so far wrong.

The second morning was clear (the previous day had been stormy) and I pulled out for the foot of Forked Lake, where I found Bill Cross, engaged as of old in hauling boats across the mile-and-a-half carry. He took my knapsack over the carry out of good nature, and I paddled leisurely down the river, and down Long Lake to the newly made Grove House, kept by Dave Helms. Dave is a well-known Long Lake guide, who, having got a little ahead, and well knowing the requirements of tourists and sportsmen, concluded to give up guiding and take the chances of keeping a woodland resort. And he does more than well. "And it will be colder than it is now if I get left on venison after the first of August," says Dave.

It is at these less pretentious houses where the landlords have mostly been guides that I find the best fare and most sport when I care to fish or hunt.

And I write this gossipy letter because I am laying off for the subsidence of a strong N. W. wind and rain. For I am not going to cruise the longest lake in the wilderness with wind and rain abeam. The *Sairy* is too light of tonnage for much extra clothing. A spare blue shirt and a pair of socks for change are all the clothing that goes on her manifest.[83]

---

83  A list of cargo

# Cruise of the *Sairy Gamp*, 4

## *FOREST AND STREAM*, AUGUST 23, 1883

Just for one day the rain held up, and a brighter morning never dawned on Raquette Lake than the one on which I paddled out for a cruise across the lake. The water was like a mirror, the air was perfect. It was a day to be marked with a white pebble.[84] I had several invitations to visit private camps, and I availed myself of them pretty largely. I found several of these camps most delightful; gotten up with the utmost care and in excellent sylvan taste. I had occasion to note that venison and trout were always forthcoming, in moderation, though the close season for deer was not quite over.

But a game constable whom I interviewed rather had the idea to my notion. He said, "I ain't here to spoil sport, but to save the deer and help sportsmen to a good time. If I catch a man slaughterin' or crustin', I'll make it red-hot for him. But if I meet one of the boys with a party who has been two or three days on the side lakes and ponds floatin', I ain't goin' through their pack-baskets." Few sportsmen kill deer enough to hurt the increase of deer. Most of the breechloaders brought into the wilderness never perforate anything more sensitive than an empty tin can. But, if there were no deer, and no fishing, how many would come to the Northern Wilderness?

And on the glorious day above mentioned, I had a taste of genuine, healthy, woodland pleasure. For once it did not rain, and I was dry—no small item for a man who runs too light for even a change of clothes, beyond a blue woolen shirt and a pair of yarn socks.

I left the Raquette for Forked Lake, and the demon of storms resumed his sway once more. I was detained by bad weather again at Fletcher's, the only

---

84  An allusion to the ancient Roman practice of marking prosperous days with a white stone on the calendar

compensation being a full supply of venison and the best of black bass. The latter have become more abundant, both in Forked and Raquette Lakes, and the pure, cold water assures the quality.

On the first morning when it did not rain, I got an early start down the lake and the Raquette River for Long Lake, via the rapids and Buttermilk Falls— since Adirondack Murray's book, called Phantom Falls. And, as on a previous occasion, I spent an hour watching the dashing, foaming water and footing up the utter impossibility of any man or boat ever tumbling over those ragged boulders and coming out anything but corpse and kindling wood.

I made the river and the three carries, sighting one deer and chasing a flock of ducks for a mile. The deer walked leisurely off. The ducks kept just ahead for a while, and finally huddled into a little cove and let me pass them within thirty yards. I carry no breechloader through the woods. My only weapon is a jackknife, and that not loaded. Deer and ducks were safe from me.

A mile below the last carry I turned in to land at the new camp of Dave Helms, erst[85] guide, and now landlord of a most pleasant camp or hotel (all the moderate-sized hotels are camps here). I found his site beautifully chosen, on a piney, breezy, sandy point, high, dry, and healthy, his charges very moderate, and, no slight item, good hunting and fishing in easy reach. Parties came across the woods from Blue Mountain, complaining that charges were high, no fishing or hunting; nothing to do but loaf around the stylish hotels or row on Blue Mountain Lake. I recommended them to try a week or two with Dave.

When a morning came that promised well, I once more paddled out, my destination being the Platt camp, three miles from the foot of Long Lake. This time I had a pleasant breeze and no rain, the wind being dead aft, a most desirable thing with a double blade. I found Senator Platt in camp, and a pleasant visit, fish, venison with open bark camp, and huge log fire in front go far to compensate for the almost daily soakings I have caught since leaving the Forge House.

---

85 Former

I ought to mention that Helms's camp is only twenty-five rods from the house of John Plumley, "Honest John," Murray's guide for several seasons.

It goes without saying that I made his acquaintance and asked him some leading questions concerning his work as Murray's guide. He said, "Murray was a good woodsman. He came in with his wife and guided himself sometimes. He could take his boat over the carries as well as I could. The big trout? Oh, yes. He caught a good many large trout. The one he caught in his 'Nameless Creek' was not the largest I saw him take. He was a capital hand with the flyrod. His 'Nameless Creek' was the inlet of Shallow Lake. It was just boiling with jumping trout that evening. As to his shooting Buttermilk Falls, any fool who takes one look at the falls knows better. But we both did run the rapids, both the upper and lower. It is a little risky, but is often done. Sometimes a man leaves all but his seats and oars, but I never broke up a boat there. I don't think Murray meant to say that he ever ran the falls. Yes, I am on the guide list yet. Have got a party as soon as I can get my hay in."

And so much for honest John Plumley, one of the experienced guides who can paddle you up to a deer by night or put you on to a spring hole where big trout abound, with the best.

On leaving the Platt camp, my good luck on weather deserted me. It was ten and a half miles to go by lake, river, and carry to Mother Johnson's. The last three miles were made in a soaking rain that left me without a dry thread. The next morning, being once more dried out, I swung out in the little *Sairy* for a seven-mile paddle down the Raquette and up Stony Creek Ponds to the Hiawatha House (Dukett's). For once I had dry weather and a pleasant trip, though the wind was high. After dinner I carried over to Corey's (three-quarters of a mile) and spent the afternoon examining some models of Adirondack boats, interviewing guides, boat builders, etc., and looking over the Upper Saranac, which looked altogether too rough for the *Sairy*. So I decided for once to relieve tired muscles by a ten-mile ride on the little steamer that navigates the lake.

I had already paddled more than the distance from side to side of the wilderness, and if it looked like dodging to avoid water on which the canoe could not live, so be it.

Paul Smith's, Adirondacks.

# Cruise of the *Sairy Gamp*, 5

## *FOREST AND STREAM*, SEPTEMBER 13, 1883

The little steamer that plies on the Upper Saranac makes the different landings in a zigzag manner that knocks the compass points endwise. Only by staying where you can watch every turn of the prow can you retain a definite notion of north and south. And that is how it happened that, being unobservant of turns, I found the sun setting in the east—a vexatious thing to a woodsman. Missing one of the turns of the boat, I was turned myself. I straightened myself out by shutting both eyes and letting a muscular guide whirl me around half a dozen times promiscuously,[86] then setting the compass without looking at the sun; then, being right on the cardinal points, I took a general average of the landscape. This brought me right.

Bartlett's Landing is a ten minutes' easy walk from the hotel. The house was well filled with boarders, and when the captain of the steamer got a little enthusiastic in describing the little canoe, nearly the entire force of the house, eager for any novelty, turned out to take a look at her. I think that not less than fifty people had a turn at lifting her. Then they wanted to see her go. So I took off boots and coat, got in, and paddled out into the lake, where there was a swell that made her dance like a cork. Then down the lake, with a whole sail breeze[87] after us, bright weather, and the principal mountain peaks in sight all the way. Very pleasant, but it came to an end.

A night at the Prospect House, and a most exasperating draw across a muddy carry of four miles, where I hung on to the canoe until my arms were numb, and I launched on Big Clear Pond, only to get caught in an ugly squall and drenching rain once more. I paddled up to honest Joe Baker's

---

86 *Promiscuously* can mean "casually" or "confusedly."

87 A common light wind

camp, wet to the skin, and got a privilege by the cookstove, which I held until bedtime.

The next day brought a steady, persistent, all-day rain, tiresome to a degree. I relieved the tedium by playing the mouth organ for Joe's children, talking to anybody who would listen, and baking my mouth with five-cent cigars. Monday, the 6th, was clear and cold. I hired Joe to take myself and canoe across the two-mile carry on a one-horse wagon, and found it the roughest, muddiest carry I had yet encountered.

Crossed the Upper St. Regis Lake to Spitfire Pond, where, for the first time, I was driven ashore by a sharp sea and a flawy wind[88] that bade fair to catch under the canoe and capsize her. I crept through the brush along shore until I reached the outlet, paddled to the Lower St. Regis, where I was again beaten off, and landed on Captain Peter's Rock in front of the hotel, where, less than half a mile off, I could see conviviality and comfort and pleasant verandas where couples were promenading and children playing about the grounds of Paul Smith's noted woodland resort.

And I was hungry and likewise thirsty. If there be creature comforts anywhere in the woods, they may be found at Paul Smith's. But there was a white-crested, topping sea between me and the comforts aforesaid. Even the stiffest guide boats shunned the rough sea from Peter's Rock to the outlet, and kept along the smoother windward shore. So I amused myself by putting a board shanty that stands on the rocky point in order, picking blueberries, cutting wild grass, and making believe I was going to camp all night within one hundred and fifty rods of a first-class hotel.

It was, on the whole, very enjoyable. The weather, barring the heavy wind, was dry and bright. I sat on the warm, mossy rock and recalled all the wild forest yarns I had heard of Cap'n Peter. I half hoped that the wind would rise

88 Brief and unexpected gusts

to a gale and hold me there all night. Once I got up my sand,[89] I "tied in" and made a straight wake for the hotel. Ten rods out a black flaw caught the *Sairy* at the garboard streak[90] and nearly lifted her over. I watched for a "smooth," turned her, and struck out again for Cap'n Peter's Rock.

Late in the afternoon, when the wind had subsided somewhat, a strong boat with two guides in her came over purposely to give me a lift "across the stormy water." At first I demurred. I would paddle over when the wind fell a little. I could "make the riffle," etc. But they said there were parties at the hotel who

89  Resolve
90  The plank at the bottom of the hull

were anxious to see the little canoe and the little old woodsman who had paddled and carried her over 118 miles. So I weakened and allowed myself to be taken in tow.

Luckily, Paul Smith happened to know me—by reputation—and he met me cordially. Grand old woodsman he is. Once a guide, and a good one. Now, the most successful landlord in the Northern Wilderness. Not so old as one who has followed the writers of the North Woods would infer. Only fifty-six, and well preserved. I am glad to have met him. More than glad to have crossed from side to side of this region without its parallel on the globed earth.

On the 12th of this month, Verplanck Colvin meets a commission at Blue Mountain to report on the expediency of preserving this grand region as a state park. May their counsels be guided by good common sense and humanitarian principles, and no politics, logrolling, or hippodroming[91] allowed the slightest consideration.

Paul Smith's, August, 1883.

---

91 Holding a race with a predetermined outcome that benefits bettors

## Little Tupper Lake, August 12

I date from Little Tupper Lake, and a finer lake it would be hard to find. No desolate lines of drowned out lands here. All as it came from the hands of nature. Have been out this morning deer hunting, so to speak. Laid off for four mortal hours waiting for a deer to attempt the crossing of Dukett's Bay. No deer came. But there came a loon, and he settled within ten rods of the canoe, raised himself on hind legs (they are very hind, and he has no others), turned his white, clean breast to me, and gave me his best weird, strange song. Clearer than a clarion, sweeter than a flute, loud enough to be heard for miles.

Never, as my soul lives, will I draw a bead on a loon. He is the very spirit of the wildwoods. Fisherman he may be. He catches his daily food after his nature. He is no trout crank. He does not catch trout at fifty cents per pound for the hotels. Don't, please don't, emulate Adirondack Murray and waste two dozen cartridges in the attempt to demolish a loon.

Every sportsman who enters the office of Paul Smith's hotel will notice the neat, well-mounted buck's head at the right, as one goes in. The head and horns are in nowise[92] remarkable. The horns are only four points to the side. I have saved a score of better heads myself. But the head is flanked on either side by an immense speckled trout. Paul Smith gave me this account of them. He said: "Mr. Hotchkiss and his partner, of New Haven, went out fishing on Big Clear Pond. Mr. Hotchkiss hooked the biggest trout, and saved him. They had a lot more, weighing from one to three pounds. I said, what are you going to do with these big trout? Give them to me and I will have them mounted. They did. I sent them to Bell, of New York, and he sent them back, as you see, with a bill for $43. I don't regret it. I have been offered $100 for them."

The success of the St. Regis is as nothing to me. But the grand old woodsman. The man who fell in love with the little canoe; who gave me points on the return trip; who talked with gusto of his guiding days, when he guided Charles Hallock[93] and many other notables of the woodland fraternity; well, I am not likely to soon forget him.

I will pause to remark that, of the two big trout, the one on the left, facing the deer's head, weighed by scale five and one-quarter pounds. The one at the right four and one-half pounds. And I have been after a big trout for fifty years, and the biggest trout I ever caught weighed less than two pounds! Well, I am no trout liar.

Paul Smith's woodland resort is rather a high-toned institution—a sort of sylvan Long Branch, a forest Newport. Coaches arrive every day quite after

---

92  In no way

93  *Forest and Stream*'s founder

the style of fifty years ago. Full inside, six on top, guard playing a loony tune on a preposterously long tin horn. Billiards, tenpins, finely kept playgrounds, good drives, good livery, and, what I did not expect, good trouting and deer hunting within easy reach of the hotel. It was on the eve of August 8. I had packed my slender duffel, had "tied in," and was promising myself an early daylight start on the following morning.

The evening was fine, the walks and piazzas were thronged, a dozen guides were gathered in front of the hotel talking dog, deer, trout, parties, etc., after the manner of guides in the North Woods. And there came from the outlet a swift, double-ended blue boat with only a guide in her, and the guide was giving her an ash breeze for all she was worth.

He ran his boat high and dry on the clean sandy beach, came quickly up to the knot of guides, and said curtly, "Boys, Joe Newell's drowned."

"Where? When? How?" were the hurried questions.

"In Follensby, Jr. Two hours ago; fell out of his boat somehow and tangled up in the lily pads."

There was silence and soberness among the guides. Finally one remarked, "Somebody ought to tell his wife."

"Jim, you go up and tell her."

"I—I can't. I've got to wash my boat and take my party up the lake. Why don't you go?"

"Wouldn't do it for a hundred dollars. Let the clerk send a boy."

Then the guides arranged for an early start over to Follensby Pond to grapple for the body, and a gloom seemed to settle on the pleasant surroundings as the news spread. And the question most often heard was "Has anyone told his wife?" I don't think I should like to be the one to carry her the news.

On the morning of the 9th at 4:30 a.m., I quietly stepped into the little canoe for the return trip by a somewhat different route. No one was astir about the hotel save the night watchman, who came down to the landing to see me off. Through the Lower St. Regis, Spitfire Pond, the Upper St. Regis, the two-mile carry, and I reached Joe Baker's in time for breakfast. Then a delightful trip of two miles across Big Clear brought me to Sweeney's, a half-mile carry to Little Clear Pond, with its bright waters and beautiful shores.

If I wanted to go into camp for a week or two for fishing and hunting, I have no ground I would prefer to the pleasant, lonely banks of Little Clear Pond. It is well stocked with both lake and brook trout. And a young Sweeney who helped me on the carry said, "Lake trout have been taken here weighing twenty-five pounds. Then, the fish commission had a hatchery just back of that point, and they turned thousands of speckled and lake trout into the pond—but few come here to fish—and there ain't a better stocked lake in the woods. Speckled trout don't do so well here, the paint[94] bothers 'em."

"The paint?"

---

94  The "paint" here is the ochre-colored precipitate of iron-eating bacteria.

"Yes, ochre paint. You can catch a tin can full in a few minutes. Good paint, too. It keeps brook trout away from the spring holes, and in the deep water the lakers gobble them. Deer are plenty. I saw a big buck in the pond last evening, but he kept so near the shore I couldn't cut him off."

Over the two-and-a-half-mile carry to the Prospect House, across the Saranac to the Sweeney Carry, and down the carry to the desolate, drowned-out shores of the once beautiful Raquette River. And get down and out of the Raquette in the quickest possible time. A sluggish, sullen stream, with miles on miles of dead timber and unnatural marsh, is not the stream to linger on, and you will be glad, as I was, that there is a little steamer to speed you out of it and land you at the head of Big Tupper in time for supper.

Half a mile above the hotel you may see a foaming sheet of water tumbling into the lake over brown, wholesome-looking boulders. This is Boy Falls, and a carry of a few rods sets the canoe afloat above and beyond dead shore lines. The cruise up Boy Stream is bright and pleasant. The carries are a little rough and muddy, but the run across Round Pond and up the channel into Little Tupper makes amends while the hunter-like welcome to be met at the Grove House inclines one to lay off for a few days and take a little hunting, as it were.

For Pliny Robins is hunter and guide, as well as landlord, and has even now started up the lake with his rifle and two eager hounds in the boat. A guide with two more hounds is just launching his boat, and it looks a good deal like a hunt. I notice a quarter of venison still left in the storeroom. I have not eaten a meal since I came here without trout or venison, one or both. Such fare is always to be had at Little Tupper. Both deer and trout are becoming more plentiful yearly, partly through better protection for the one and judicious restocking for the other.

The number of beautiful lakes and ponds in this wonderful region, no man knows, and Little Tupper is among the finest. Gamy as the gamiest, clear as the clearest, and seldom rough. Where there are so many delightful sheets of water, each with its own peculiar beauties, it is idle to claim any one as *par excellence* the finest.

The *Sairy* has been fairly paddled up to date. I am called on about every day to take her out and show her paces for the benefit of the curious or skeptical. I mostly comply. I am pleased to show people how light a boat will carry a man safely and comfortably. She is to go back by the Slim Pond route, and Long Lake, Forked, Raquette, etc., to my favorite stamping ground, the waters of the Moose.

# Cruise of the *Sairy Gamp*, 7

*FOREST AND STREAM*, SEPTEMBER 20, 1883

One of the puzzles that will be apt to fog the lone canoeist is the repetition of names as applied to ponds, lakes, and streams. For instance, take Stoddard's map.[95] You will find nine "Clear Ponds," seven "Mud Ponds," six "Long Ponds," six "Wolf Ponds," four "Rock Ponds," several "Round Ponds," etc., etc. And you will find these names repeated in many localities where no ponds or lakes are indicated on the map. To the man who has studied the wilderness, these repetitions are of little account. But I was surprised when old guides of twenty-five years' standing coolly disputed me on this point and were hardly convinced by reference to the map. But this was to be expected.

The Forge House guide is bound to know the waters of the Moose River, north and south branches, with the Fulton Chain, side lakes, spring holes, and all places where trout do most abound or deer are successfully floated. He has camps thereon and takes his parties thereunto. So of the Beaver guide, the Saranac guide, Long Lake, etc., etc. But none of them are guides for the whole wilderness, and never can be.

Life is not long enough to learn this mystic region in its entirety. A few of the oldest have a knowledge of this region that is wonderful, and only to be acquired by a life devoted to guiding. Among them are such men as Mitchell Sabattis, Sam Dunakin, Alvah Dunning, Lon Wood, Paul Jones, John Brinkerhoff, and Pliny Robins. Most of these are waxing old. Alvah Dunning is sixty-eight. Many of the best guides are on the wrong side of fifty, and the younger guides cannot fill their places, though willing and strong.

---

95 Seneca Ray Stoddard, a writer, photographer, and conservationist, wrote the guidebook *The Adirondacks* and created a number of maps of the area.

Sportsmen understand this but too well. Recently, while young guides at Blue Mountain were waiting in vain for parties, Sabattis had thirty applications in one day from parties who knew the famous old Indian guide by reputation, and a dozen guides, just as good, were waiting for employment. It is right that the older guides have first choice of parties. They have knowledge of spring holes where large trout may be taken by the tyro. They know unmapped, nameless lakes where any greenhorn can get a shot at a deer within twenty yards. They are all good cooks. It is their religion to take care of their parties. Once you employ a guide, he is yours. His platform is simple—to care for his party as a mother cares for her child; not to wet you, and to die sooner than leave you on a long, dismal carry. I have known a guide to pack a sick man over three hard carries by the light of a lantern; then go back and double-trip the carries for his fool duffel of rods, guns, etc., etc., with no extra charge.

N.B.—When you take a guide, tie to him.

The man who finds himself at the camp of Pliny Robins, with an intention of going out to the westward, will do well to study the routes by which he can "make the riffle." Firstly, there is the route by Smith and Albany Lakes, Charley Pond, the stiff carry over to Twitchell Lake, over to Big Moose, down the North Branch, through the North Branch Lake, over the carry to Fourth Lake. Fourteen miles of carries. Not so very interesting, and pretty hard, as all agreed. Then, there was the route by Rock and Bottle Ponds. This promised better. There was good fishing. The scenery was very fine. The route would bring me to the head of Little Forked Lake, within six miles of Forked Lake Landing, which is within twelve miles of Raquette Lake.

I had nearly made up my mind to take this route, but Pliny Robins said, "Have you ever thought of the Slim Ponds route? Strikes me as the most interesting route, and I have traveled them all. Suppose you go over to Big Slim tomorrow, and come back. If you don't like it take Rock and Bottle Pond route." I did. When I was well fed on trout and venison, and the weather for once was too fine for description, I paddled across Little Tupper Lake, left the big leaning pine on the left, rounded the sharp point, paddled up to the head of the bay, and found the landing easily.

There I hung up coat and boots, deciding to go through in stocking feet, for my feet are tough and perfect; I have no corns or bunions. I made the carry easily, "tied out," and was making for the easily seen landing, sixty rods away, when an innocent bear paddled out from an island forty rods to the right and headed for a barren hill, half a mile distant. In an instant I froze down solid. Not a motion. I did not want to kill him or save him. But I thought to get up a little racket in the way of fun. He was too sharp. He had probably seen the canoe. He rounded the point of the island, and although I gave him my best spruce breeze, I saw him no more. He might as well have kept on his course. I had nothing with which to hurt him more dangerous than a light pine paddle.

Then I took the carry from Stony Pond to Big Slim, going for a hundred rods on an easy path, then turning sharp to the right and taking the path down to a shaking bog,[96] to the narrow, muddy ditch, which they call on the eastern side a "slang."

This "slang" was a mile long and so narrow that I brought in the paddle, laid it alongside, and made my way by pulling the canoe along by the weeds and water shrub on either side. It was a tedious job, but when I came out into the clear, bright waters and entire solitude of Big Slim Pond, I was well rewarded.

They have a way on the eastern side of calling a lake a pond. Big Slim Pond is a beautiful lake, narrow, long, and lonely. One may here catch all the trout

---

96 A quagmire

any reasonable sportsman may desire, and all of good size. Deer may be floated successfully on either Big or Little Slim. Halfway down Big Slim there is a point jutting out to the right on which there is a pine bark camp, and just at this point one may catch fine trout at the mouth of the cold spring brook that comes brattling[97] down by the camp. I noted all this for future reference and then made my way back to Pliny Robins's hotel.

The next day was fair, and as is my way, I paddled out at 5:00 a.m. I take the early day in canoeing when the winds are low. I lay my course the day before. If a dense fog covers the waters, as it often does, I lay the compass on the keelson before me and steer by the points. Men and women have deceived me often, the compass never. And so across Little Tupper by Stoney Pond, Big Slim, Little Slim, Mud Pond, the three-mile carry, across Clear Pond, the one-mile carry to Long Lake, and three miles up the lake I came again to the camp of honest Dave Helms. Rather glad to get there, I may say. I had camped overnight on Big Slim and caught—just one trout. He was fourteen inches long. I reeled up and quit at once. I wanted no more. Was I fishing for creels,[98] counts, or hotels? Rather not, I should remark. I take what I need, no more; I do not fish for hotels.

It was on the 15th of August that I reached the camp of Dave Helms. The law on hounding deer "runs out" on that day. There is a gentleman on an island in Raquette Lake—(or was), Mr. William Durant, of Adirondack Railroad notoriety. This gentleman has a camp on Raquette Lake that looks like a Swiss villa. Having no excuse for obtruding myself upon him, I did not land at his camp, but I "laid off" and took stock of the camp as I passed up the lake; and if, as was said, the camp cost $15,000, I think it was reasonable, and cheap—for the man who could afford it.

Now, Mr. Durant had organized a hunt of feudal proportions, to come off on the 16th of August. Just the day I was going up from Long Lake to Raquette.

---

97  Moving with a clattering sound
98  Baskets that are used to hold fish

I had, and have, a theory that I can gaff the largest deer in a light canoe and handle him as easily as I can a large trout. And so, on the morning of the 16th, with line and gaff in readiness, I paddled slowly up the head of Long Lake listening for hounds, but hearing none.

Going up the Raquette River and over the three carries, I rather made time. But once on Forked Lake I took it easy and looked for deer. I saw several blue boats along shore with guides and sportsmen ready to strike out and "cut off" the hapless deer that might take water. But I saw no deer, though I twice heard hounds in full cry. Resting, laying off, and slowly working my way to the Forked Lake House, I laid up the canoe a little before sundown and awaited reports. The reports began to come in about dark and continued until midnight. There had been thirty-six sportsmen in the hunt, with nineteen guides and thirty hounds, more or less. The results were, one fine buck and a small yearling. Eleven guides, who could find no room to spread their blankets at Durant's camp, rowed down to the Forked Lake House for quarters, and they rather made it lively. And there was high jinks at the Durant camp until "the wee short hour ayont the twal."

Gossip said that the hunt cost the originator of it $1,000. If so, he probably does not regret it. He might as easily have invested it on a single hand of draw poker; with not a tithe of the sport.

Crossing Raquette Lake once more, I found Ed Bennett's place, "Under the Hemlocks," well stocked with guides, tourists, sportsmen, and summer boarders all eager for any little excitement or novelty. Whence it happened, I suppose, that nearly all the force turned out to have a look at the little canoe. To lift her and exclaim on her lightness. To ask questions of the rough-looking little old duffer who had cruised her from side to side of the wilderness, and pretty well back again by a different route. Ed Bennett, who weighs 170 pounds, was bound to paddle the *Sairy*. He took his shoes off to get in.

"You promised to let me ride in her when you came back," said he.

"Not for twice her value. She might collapse like an eggshell. She is within forty-seven miles of the Moose River House. I know the route as well as any guide. If her frail siding should get broken now, I had as lief[99] you broke my neck."

And I ported the double blade, tied in strongly, and took the canoe up to the porch, "under the hemlocks."

At the landing I met honest Joe Whitney, who was en route for Blue Mountain Lake. Finding I was bound for his camp, he put me in care of Billy Cornell, a young guide who takes charge in his absence, saying, "Take good care of him, and keep him until I get back." And we walked over the point, crossed the beautiful bay, and were once more in the quiet, breezy camp of Joe Whitney.

Now, I was very glad of a chance for a visit and a talk with young Cornell. It happened that when I was at this same camp the last week in July, that Billy Cornell and another young man were off on a rather peculiar expedition, and Joe seemed very anxious about their return. He was looking for them the night of my arrival. They did not come until the next evening as the sun was sinking below the hills. They came up the bay wearily with oars and paddle, pretty well fagged out. They had two pack baskets, one containing about twenty pounds of large trout, the other holding the meat of a yearling buck. They had toted boat and baskets ten miles through tangled woods where there was no trail and were too tired for much talk. They left me a couple of large trout, with some venison, and took the balance to Hathorn's camp, across the bay. It struck me as paying pretty dearly for the whistle, putting in three days of such work for a small deer and a basket of trout, and I said so.

"Well," said Joe, "the trout and venison were in order, seeing they were there and might as well take them in. But that wasn't what they went for. They went over to educate the deer."

---

99  As soon

I had a pretty close notion of what he meant, but was not going to ask questions, lest I give myself away. And, as I left at 5:00 a.m. the next morning, while the boys were sleeping like the dead, there was no chance for explanations.

But now that Billy Cornell had me in his care to feed, warm, and look after; that the out-of-door fire was burning brightly; that he had paddled the *Sairy* about the bay as well as I could—his weight is just 141½ pounds—I thought it in order to ask, "By the way, how did you make it, educating the deer, and what was the object anyhow?"

Billy adjusted the fire, settled himself on his block, and thus explained: "You see, there are two ponds about ten miles from here that you won't find laid down on any map. And I doubt if you can find two ponds in the North Woods where more deer come to feed than right there. It is on the ground where my partner and I still hunt in the fall and early winter, but is too far off for floating from this side. We can get good floating in a quarter of the distance.

"But on the other side there is a gang of half-breeds who make it a part of their religion to get in on the ponds on the last day of July and just go for slaughter. Last year they floated two nights and dragged off fifteen deer. This year we thought it might be well to cut them off. So we packed boat and baskets ten miles through the woods and spent three days 'educating' deer. The ponds were swarming with them, and they were tamer than sheep. We would paddle up to the deer, and when within thirty or forty feet cut loose with four drams[100] of powder and just a pinch of number thirteen shot, to sting him, so he wouldn't forget his lesson. We educated over a dozen the first night. The second night we took the other pond and gave free lessons to as many more. Not a deer of them will ever stand for a light again. Of course, the gang will come in and get a few deer this season, but they won't make slaughter-yards of the ponds as they did last year.

"We saved one little yearling buck. What moral difference was there between killing him on the night of the 20th or the 31st of July? And the camps all need

---

100  A dram is a measure equal to one-sixteenth of an ounce.

venison. We saved every pound of the meat, and it was more than it was worth to pack it out. Yes, the best speckled trout fishing, and the best floating is on ponds, lakes, and streams not down on the maps."

"And there are many of these?"

"Scores of them. Perhaps hundreds. I could take you, if you didn't mind some hard travel, to ponds where you could get half a dozen shots in a night, or catch all the trout you cared to pack out; and I don't set up for much of a guide."

It is true that along the traveled routes and where camps do most abound, deer have become wary and rather scarce, while trout are hard to get.

But, on the secluded lakes and ponds, far in the woods, away from frequented trails, deer and trout are most abundant.

# Cruise of the *Sairy Gamp*, 8

## *FOREST AND STREAM*, SEPTEMBER 27, 1883

It was on the morning of August 17, at 5:00 a.m., that I paddled out from the Whitney camp, intending to make the Forge House by evening, distance twenty-seven miles, about four miles of it carries. I made the first eight miles before stopping for breakfast but was caught in a shower and spent a couple of hours drying out.

I had stopped at Alvah Dunning's island on Eighth Lake and had depended on finding the key to his camp, as he told me where to look for it when I met him at Raquette Falls. But the key was gone and I was obliged to take an outside ticket. So I stole a couple of Alvah's shooks,[101] improvised a dry platform, made a rousing fire on the lee side of his camp, also a pot of green tea—the kind that raises the hair—got out the old shelter tent for a bed, and, having had breakfast, was lounging and smoking, when, at the landing above, I saw a blue boat on a pair of blue legs walk down to the water and prepare to launch out. The legs had the balance of a guide-looking man above them, and the man shipped his oars in a businesslike way, headed for the island, and came speedily abreast of the camp.

I hailed, "Would he land?"

He hesitated for a moment, backed water, and came to the landing. He proved to be Fred Loveland, landlord of the Boreas River House and one of the old-time guides. He was bound for the Forge House and was in no hurry. That was just my case. I proposed that we keep company, and he readily agreed. And so, by the bright green solitary shores of the Eighth Lake and over to the clean sandy landing, we went together, or rather he went ahead, and I followed after

---

101  A collection of wood parts

with such speed as a nine-foot canoe can make, with a head wind and a short snappy sea to beat with the broad double blade.

At the landing he tied in and asked me to hold up the stern while he crept under and adjusted the neck-yoke. "She is a brute of a boat," he added. "In twenty-five years of guiding I never carried but one such boat, and I never will carry another. Once I get her to the Forge, she may go to—the fool that built her. She weighs over one hundred pounds." And she did. Once we stopped to rest on the mile carry from Eighth down to Seventh, and, as I held up the prow again, his remarks were terse and sharp on a "boat that it took two men to shoulder."

Over the carry, down the dismal swamp (where I hung up all night two years ago), sometimes in the channel, sometimes out, and we began to feel the swell at the head of Seventh.

I had kept good pace with the guide down the crooked channel, but when I saw the white caps on the Seventh it struck me as rather an unsocial way of traveling, that one should go ahead with a long, sharp boat, and his companion come puffing along in the rear with a canoe little larger than a bread tray. Wherefore I fell in readily with the suggestion that the larger boat would "trim" better with two than one. Also, I may have had some doubts as to whether I could make the opposite shore at all.

Loveland adjusted his seats for two, and I got into the stern and took hold of the bit of fish-line that serves the *Sairy* for a painter. She danced along like a cork, and we crossed the Seventh, with its dreary shorelines of dead timber, with scarcely a spoken word. Down the crooked outlet to the more dismal Sixth, with its accursed, ill-smelling dam. Here we "took out" for the last carry, from Sixth to Fifth. It is nearly three-quarters of a mile, but is rocky, tortuous, and hilly. One thing can be said of the Fifth: it is still about as nature formed it. Also, it is good "frogging" ground, but only a pughole[102] of nine acres.

---

102  Possibly a sinkhole

Coming down the shallow outlet of the Fifth, the wisdom of having good company became very apparent to me at least. There was a stiff topsail breeze blowing directly up the lake, and the white-crested waves at the head of the "Stormy Fourth" were piling up in a way that would have made it impossible for the *Sairy* to advance a rod in an hour. Not that I think the sea would have swamped her. But every wave would have lifted half her length out of water, the wind would have caught under her full bearings, also on the broad blades, and any progress would have been out of the question. Even the sturdy guide, with a well-handled pair of oars and a sharp, narrow boat, was sometimes brought to a standstill as we rounded an exposed point. Then there would come a lull and we would go ahead again. I think we were nearly two hours making the first three miles. There was no boat in sight but ours. Boats mostly avoid the head of the Fourth in a stiff wind.

When about halfway down the lake we swung into a shallow bay to avoid the wind, and I saw, on the port bow, a neat, fresh-looking bark camp that appeared unoccupied. I called Loveland's attention to it, and, giving it one look, he turned and pulled straight for the landing without a word.

In ten minutes the boats were hauled up, I had a bright fire burning, and we had cleaned up an empty quart can for tea. He went to his boat and took out an oblong package that I noticed he had been very careful of, and the package developed into sandwiches, bread, and cheese. My knapsack was capable of tea, sugar, butter, and bacon, with tinware for cooking. There was a bed of fresh browse in the camp, and a fine spring nearby, with a rough table outside. Best of all, we were both wolf-hungry.

It was one of the impromptu, wholesome woodland dinners that are remembered through life, while the memory of more pretentious feasts have

Gone, like the tenants that left without warning,

Down the back entry of Time.

After dinner I suggested that we spend an hour or so smoking, lounging on the browse, and waiting for the wind to go down with the sun, and we did. There was no hurry. We had all the time there was, and the evening was almost certain to be fine, with a full moon. So we possessed our souls in patience and took turns smoking the only pipe we had between us.

"When the sun was very low, and wild winds bound within their Cell,"[103] we pulled over the remaining three miles of the now-placid Fourth, and I stopped at the foot to land at my old camp of three years ago, while Loveland rowed to Perrie's camp on Third Lake.

At Third Lake I found him and he urged me to take a seat in his boat to the Forge House, just for sociability, but I declined. I wanted to visit a little with old acquaintances, and also I had a fancy for taking in the lower three lakes by moonlight once more, for I had a presentiment that I was likely to go over them no more.

---

103  From Alfred, Lord Tennyson's poem "Mariana," though in the original it is the moon, not the sun.

And when the moon rose, orange-red and large and full, I paddled, very quietly and a little sadly, over the Third, by the Eagle's Nest, across the Second, by the Stickney camp and over the First, and so down by the Indian Rock and down the channel until I made the lights of the Forge House. I landed at the boathouse, tied in, and at 8:30 o'clock the *Sairy* was resting by the maple tree where my canoes have so often found a safe resting place.

It had been a part of my program to take in about two weeks of deer hunting on the branches of Moose River: wherefore I had left the old hair-triggered, nail-driving muzzle loader at the Forge House in charge of Charley Barrett.

For the first twenty-one days after leaving the Forge House for Paul Smith's, I had nineteen rainy days, and all cold. This, with an accident that nearly paralyzed my right arm, made the cruise a slow affair. And it was not strange that I found my vacation of six weeks all gone. But I still lingered, stealing one more week. I had been just one month crossing the wilderness and returning. It was as well so. I was not running on time. I stopped wherever and whenever I found objects of interest or saw a chance to pick up useful knowledge of the noted North Woods. And now my time was up.

On the morning of August 24, I picked up the *Sairy* at 5:00 a.m. and started for the last day's cruise I shall probably make in her. By way of the Stillwater and Jones's camp, it is twenty miles to Moose River Tannery. And the route is not what it was three or even two years ago. It has fallen into disuse. The bridge at the old Arnold place has succumbed to time and now blocks the course, a dismal-looking wreck. Huge trees have fallen across the stream and remain as they fell. And there are two ugly flood-jams that are so many terrors to a light canoe.

Cautiously and slowly I worked by all these, and then there was the Little Rapids. Two years ago I paddled the *Nipper* up these rapids and never took out until I reached the Forge House landing. It was not so now. The gate at the foot of First Lake was raised, and a black and white torrent was rushing and roaring over the ragged sandstone boulders, looking a trifle dangerous for such a light craft. While I was hanging on at the head of the rapids, back-paddling and making up my mind whether to "shoot" them or carry around, fate decided the question. One of those colorless boulders caught the prow of the canoe, whirled her broadside on, and the next instant I was shooting the rapids, stern foremost. I think it was not five seconds until I was safely by the rocks and on the level, foamy current below. One bump and a jump on a rock that nearly threw me out, and I was calmly floating on deep, clear water.

Feeling a little faint, I headed downstream and paddled leisurely to Jones's camp, thinking what a neat adventure it would have been had I been capsized and the canoe gone down the river without me. Aye. But you see, she couldn't do it. The double-bladed paddle was tied to her ribbing with six feet of strong trolling line. I never let go of the paddle in an upset. I hang to the paddle. Paddle holds the canoe. See?

Jones's camp was deserted and desolate. A lively red squirrel was the only live thing in sight or hearing. He had wired his way into Jones's horse barn and was living at free quarters. I was glad of it. I hope he will eat up ten bushels of chop-stuff and oats and call in his sisters, his cousins, and his aunts. For Eri Jones flatly declined to "put me on" to the hiding place of his camp key. I stood about one chance in fifty of needing it. But if I did need it, I should need it badly. Luckily, it would have been of no use.

I took a half hour's rest, nibbled a bread crust, and tied in for the last long carry of nine miles. Up and down, rocks, fallen trees, and mud holes, brush and briers, slippery corduroys and slimy logs. It was a wearisome carry, but I made it. I had started at 5:00 a.m.; I sighted the Tannery at 1:30 p.m.

Declining the offer of a friend to "set" me across, I took out, launched, and ferried myself over, landed in the Tannery ooze, drew the *Sairy* up into the fresh, green grass, wiped her frail siding clean, and "tied in" neatly and carefully. Then, amid the questions and congratulations of a dozen good-natured friends, I mounted her on my head for a last short carry to the hotel and walked wearily up to the hospitable door of the Moose River House. I laid her down carefully on the shady porch, as a mother would a tired infant, and the cruise of the *Sairy Gamp* was ended.

I have little more to add. I had cruised her, by paddle and carry, 118 miles on the outward trip, and, by a different route, 148 miles on the return. She had been a surprise to me. It required care and caution to get into or out of such a light, limber boat. But, once seated fairly, she was steady as a whole-boat. Her builder thought her too small and light for a working boat. He was a trifle mistaken. I would as soon take her to float a deer or handle a large fish as any canoe I have ever owned, but her carrying capacity is, of course, small. She "trims" best at 140 pounds. Say 110 pounds at the seat and fifteen pounds at each stem.

At another time and place I shall have more to say on the open canoe and double blade. But my outing is over for this year. I have brought the *Sairy* home without a check in her frail siding. She sits lightly on a shelf, where I can rest my eyes on her, as

> *I turn and raise the load,*
> *With weary shoulders bending;*
> *And take the old, well-beaten road,*
> *That leads—unto the ending.*
> *NESSMUK*

P.S.—To the oft-recurring question of my friends, "What luck fishing and hunting?" I answer I have not been fishing and hunting. I fished a little, incidentally; hunted not at all. To those who assume that I have been straggling and cruising through the Northern Wilderness for six weeks, that I may say I have cruised the lightest working cedar canoe ever built, I can only say they are badly mistaken. I don't know that she is the lightest, and there are scores of canoeists who can handle her as well or better than her present owner. The few who call me a "canoe crank" and "hobby rider" come nearer the mark. I think myself it is a hobby—but a mighty pleasant one to ride.

N.

The editor of *Forest and Stream* added the following postscript to the above letter:

Mr. Rushton sends us a letter received from "Nessmuk" from which we quote: "To-day I send you back the *Sairy Gamp*. She is of no further use to me. There is not a lake in Tioga County, and I am not going to rattle her over the stones of Pine Creek. She has astonished me; she will be more of a surprise to you. Remember the advice you gave me about bracing, etc. Remember you said you 'would not warrant her for an hour; she may go to pieces like an eggshell.' That's what you said; she don't go to pieces worth a cent. I have snagged her, rocked her, got her onto spruce knots, and been rattled down rapids stern foremost; and I send her back, as tight and staunch as the day I took her at Boonville. There are more than a hundred cuts, scratches, and abrasions on her thin siding, there are red and green blotches on her strips, from contact with amateur boats, and longer streaks of blue from collisions, with the regulation guide boat, but she does not leak a drop. I once said in *Forest and Stream* I was trying to find out how light a canoe it took to drown a man. I never shall know. The *Sairy Gamp* has only ducked me once in a six weeks' cruise, and that by my own carelessness."

## Light vs. Heavy Canoes

### AUGUST 10, 1884

I N *FOREST AND STREAM* FOR JULY 13 APPEARS AN article by "J.R. Jr." in which he alludes to the little canoe against which he kicked his toe, at Perrie's camp on Third Lake, Fulton Chain, Bronson's Tract. The canoe was the worse for wear. He turned it over and read the name "Nessmuk." He says, "Ah! I see hoe it is now. 'Nessmuk' paddled around the waters in that miserable little cheese box, cramped up, sitting on the damp bottom of this boat. No wonder he told us such pitiful tales of his coughing continually, being sick all the time, finally growing out of the woods disgusted, and determined to cry down the Adirondacks as a fraud and a humbug. Now Mr. 'Nessmuk,' when you go into the Adirondacks again, go in a boat—take one of the new double-enders that weigh about sixty pounds, and as you get into it sit down on a seat—stretch out your feet, and row like a man, let the Indians keep to the paddle if they like, then you may be able to shake off that cough, etc."

I rise for a few explanatory remarks.

The canoe against which "J.R. Jr." kicked his toe last June at Third Lake was not the cause I cruised in last summer. I cruised in the *Nipper*, larger, longer, and two pounds lighter than the *Nessmuk*. I cruised in the latter about six or seven weeks and 550 miles, the previous summer.

That healthy men and women are, in our changeable climate, subject to sudden and dangerous colds, is mournfully true. Deaths by pneumonia, pleurisy, and kindred diseases are sadly frequent, as well as in city as country, and sickness is more apt to strike the comfortable, well-fed citizen than the dweller in forest camps. That thorough exposure to storms and an all-night soaking in a submerged forest I contracted a cough that was hard to beat was no marvel, and might easily happen to a younger and stronger man. Just how it would have helped my case to have been chilled through in a heavier boat is one of the things I shall never find out, I am always a little ashamed of being sick. I have a sort of blue water notion that no man has any business to be sick. "Nobody ships for nurse," as old sailors say. However, I stuck to the cruise for over 200 miles, taking my canoe over all the carries. She only weighed sixteen pounds. Had she been a double-ender of sixty—well, I shouldn't have been there.

As to the superior comfort of riding in such a boat such as "J.R." recommends, he has simply got the cart before the horse. The comfort is all on the side of the canoe. The boat he recommends is the regular Long-Laker—the guide boat of the wilderness. In her you sit all day (you dare not stand up) on a hard, painted board, with no choice or change of position. The position becomes very tiresome in an all-day ride. You are even glad of the relief afforded by a "carry." Now, if you would be a genuine canoeist, you reserve all this; you go as you like, and you sit on a soft cushion with four or five changes of "posish," and consequent relief to stiff, tired muscles. To wit: You are provided with a seat, made by stitching the two ends of one yard of unbleached sheeting together, and closing one end with a circular piece of the same twelve inches in diameter, sewed in strongly. This makes a round bag a little more than two feet long and one foot across. To convert it into a cushion, fill it to the desired height with hemlock browse, grass and leaves, dry moss, or grass. About four or five inches suits me. A taller man may prefer a seat an inch or two higher. Pack the stuffing as solid as possible, and turn in the loose cloth at the top. Shape and flatten it to your notion, and you have a seat that adapts itself to the lines of the canoe—and the canoeist— perfectly. It is never hard or tiresome, and, on making a carry, you throw out the filling, put the bag in your pocket, and fill it again in five minutes, when wanted. At night it makes a capital pillow; or, if not needed for that, an excellent and safe depository for the loose duffel that is always getting lost in the leaves and debris of an improvised camp.

When tired of the one position, push the seat back, double a coat or blanket, and sit down.

Next, paddle in a kneeling posture, varying it by sitting back on your heels, when tired.

Then try the squatting position, as a relief.

Finally, go back to the bag cushion, which is the first and best position. The others are, each one, a rest—just what you do not get in a crank Long-Laker, as you "row like a man" with "room to stretch out your feet, swell out your lungs, and fill them full of the health-giving air, etc."

The pulling of oars is not new to me. When I was twelve years of age, it was my daily task to pull an oar (not a swivel oar, but loose in hole pins) from East Dennis, on the fishhook end of Cape Cod, straight out to sea, in a secondhand whale boat, for fish. In my young manhood I "pulled stroke" in the waist boat[104] of old Rajah, of and from New Bedford, West, master. The dog's life of a sailor sickened me for over a life "before the mast."

I have plied the round-bladed paddle of the *Muris* and *Mundrucus* on the Amazon River; the Madeira, the Rio Negro, and the Tocantins, in Brazil; and the narrow blade of the Chippewas in a light pine dugout on the upper waters of the Mississippi. I have at last come to accept the light, double-bladed paddle as the *ne plus ultra*[105] of propulsion in a light canoe.

I have never gone on a cruise in which I did not learn something new. I am always open to advice. But in return perhaps I can give a useful hint or two; at least I can try.

First. If you love nature in undress learn to go alone. You can study your route and the courses of streams, and you carry a compass? Be self-reliant. Go alone. If, in the grand old forest, you are not sufficient unto yourself, select a partner, and take a thirty-five-pound clinker-built cedar canoe. Two men make lighter carries, and some men must have company (I prefer to be alone).

Second. While breech-loading guns and bamboo rods have been brought to something like perfection, nobody seems to have made a study of light, single, paddling canoes. The question of the ounces and pounds of the canoe in proportion to weight of the canoeist I have not seen agitated as yet. In boats and canoes we run all too heavy and trust too much to guides. Careful experiment, covering months or at least weeks, through several seasons, leads me to put in type a few general rules—approximatively only, but mainly correct. As thus: For a lightweight canoeist, one pound of canoe to six pounds of canoeist.

---

104  A smaller boat carried aboard a whaling ship
105  The best

This gives a canoe of 20 pounds to a 120-pound man. It is more than is needed. The dimensions of such a canoe should be: length, 10½ feet; beam, 27 inches; rise at center, 7 to 8 inches.

For a heavier man, increase weight and size of canoe slowly. For instance, weight of canoeist, 150 pounds. For such a man, a canoe 10 feet, 9 inches in length, 28 inches beam. Weight, 22 pounds. (The canoe will carry the man and a light passenger of 100 pounds.)

For a muscular, strong welter[106] of 180 pounds, or thereabouts, a canoe 11 feet long 28 inch beam, 9 inches rise at center, steep fore foot, and 14 inches shear at stem; weight, about 26 pounds.

Strength of each of the above canoes, mainly on keel, keelson, and garboard streaks, with pretty strong and well-guarded stems.

(As boatmen and canoeists, my dear "J.R. Jr.," we mostly go overweighted. Remember it.)

As to the well-worn "cheese box," against which you kicked your toe last June, I sold her to Perrie last summer. But, as regards her, Harry Bronker, a muscular young cheery Baltimorean, paddled her from the Forge House last July, through three first lakes of the Fulton Chain, at a rate that left me, in the *Nipper*, out of sight. His weight was 175 pounds.

Mrs. Sperry, who has a camp on Fourth Lake, used to borrow the *Nessmuk*, and paddle her around the lakes, delivering supplies. Mrs. Sperry weighs over 130 pounds.

No, I cannot, as yet, say just what the proportions of canoe and canoeist ought to be, to get the proper combination of relative weight, with safety, pleasure, and convenience.

---

106  Or welterweight, a boxing weight division

But, I am going to know.

I have ordered another canoe of Rushton to weigh 12 pounds (I think 10 pounds would do). Under date of June 9, he says, "Can build you a boat of any size. Whether it would float you or not cannot say. I will build it awful light, but won't say how much racket it will stand. I expect it will drown you, yet. So far as I know no one has ever seen a 12 pound boat of any make, fairly afloat, with a man in her."

Under date of 26th June, he writes, "I'll make it. I'll make it light. But you just go in it in shallow water for a spell. I don't dare guarantee anything for strength. It may go to pieces like an egg shell."

Mr. Rushton builds better than he knows. He can build a 10-pound canoe that I can ride. I am astonished and rigged that even my personal friends should say, "Ah! Your light canoes are for notoriety, and a trifle of bluff, eh?" Now, I am no gambler—never was. But I am no moralist. I had as lief back an opinion with a wager as an argument. And I will wager $100 or $200 that J. H. Rushton makes me a canoe to weigh less than 10 pounds and less than 8 feet in length. That I take the canoe at Tom Nightingale's door (Moose River House) and paddle and carry the same through the Fulton Chain to the Raquette Lake, register at Ed Bennett's, at Leavitt's on Forked Lake, go through to Paul Smith's, come back by way of the Tuppers, Smith, and Albany Lakes, to Ed Dunbur's on the Beaver; from there by the Beaver and the seven-mile carry to Twitchell Lake, thence to Big Moose and down by the three carries to Fourth Lake, and down from thence to the Forge House. All is to be done by a lightweight who has never been over the route before farther than Long Lake. My duffel shall not exceed 20 pounds. Less is better.

Rowboats are good; sailing canoes splendid for those who delight in canvas.

We all have our hobbies. My hobby is the lightest possible clinker-built cedar canoe and the double paddle. I do not quarrel with other men's hobbies. I like them, rather.

One word as to my decrying the Adirondacks as "a fraud and a humbug." Never. "Where do you get that?" A better, manlier, sturdier class of men than the guides of the North Woods I have not seen. All the same I am no baby. I have read "Adirondack Murray" and "Camp Lou." Bismillah! It is bosh! There were twenty-three deaths from lung diseases in the St. Regis country and the Saranac region; many more barely crept out alive to die at home, last summer. Don't tie to a vain thing.

The entire North Woods region is exceptionally healthy, but it won't quite bring the dead to life, "Adirondack Murray" and "Camp Lou" to the contrary notwithstanding.

But it is the best region on this earth for a cruise by a lone, self-reliant canoeist. Never again when I'm sick will I own up.

Verplanck Colvin and other writers have put up the value of the Adirondacks as a park, so to speak, a national or state park. Just so. And on a score of the main stream, without let or hindrance, dams have been placed, and the bright, green shorelines have been converted into lines of desolation and death.

Time passes. I am one of the great army who are always working. But I have time for a cruise. Does "J.R. Jr." mean what he says? Will he meet me for a cruise of a month or more at any point between "Paul Smith's" and the Forge House? I in a 12-pound canoe, he in such boat as he pleases. Address "Nessmuk," care of *Forest and Stream*.

### FOREST AND STREAM, JULY 16, 1885

Monday, May 18, was a good day for canoes. It was barely sunrise, and I was monkeying around the fire with a condensed milk can by way of coffee pot, when Jake, the darky carter, passed within ten rods of camp with an oblong box on his cart, beading straight for Kendall's ranch. He hailed me with, "I'se got a little boat here fer de cap'n; come ober an' see her."

"All right, Jake, you've got a little boat there for me, too, I reckon?"

"No, sah. Box ain' big enough for two boats," and he drove on.

Now, the captain's ranch is just about seventy rods from my camp, and before the leaves grew so dense on the blackjacks the camps were in sight of each other. Even now I catch glimpses of light from his windows at night, while he can always see my blazing campfires of a dark evening. And as I leisurely drank a cup of black coffee (which is the proper thing to do of a morning in this climate), I heard a hammering and rending clatter over at the captain's house, as of one who opens a dry goods box with a store hatchet, and there came a clear ringing hail, which I answered, and then walked over to the ranch. I found the captain contemplating the contents of the open box with a smile of grim satisfaction, while Mrs. K was actually dancing with delight like an excited schoolgirl. Her little canoe, the long looked for, clinker-built cedar, had come at last and was nestling snugly and safely in its packing without scratch or crack. Well, she was a beauty, and light as a cork, turning the scales at sixteen and a half pounds barely. Finished in oil and varnish, and of a different model from any of the light open canoes I have seen, though the difference is slight. On the whole I prefer her model to that of the *Bucktail*, though the latter was built strictly on the dimensions given by myself. Her length is 10½ feet, beam 26 inches, with 9 inches rise at center, 12 inches at stems.

But what interested me most was another and lighter canoe nested neatly and safely inside the first. This was the little *Rushton* ordered nearly a year ago, with no directions save as to name and weight. She must in any case weigh less than ten pounds. And the name to be painted neatly on each side of one stem in gold and scarlet letters. This was meant as a slight compliment to the man who has done more and better canoe work for me than any man living. Other makers might have done just as well, but they all, I believe, use white lead or some other waterproof material to make close joints. Other things being equal, I prefer naked wood to wood; close joints by close work. When I have rattled my canoes until they leak, I can do the daubing myself. The *Rushton Fairbanks* at just 9 pounds, 15 ounces, is 8½ feet long and has a 23-inch beam, with 8 inches rise at center, and 10¼-inch rise at stems. I thought she had rather a tubby look when first placed on the water. Her very flat bearings, with the way she carried her width out toward the stems, made her look like the model of a Dutch galliot,[107] but turning her keel up, she showed lines and curves that looked like gliding over water very fairly. Balancing her on the end of a finger, she really did seem too frail—too trifling for real work. But I remembered the handsome behavior of the *Sairy Gamp* (only 9 ounces heavier) and decided to test her fairly.

We formed a procession of three down to the landing, Mrs. K leading, and jubilant at the thought that she could make her own carries without help from the male element, whereat the M. E. gave me a side wink and grinned sardonically.

I do not like Kendall's landing—not for an open canoe. The water is too deep and the bank too steep. I prefer a gentle slope of soft sand where the canoe can glide up to a stop easily, and I may walk out or in on the keelson. It was agreed that Mrs. K should launch out first, and with some trepidation and a little help from the captain, she got safely off and began to ply the double blade. Gingerly at the start but finding the canoe steady and easy under paddle she grew confident and put on muscle, paddling up and down the river, in and out of bayous, and handling the light craft skillfully as a squaw. Finally she landed and lifted the canoe out of water, saying, "Oh, she is just lovely; worth half a dozen spring bonnets." Then the captain hinted he would like to see the Rushton "go," and I dropped her into the water with a spat, dropped a folded blanket into her for a seat, and crept in, rather carefully it must be owned.

But once in and fairly seated I found her, to my surprise, steadier than the *Bucktail* of more than twice her size (i.e., she did not tip or rock so easily, and she required less propelling to the mile than any boat or canoe I had ever handled). I saw that she would trim with fifteen or twenty pounds in addition

---

107  A lightweight boat with a shallow draft

to my own weight, and I had not paddled her half an hour before deciding that, if she would stay in a lumpy sea, I would adopt her as my cruising canoe.

We went down to the Springs, the captain, Mrs. K, and I. It is only a mile as the crow flies. By the tortuous channel of river and bayou it is nearly three, and a pleasant trip we made of it. Of course, the light canoes attracted a crowd; they always do that, even in towns where canoes are common, but the crowd was not a large one. The Northern tourists had flitted, and the permanent population of the Springs is less than one hundred. We paddled back in the cool of the evening and agreed that it was good to be there.

"It's the first time three double-bladers ever hauled in at one landing on this coast," said the captain. And I think he was right.

This was more than a month ago, and I have kept the Rushton pretty well in use since.

Every well-built canoe, yacht, or ship has some individuality, some peculiar trait of its own. The peculiar trait of the Rushton is to take in spray heavily

when going to windward, say four points off. This is owing to her sharp, short curved lines. We went outside, Tarpon and I, to test her against a brisk sea breeze—he to lie off, watch her closely, and give his opinion as canoeist, builder, and sailor. For he is all these. I put her straight in the wind's eye with a choppy lump of sea against her, and she rode it like a duck. I turned and ran before it, and she got away from the seas like a whale boat. Then I laid her beam on, and—well, it took some balancing, but she kept dry. Lastly I tried her with the wind about four points abaft[108] the stem, and she slashed the spray in, a few spoonsful at a time, until I was obliged to creep under Tarpon's lee and sponge out.

Then he gave his opinion: "Let me deck her and you can stay out as long as the seas don't break under you. That will swamp any canoe." So she is to have a light cloth decking and a cockpit withal, like the able-bodied canoes of the A.C.A.[109]

---

108  Toward the stern of

109  American Canoe Association

# MY FOREST CAMP

*I have a camp in Yamel Glen,*
*A hunter's cabin, roofed with bark,*
*Far from the noisy haunts of men.*
*Where song of thrush or meadow lark*
*Floats never on the somber air.*
*When summer suns are fiercely hot*
*And birds sit mute with drooping wing,*
*Ofttimes I seek this lonely spot,*
*My cabin by the mountain spring,*
*And spend my days of leisure there.*
*Perchance[110] some book of pleasant vein*
*May wile an hour of idle time.*
*Perchance I choose the quaint refrain*
*Of Chaucer or of Spenser's rhyme,*
*Nor heed the failing day's decline.*
*At night my forest bed I make*
*On fragrant boughs, and sweetly dream*

*Of deer or trout that I may take*

*On mountain side or forest stream,*

*With rifle true or silken line.*

*When autumn frosts have clothed the woods*

*In hues of gold and crimson red,*

*Again I seek these solitudes,*

*The moss-grown spring and forest bed.*

*Again I breathe the mountain air.*

*Then give me but my forest home,*

*My rifle, rod, and buoyant health,*

*With freedom where I please to roam;*

*And take who will the banker's wealth,*

*His sleepless nights of anxious care.*

# WOODCRAFT

Woodcraft is dedicated
to the Grand Army of "Outers,"
as a pocket volume of reference
on—woodcraft.

## CHAPTER I

# OVERWORK AND RECREATION– OUTING AND OUTERS– HOW TO DO IT, AND WHY THEY MISS IT

IT DOES NOT NEED THAT HERBERT SPENCER[111] should cross the ocean to tell us that we are an overworked nation; that our hair turns gray ten years earlier than the Englishman's; or "that we have had somewhat too much of the gospel of work," and "it is time to preach the gospel of relaxation." It is all true. But we work harder, accomplish more in a given time, and last quite as long as slower races. As to the gray hair—perhaps gray hair is better than none, and it is a fact that the average Briton becomes bald as early as the American turns gray. There is, however, a sad significance in his words when he says: "In every circle I have met men who had themselves suffered from nervous collapse due to stress of business, or named friends who had either killed themselves by overwork, or had been permanently incapacitated, or had wasted long periods in endeavors

---

111 An English sociologist and philosopher

to recover health." Too true. And it is the constant strain, without let-up or relaxation, that, in nine cases out of ten, snaps the cord and ends in what the doctors call "nervous prostration"—something akin to paralysis—from which the sufferer seldom wholly recovers.

Mr. Spencer quotes that quaint old chronicler Froissart[112] as saying, "The English take their pleasures sadly, after their fashion" and thinks if he lived now, he would say of Americans, "they take their pleasures hurriedly, after their fashion." Perhaps.

It is an age of hurry and worry. Anything slower than steam is apt to "get left." Fortunes are quickly made and freely spent. Nearly all busy, hard-worked Americans have an intuitive sense of the need that exists for at least one period of rest and relaxation during each year, and all—or nearly all—are willing to pay liberally, too liberally in fact, for anything that conduces to rest, recreation, and sport. I am sorry to say that we mostly get swindled. As an average, the summer outer who goes to forest, lake, or stream for health and sport, gets about ten cents' worth for a dollar of outlay. A majority will admit—to themselves at least—that after a month's vacation, they return to work with an inward consciousness of being somewhat disappointed—and beaten. We are free with our money when we have it. We are known throughout the civilized world for our lavishness in paying for our pleasures, but it humiliates us to know we have been beaten, and this is what the most of us know at the end of a summer vacation. To the man of millions it makes little difference. He is able to pay liberally for boats, buckboards, and "body service," if he chooses to spend a summer in the North Woods. He has no need to study the questions of lightness and economy in a forest and stream outing. Let his guides take care of him, and unto them and the landlords he will give freely of his substance.

I do not write for him and can do him little good. But there are hundreds of thousands of practical, useful men, many of them far from being rich; mechanics, artists, writers, merchants, clerks, businessmen—workers, so to

---

112 Jean Froissart, a French author in medieval times

speak—who sorely need and well deserve a season of rest and relaxation at least once a year. To these, and for these, I write.

Perhaps more than fifty years of devotion to "woodcraft" may enable me to give a few useful hints and suggestions to those whose dreams, during the close season of work, are of camp-life by flood, field, and forest.

I have found that nearly all who have a real love of nature and out-of-door camp-life, spend a good deal of time and talk in planning future trips, or discussing the trips and pleasures gone by, but still dear to memory.

When the mountain streams are frozen and the Nor'land winds are out; when the winter winds are drifting the bitter sleet and snow; when winter rains are making out-of-door life unendurable; when season, weather, and law combine to make it "close time" for beast, bird, and man, it is well that a few congenial spirits should, at some favorite trysting place, gather around the glowing stove and exchange yarns, opinions, and experiences. Perhaps no two will exactly agree on the best ground for an outing, on the flies, rods, reels, guns, etc., or half a dozen other points that may be discussed. But one thing all admit. Each and every one has gone to his chosen ground with too much impedimenta, too much duffel, and nearly all have used boats at least twice as heavy as they need to have been. The temptation to buy this or that bit of indispensable camp-kit has been too strong, and we have gone to the blessed woods, handicapped with a load fit for a pack-mule. This is not how to do it.

Go light; the lighter the better, so that you have the simplest material for health, comfort, and enjoyment.

Of course, if you intend to have a permanent camp and can reach it by boat or wagon, lightness is not so important, though even in that case it is well to guard against taking a lot of stuff that is likely to prove of more weight than worth—only to leave it behind when you come out.

# Clothing

As to clothing for the woods, a good deal of nonsense has been written about "strong, coarse woolen clothes." You do not want coarse woolen clothes. Fine woolen cassimere[113] of medium thickness for coat, vest, and pantaloons, with no cotton lining. Color, slate gray or dead-leaf (either is good). Two soft, thick woolen shirts; two pairs of fine, but substantial, woolen drawers;[114] two pairs of strong woolen socks or stockings; these are what you need, and all you need in the way of clothing for the woods, excepting hat and boots, or gaiters. Boots are best—providing you do not let yourself be inveigled into wearing a pair of long-legged heavy boots with thick soles, as has been often advised by writers who knew no better. Heavy, long-legged boots are a weary, tiresome encumbrance on a hard tramp through rough woods. Even moccasins are better. Gaiters, all sorts of high shoes, in fact, are too bothersome about fastening and unfastening. Light boots are best. Not thin, unserviceable affairs, but light as to actual weight. The following hints will give an idea for the best footgear for the woods;

---

113  A material of smooth, tight knit
114  Underwear

let them be single soled, single backs, and single fronts, except light, short foot-linings. Back of solid "country kip";[115] fronts of substantial French calf; heel one inch high, with steel nails; countered outside; straps narrow, of fine French calf put on "astraddle"[116] and set down to the top of the back. The outsole stout, Spanish oak, and pegged rather than sewed, although either is good. They will weigh considerably less than half as much as the clumsy, costly boots usually recommended for the woods, and the added comfort must be tested to be understood.

The hat should be fine, soft felt with moderately low crown and wide brim; color to match the clothing.

The proper covering for head and feet is no slight affair and will be found worth some attention. Be careful that the boots are not too tight or the hat too loose. The above rig will give the tourist one shirt, one pair of drawers, and a pair of socks to carry as extra clothing. A soft, warm blanket-bag, open at the ends, and just long enough to cover the sleeper, with an oblong square of waterproofed cotton cloth 6×8 feet, will give warmth and shelter by night and will weigh together five or six pounds. This, with the extra clothing, will make about eight pounds of dry goods to pack over carries, which is enough. Probably, also, it will be found little enough for comfort.

During a canoe cruise across the Northern Wilderness in the late summer, I met many parties at different points in the woods, and the amount of unnecessary duffel with which they encumbered themselves was simply appalling. Why a shrewd businessman, who goes through with a guide and makes a forest hotel his camping ground nearly every night, should handicap himself with a five-peck[117] pack basket[118] full of gray woolen and gum blankets, extra clothing, pots, pans, and kettles, with a nine-pound ten-bore, and two rods—yes, and an extra pair of heavy boots hanging astride of the gun—well,

---

115 A type of leather made from a young animal's hide
116 Running side to side
117 One peck is equal to two gallons.
118 A basket worn like a backpack

it is one of the things I shall never understand. My own load, including canoe, extra clothing, blanket-bag, two days' rations, pocket-axe, rod, and knapsack, never exceeded twenty-six pounds, and I went prepared to camp out any and every night.

## Preparations

People who contemplate an outing in the woods are pretty apt to commence preparations a long way ahead and to pick up many trifling articles that suggest themselves as useful and handy in camp; all well enough in their way but making at least a too heavy load. It is better to commence by studying to ascertain just how light one can go through without especial discomfort. A good plan is to think over the trip during leisure hours and make out a list of indispensable articles, securing them beforehand, and have them stowed in handy fashion, so that nothing needful may be missing just when and where it cannot be procured. The list will be longer than one would think but need not be cumbersome or heavy. As I am usually credited with making a cruise or a long woods tramp with exceptionally light duffel, I will give a list of the articles I take along—going on foot over carries or through the woods.

## CHAPTER II

# KNAPSACK, HATCHET, KNIVES, TINWARE, RODS, FISHING TACKLE, DITTY BAG

T HE CLOTHING, BLANKET-BAG, AND SHELTER-cloth are all that need be described in that line. The next articles that I look after are knapsack (or pack basket); rod with reel, lines, flies, hooks, and all my fishing gear; pocket-axe; knives; and tinware. Firstly, the knapsack; as you are apt to carry it a great many miles, it is well to have it right and easy-fitting at the start. Don't be induced to carry a pack basket. I am aware that it is in high favor all through the Northern Wilderness and is also much used in other localities where guides and sportsmen most do congregate. But I do not like it. I admit that it will carry a loaf of bread, with tea, sugar, etc., without jamming; that bottles, crockery, and other fragile duffel is safer from breakage than in an oil-cloth knapsack. But it is by no means waterproof in a rain or a splashing head sea,[119] is more than twice as heavy—always growing heavier as it gets wetter—and I had rather have bread,

---

119  Waves that come straight toward the bow of the boat

tea, sugar, etc., a little jammed than water-soaked. Also, it may be remarked that man is a vertebrate animal and ought to respect his backbone. The loaded pack basket on a heavy carry never fails to get in on the most vulnerable knob of the human vertebrae. The knapsack sits easy and does not chafe. The one shown in the engraving is of good form, and the original—which I have carried for years—is satisfactory in every respect. It holds over half a bushel[120] and carries blanket-bag, shelter-tent, hatchet, ditty bag, tinware, fishing tackle, clothes, and two days' rations. It weighs, empty, just twelve ounces.

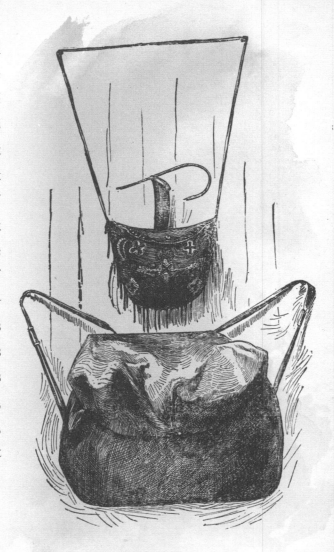

## Hatchet and Knives

The hatchet and knives shown in the engraving will be found to fill the bill satisfactorily so far as cutlery may be required. Each is good and useful of its kind, the hatchet especially, being the best model I have ever found for a "double-barreled" pocket-axe. And just here let me digress for a little chat on the indispensable hatchet; for it is the most difficult piece of camp-kit to obtain in perfection of which I have any knowledge. Before I was a dozen years old, I came to realize that a light hatchet was a sine qua non[121] in woodcraft, and I also found it a most difficult thing to get. I tried shingling hatchets, lathing hatchets, and the small hatchets to be found in country hardware stores, but none of them were satisfactory. I had quite a number made by blacksmiths

---

120  A bushel is equal to eight gallons.

121  Indispensable

who professed skill in making edge tools, and these were the worst of all, being like nothing on the earth or under it—murderous-looking, clumsy, and all too heavy, with no balance or proportion. I had hunted twelve years before I caught up with the pocket-axe I was looking for. It was made in Rochester, by a surgical instrument maker named Bushnell. It cost time and money to get it. I worked one rainy Saturday fashioning the pattern in wood. Spoiled a day going to Rochester, waited a day for the blade, paid $3.00 for it, and lost a day coming home. Boat fare $1.00, and expenses $2.00, besides three days lost time, with another rainy Sunday for making leather sheath and hickory handle.

My witty friends, always willing to help me out in figuring the cost of my hunting and fishing gear, made the following businesslike estimate, which they placed where I would be certain to see it the first thing in the morning. Premising that of the five who assisted in that little joke, all stronger, bigger fellows than myself, four have gone "where they never see the sun,"[122] I will copy the statement as it stands today, on paper yellow with age. For I have kept it over forty years.

A WOODSMAN,

Aug. 15, 1843

DR.

To getting up one limber-go-shiftless pocket-axe:

Cost of blade $3.00

Fare on boat 1.00

Expenses for 3 days 3.00

---

122  From Robert Browning's poem "A Toccata of Galuppi's"

**Three days lost time at $1.25 per day 3.75**

**Two days making model, handle and sheath, say 2.00**

**Total $12.75**

**Per contra,[123] by actual value of axe 2.00**

**Balance $10.75**

Then they raised a horse laugh, and the cost of that hatchet became a standing joke and a slur on my "business ability." What aggravated me most was that the rascals were not so far out in their calculation. And was I so far wrong? That hatchet was my favorite for nearly thirty years. It has been "upset"[124] twice by skilled workmen, and if my friend "Bero" has not lost it, is still in service.

Would I have gone without it any year for one or two dollars? But I prefer the double blade. I want one thick, stunt edge for knots, deers' bones, etc., and a fine, keen edge for cutting clear timber.

A word as to knife, or knives. These are of prime necessity and should be of the best, both as to shape and temper. The "bowies" and "hunting knives" usually kept on sale, are thick, clumsy affairs, with a sort of ridge along the middle of the blade, murderous-looking, but of little use; rather fitted to adorn a dime novel or the belt of "Billy the Kid" than the outfit of the hunter. The one shown in the cut is thin in the blade and handy for skinning, cutting meat, or eating with. The strong double-bladed pocketknife is the best model I have yet found, and in connection with the sheath knife, is all sufficient for camp use. It is not necessary to take table cutlery into the woods. A good fork may be improvised from a beech or birch stick, and the half of a freshwater mussel shell, with a split stick by way of handle, makes an excellent spoon.

---

123  On the contrary

124  In this sense, "upset" refers to the process of re-forming the hatchet head by hammering or forging.

## Cooking Utensils

My entire outfit for cooking and eating dishes comprises five pieces of tinware. This is when stopping in a permanent camp. When cruising and tramping, I take just two pieces in the knapsack.

I get a skillful tinsmith to make one dish as follows: 6 inches on bottom, 6¾ inches on top, side 2 inches high. The bottom is of the heaviest tin procurable, the sides of lighter tin, and seamed to be watertight without solder. The top simply turned, without wire. The second dish to be made the same but small enough to nest in the first, and also to fit into it when inverted as a cover. Two other dishes made from common pressed tinware, with the tops cut off and turned, also without wire. They are fitted so that they all nest, taking no more room than the largest dish alone, and each of the three smaller dishes makes a perfect cover for the next larger. The other piece is a tin camp-kettle, also of the heaviest tin, and seamed watertight. It holds two quarts, and the other dishes nest in it perfectly, so that when packed, the whole takes just as much room as the kettle alone. I should mention that the strong ears[125] are set below

125  Lugs

the rim of the kettle, and the bale[126] falls outside, so, as none of the dishes have any handle, there are no aggravating "stick-outs" to wear and abrade. The snug affair weighs, all told, two pounds. I have met parties in the North Woods whose one frying pan weighed more—with its handle three feet long. How ever did they get through the brush with such a culinary terror?

It is only when I go into a very accessible camp that I take so much as five pieces of tinware along. I once made a ten days' tramp through an unbroken wilderness on foot, and all the dish I took was a ten-cent tin; it was enough. I believe I will tell the story of that tramp before I get through. For I saw more game in the ten days than I ever saw before or since in a season, and I am told that the whole region is now a thrifty farming country, with the deer nearly all gone. They were plenty enough thirty-nine years ago this very month.

# Rods

I feel more diffidence in speaking of rods than of any other matter connected with outdoor sports. The number and variety of rods and makers, the enthusiasm of trout and fly "cranks"; the fact that angling does not take precedence of all other sports with me, with the humiliating confession that I am not above bucktail spinners, worms, and sinkers, minnow tails and white grubs—this and these constrain me to be brief.

But, as I have been a fisher all my life, from my pinhook days to the present time, as I have run the list pretty well up, from brook minnows to hundred-pound albacores, I may be pardoned for a few remarks on the rod and the use thereof.

A rod may be a very high-toned, high-priced aesthetic plaything, costing $50 to $75, or it may be—a rod. A serviceable and splendidly balanced rod can be obtained from first-class makers for less money. By all means let the man of money indulge his fancy for the most costly rod that can be procured. He might do worse. A practical everyday sportsman whose income is limited will

---

126 Handle

find that a more modest product will drop his flies on the water quite as attractively to *Salmo fontinalis*.[127] My little 8½-foot, 4¾-ounce split bamboo, which the editor of *Forest and Stream* had made for me, cost $10.00. I have given it hard usage and at times large trout have tested it severely, but it has never failed me. The dimensions of my second rod are 9½ feet long and 5¾ ounces in weight. This rod will handle the bucktail spinners, which I use for trout and bass, when other things have failed. I used a rod of this description for several summers both in Adirondack and western waters. It had a handmade reel seat, agate first guide, was satisfactory in every respect, and I could see in balance, action, and appearance no superiority in a rod costing $25.00, which one of my friends sported. Charles Dudley Warner, who writes charmingly of woods life, has the following in regard to trout fishing, which is so neatly humorous that it will bear repeating:

"It is well known that no person who regards his reputation will ever kill a trout with anything but a fly. It requires some training on the part of the trout to take to this method. The uncultivated trout in unfrequented waters prefers the bait; and the rural people, whose sole object in going a-fishing appears to be to catch fish, indulge them in their primitive state for the worm. No sportsman, however, will use anything but a fly—except he happens to be alone."

Speaking of rods, he says:

"The rod is a bamboo weighing seven ounces, which has to be spliced with a winding of silk thread every time it is used. This is a tedious process; but, by fastening the joints in this way, a uniform spring is secured in the rod. No one devoted to high art would think of using a socket joint."

One summer during a seven weeks' tour in the Northern Wilderness, my only rod was a 7½-foot Henshall. It came to hand with two bait-tips only, but I added a fly-tip, and it made an excellent "general fishing rod." With it I could

---

127  Brook trout, now known as *Salvelinus fontinalis*

handle a large bass or pickerel; it was a capital bait-rod for brook trout; as fly rod it has pleased me well enough. It is likely to go with me again. For reel casting, the 5½-foot rod is handier. But it is not yet decided which is best, and I leave every man his own opinion. Only, I think one rod enough, but have always had more.

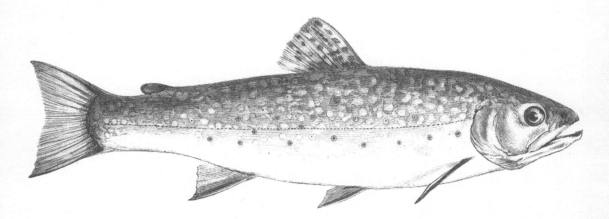

And don't neglect to take what sailors call a "ditty bag." This may be a little sack of chamois leather about 4 inches wide by 6 inches in length. Mine is before me as I write. Emptying the contents, I find it inventories as follows: a dozen hooks, running in size from small minnow hooks to large Limericks; four lines of six yards each, varying from the finest to a size sufficient for a 10-pound fish; three darning needles and a few common sewing needles; a dozen buttons; sewing silk; thread and a small ball of strong yarn for darning socks; sticking salve; a bit of shoemaker's wax; beeswax; sinkers; and a very fine file for sharpening hooks. The ditty bag weighs, with contents, 2½ ounces, and it goes in a small buckskin bullet pouch, which I wear almost as constantly as my hat. The pouch has a sheath strongly sewed on the back side of it, where the light hunting knife is always at hand, and it also carries a 2-ounce vial of fly medicine, a vial of "painkiller," and two or three gangs[128] of hooks on brass wire snells—of which, more in another place. I can always go down into that pouch for a waterproof match safe, strings, compass, bits of linen and scarlet flannel (for frogging), copper tacks, and other light duffel. It is about as handy a piece of woods-kit as I carry.

---

128 Sets

I hope no aesthetic devotee of the fly rod will lay down the book in disgust when I confess to a weakness for frogging. I admit that it is not high-toned sport, and yet I have got a good deal of amusement out of it. The persistence with which a large batrachian[129] will snap at a bit of red flannel after being several times hooked on the same lure, and the comical way in which he will scuttle off with a quick succession of short jumps after each release; the cheerful manner in which, after each bout, he will tune up his deep, bass pipe—ready for another greedy snap at an ibis fly or red rag—is rather funny. And his hind legs, rolled in meal and nicely browned, are preferable to trout or venison.

---

129 Amphibian

# GETTING LOST– CAMPING OUT– ROUGHING IT OR SMOOTHING IT– INSECTS–CAMPS, AND HOW TO MAKE THEM

WITH A LARGE MAJORITY OF PROSPECTIVE tourists and outers, "camping out" is a leading factor in the summer vacation. And during the long winter months they are prone to collect in little knots and talk much of camps, fishing, hunting, and "roughing it." The last phrase is very popular and always cropping out in the talks on matters pertaining to a vacation in the woods. I dislike the phrase. We do not go to the green woods and crystal waters to rough it, we go to smooth it. We get it rough enough at home; in towns and cities; in shops, offices, stores, banks—anywhere that we may be placed—with the necessity always present of being on time and up to our work; of providing for the dependent ones; of keeping up, catching up, or getting left. "Alas for the life-long battle, whose bravest slogan is bread."

As for the few fortunate ones who have no call to take a hand in any strife or struggle, who not only have all the time there is, but a great deal that they cannot dispose of with any satisfaction to themselves or anybody else—I am not writing for them but only to those of the world's workers who go, or would like to go, every summer to the woods. And to these I would say, don't rough

it; make it as smooth, as restful, and pleasurable as you can.

To this end you need pleasant days and peaceful nights. You cannot afford to be tormented and poisoned by insects, nor kept awake at night by cold and damp, nor to exhaust your strength by hard tramps and heavy loads. Take it easy, and always keep cool. Nine men out of ten, on finding themselves lost in the woods, fly into a panic, and quarrel with the compass. Never do that. The compass is always right, or nearly so. It is not many years since an able-bodied man—sportsman of course—lost his way in the North Woods, and took fright, as might be expected. He was well armed and well found for a week in the woods. What ought to have been only an interesting adventure became a tragedy. He tore through thickets and swamps in his senseless panic, until he dropped and died through fright, hunger, and exhaustion.

A well-authenticated story is told of a guide in the Oswegatchie region, who perished in the same way. Guides are not infallible; I have known more than one to get lost. Wherefore, should you be tramping through a pathless forest on a cloudy day, and should the sun suddenly break from under a cloud in the northwest about noon, don't be scared. The last day is not at hand, and the planets have not become mixed; only, you are turned. You have gradually swung around, until you are facing northwest when you meant to travel south. It has a muddling effect on the mind—this getting lost in the woods. But if you can collect and arrange your gray brain matter, and suppress all panicky feeling, it is easily got along with. For instance, it is morally certain that you commenced swinging to southwest, then west, to northwest. Had you kept on until you were heading directly north, you could rectify your course simply by following a true south course. But, as you have varied three-eighths of the circle, set your compass and travel by it to the southeast, until, in your judgment, you have about made up the deviation; then go straight south, and you will not be far wrong. Carry the compass in your hand and look at it every few minutes; for the tendency to swerve from a straight course when a man is once lost—and nearly always to the right—is a thing past understanding.

## Insect Pests

As regards poisonous insects, it may be said that, to the man with clean, bleached, tender skin, they are, at the start, an unendurable torment. No one can enjoy life with a smarting, burning, swollen face, while the attacks on every exposed inch of skin are persistent and constant. I have seen a young man after two days' exposure to these pests come out of the woods with one eye entirely closed and the brow hanging over it like a clamshell, while face and hands were almost hideous from inflammation and puffiness. The St. Regis and St. Francis Indians, although born and reared in the woods, by no means make light of the black fly.

It took the man who could shoot Phantom Falls to find out, "Its bite is not severe, nor is it ordinarily poisonous. There may be an occasional exception to this rule; but beside the bite of the mosquito, it is comparatively mild and harmless." And again: "Gnats…in my way of thinking, are much worse than the black fly or mosquito." So says Murray. Our observations differ. A thousand mosquitoes and as many gnats can bite me without leaving a mark, or having any effect save the pain of the bite while they are at work. But each bite of the black fly makes a separate and distinct boil that will not heal and be well in two months.

While fishing for brook trout in July last, I ran into a swarm of them on Moose River and got badly bitten. I had carelessly left my medicine behind. On the first of October the bites had not ceased to be painful, and it was three months before they disappeared entirely. Frank Forester[130] says, in his *Fish and Fishing*, page 371, that he has never fished for the red-fleshed trout of Hamilton County, "being deterred therefrom by dread of that curse of the summer angler, the black fly, which is to me especially venomous."

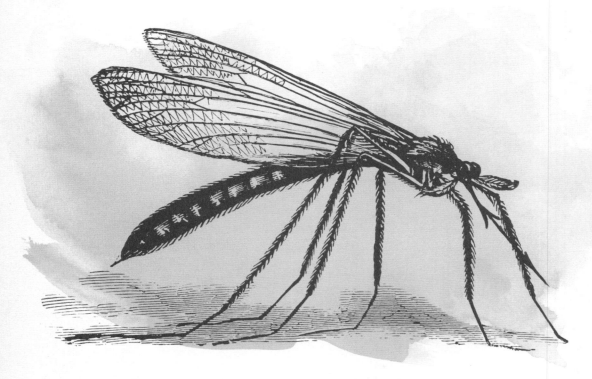

"Adirondack Murray" gives extended directions for beating these little pests by the use of buckskin gloves with chamois gauntlets, Swiss mull,[131] fine muslin, etc. Then he advises a mixture of sweet oil and tar, which is to be applied to face and hands, and he adds that it is easily washed off, leaving the skin soft and smooth as an infant's; all of which is true. But more than forty years' experience in the woods has taught me that the following recipe is infallible anywhere that sancudos,[132] moquims,[133] or our own poisonous insects do most abound.

---

130 The pen name of Henry William Herbert, an English writer and poet
131 A sheer muslin fabric
132 *Zancudos* is a Spanish word for "mosquitoes."
133 A type of mite

It was published in *Forest and Stream* in the summer of 1880, and again in '83. It has been pretty widely quoted and adopted, and I have never known it to fail: Three ounces pine tar, two ounces castor oil, one ounce pennyroyal oil. Simmer all together over a slow fire, and bottle for use. You will hardly need more than a two-ounce vial full in a season. One ounce has lasted me six weeks in the woods. Rub it in thoroughly and liberally at first, and after you have established a good glaze, a little replenishing from day to day will be sufficient. And don't fool with soap and towels where insects are plenty. A good safe coat of this varnish grows better the longer it is kept on—and it is cleanly and wholesome. If you get your face and hands crocky[134] or smutty about the campfire, wet the corner of your handkerchief and rub it off, not forgetting to apply the varnish at once, wherever you have cleaned it off. Last summer I carried a cake of soap and a towel in my knapsack through the North Woods for a seven weeks' tour, and never used either a single time. When I had established a good glaze on the skin, it was too valuable to be sacrificed for any weak whim connected with soap and water. When I struck a woodland hotel, I found soap and towels plenty enough. I found the mixture gave one's face the ruddy tanned look supposed to be indicative of health and hard muscle. A thorough ablution in the public washbasin reduced the color but left the skin very soft and smooth; in fact, as a lotion for the skin it is excellent. It is a soothing and healing application for poisonous bites already received.

I have given some space to the insect question, but no more than it deserves or requires. The venomous little wretches are quite important enough to spoil many a well-planned trip to the woods, and it is best to beat them from the start. You will find that immunity from insects and a comfortable camp are the two first and most indispensable requisites of an outing in the woods. And just here I will briefly tell how a young friend of mine went to the woods, some twenty-five years ago. He was a bank clerk, and a good fellow withal, with a leaning toward camp-life.

---

134  Dirty

For months, whenever we met, he would introduce his favorite topics, fishing, camping out, etc. At last in the hottest of the hot months, the time came. He put in an appearance with a fighting cut on his hair, a little stiff straw hat, and a soft skin, bleached by long confinement in a close office. I thought he looked a little tender, but he was sanguine. He could rough it, could sleep on the bare ground with the root of a tree for a pillow; as for mosquitoes and punkies, he never minded them.

## Beware the Black Fly

We went in a party of five, two old hunters and three youngsters, the latter all enthusiasm and pluck—at first. Toward the last end of a heavy eight-mile tramp, they grew silent, and slapped and scratched nervously. Arriving at the camping spot, they worked fairly well but were evidently weakening a little. By the time we were ready to turn in, they were reduced pretty well to silence and suffering—especially the bank clerk, Jean L. The punkies were eager for his tender skin, and they were rank poison to him. He muffled his head in a blanket and tried to sleep, but it was only a partial success. When, by suffocating himself, he obtained a little relief from insect bites, there were stubs and knotty roots continually poking themselves among his ribs or digging into his backbone.

I have often had occasion to observe that stubs, roots, and small stones, etc., have a perverse tendency to abrade the anatomy of people unused to the woods. Mr. C. D. Warner has noticed the same thing, I believe.

On the whole, Jean and the other youngsters behaved very well. Although they turned out in the morning with red, swollen faces and half-closed eyes, they all went trouting and caught about 150 small trout between them. They did their level bravest to make a jolly thing of it, but Jean's attempt to watch a deerlick, resulted in a wetting through the sudden advent of a shower, and the shower drove about all the punkies and mosquitoes in the neighborhood under our roof for shelter. I never saw them more plentiful or worse. Jean gave in and varnished his pelt thoroughly with my "punkie dope," as he called it, but too late; the mischief was done. And the second trial was worse to those youngsters than the first. More insects. More stubs and knots. Owing to these little annoyances, they arrived at home several days before their friends expected them—leaving enough rations in camp to last Old Sile and the writer a full week. And the moral of it is, if they had fitted themselves for the woods before going there, the trip would have been a pleasure instead of a misery.

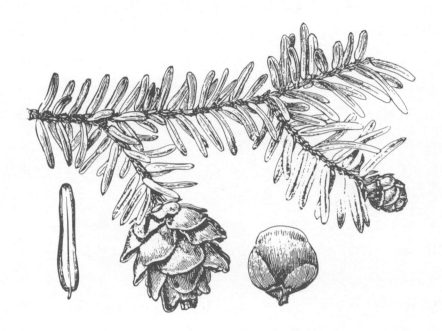

One other little annoyance I will mention, as a common occurrence among those who camp out; this is the lack of a pillow. I suppose I have camped fifty times with people, who, on turning in, were squirming around for a long time, trying to get a rest for the head. Boots are the most common resort. But when you place a bootleg—or two of them—under your head, they collapse and make a headrest less than half an inch thick. Just why it never occurs to people that a stuffing of moss, leaves, or hemlock browse would fill out the bed-leg and make a passable pillow is another conundrum I cannot answer. But there is another and better way of making a pillow for camp use, which I will describe further on.

And now I wish to devote some space to one of the most important adjuncts of woodcraft—camps; how to make them and how to make them comfortable. There are camps, and camps. There are camps in the North Woods that are really fine villas, costing thousands of dollars, and there are log-houses, and shanties, and bark camps, and A tents, and walled tents, shelter-tents, and

shanty-tents. But I assume that the camp best fitted to the wants of the average outer is the one that combines the essentials of dryness, lightness, portability, cheapness, and is easily and quickly put up. Another essential is that it must admit of a bright fire in front by night or day. I will give short descriptions of the forest shelters (camps) I have found handiest and most useful.

Firstly, I will mention a sort of camp that was described in a sportsman's paper and has since been largely quoted and used. It is made by fastening a horizontal pole to a couple of contiguous trees and then putting on a heavy covering of hemlock boughs, shingling them with the tips downward, of course. A fire is to be made at the roots of one of the trees. This, with plenty of boughs, may be made to stand a pretty stiff rain, but it is only a damp arbor, and no camp, properly speaking. A forest camp should always admit of a bright fire in front, with a lean-to or shed roof overhead, to reflect the fire heat on the bedding below. Any camp that falls short of this lacks the requirements of warmth, brightness, and healthfulness. This is why I discard all close, canvas tents.

## The Indian Camp

The simplest and most primitive of all camps is the "Indian camp." It is easily and quickly made, is warm and comfortable, and stands a pretty heavy rain when properly put up. This is how it is made: Let us say you are out and have slightly missed your way. The coming gloom warns you that night is shutting down. You are no tenderfoot. You know that a place of rest is essential to health and comfort through the long, cold November night. You dive down the first little hollow until you strike a rill[135] of water, for water is a prime necessity. As you draw your hatchet, you take in the whole situation at a glance. The little stream is gurgling downward in a half-choked frozen way. There is a huge sodden hemlock lying across it. One clip of the hatchet shows it will peel. There is plenty of smaller timber standing around, long, slim poles, with a tuft of foliage on top. Five minutes suffice to drop one of these, cut a twelve-foot pole from it, sharpen the pole at each end, jam one end into the ground and the other into the rough back of a scraggy hemlock, and there is your ridge pole. Now go—with your hatchet—for the bushiest and most promising young hemlocks within reach. Drop them and draw them to camp rapidly. Next, you need a fire. There are fifty hard, resinous limbs sticking up from the prone hemlock; lop off a few of these and split the largest into match timber; reduce the splinters to shavings, scrape the wet leaves from your prospective fireplace, and strike a match on the balloon part of your trousers. If you are a woodsman, you will strike but one. Feed the fire slowly at first; it will gain fast. When you have a blaze ten feet high, look at your watch. It is 6:00 p.m. You don't want to turn in before ten o'clock, and you have four hours to kill before bedtime. Now, tackle the old hemlock; take off every dry limb, and then peel the bark and bring it to camp. You will find this takes an hour or more.

---

135  A tiny brook

Next, strip every limb from your young hemlocks, and shingle them onto your ridge pole. This will make a sort of bear den, very well calculated to give you a comfortable night's rest. The bright fire will soon dry the ground that is to be your bed, and you will have plenty of time to drop another small hemlock and make a bed of browse a foot thick. You do it. Then you make your pillow. Now, this pillow is essential to comfort and very simple. It is half a yard of muslin, sewed up as a bag, and filled with moss or hemlock browse. You can empty it and put it in your pocket, where it takes up about as much room as a handkerchief. You have other little muslin bags—an'[136] you be wise. One holds

a couple of ounces of good tea; another, sugar; another is kept to put your loose duffel in: money, match safe, pocketknife. You have a pat of butter and a bit of pork, with a liberal slice of brown bread, and before turning in you make a cup of tea, broil a slice of pork, and indulge in a lunch.

Ten o'clock comes. The time has not passed tediously. You are warm, dry, and well fed. Your old friends, the owls, come near the firelight and salute you with their strange wild notes; a distant fox sets up for himself with his odd, barking cry and you turn in. Not ready to sleep just yet.

But you drop off, and it is two bells in the morning watch[137] when you waken with a sense of chill and darkness. The fire has burned low, and snow is falling. The owls have left, and a deep silence broods over the cold, still forest. You rouse the fire, and as the bright light shines to the farthest recesses of your forest den, get out the little pipe, and reduce a bit of navy plug[138] to its lowest denomination. The smoke curls lazily upward; the fire makes you warm and drowsy, and again you lie down—to again awaken with a sense of chilliness— to find the fire burned low and daylight breaking. You have slept better than you would in your own room at home. You have slept in an "Indian camp."

You have also learned the difference between such a simple shelter and an open-air bivouac under a tree or beside an old log.

Another easily made and very comfortable camp is the "brush shanty," as it is usually called in northern Pennsylvania. The frame for such a shanty is a cross-pole resting on two crotches about six feet high, and enough straight poles to make a foundation for the thatch. The poles are laid about six inches apart, one end of the ground, the other on the cross-pole, and at a pretty sharp angle. The thatch is made of the fan-like boughs cut from the thrifty young hemlock and are to be laid bottom upward and feather end down. Commence to lay them from the ground and work up to the cross-pole,

---

137  5:00 a.m.

138  An inch-thick roll of tobacco

shingling them carefully as you go. If the thatch be laid a foot in thickness, and well done, the shanty will stand a pretty heavy rain—better than the average bark roof, which is only rainproof in dry weather.

A bark camp, however, may be a very neat sylvan affair, provided you are camping where spruce or balsam fir may be easily reached, and in the hot months when bark will "peel," and you have a day in which to work at a camp. The best bark camps I have ever seen are in the Adirondacks. Some of them are rather elaborate in construction, requiring two or more days' hard labor by a couple of guides. When the stay is to be a long one, and the camp permanent, perhaps it will pay.

## The Shanty-Tent

As good a camp as I have ever tried—perhaps the best—is the "shanty-tent," shown in the illustration. It is easily put up, is comfortable, neat, and absolutely rainproof. Of course, it may be of any required size, but for a party of two, the following dimensions and directions will be found all sufficient:

Firstly, the roof. This is merely a sheet of strong cotton cloth 9 feet long by 4 or 4½ feet in width. The sides, of the same material, to be 4½ feet deep at front, and 2 feet deep at the back. This gives 7 feet along the edge of the roof, leaving 2 feet for turning down at the back end of the shanty. It will be seen that the sides must be "cut bias," to compensate for the angle of the roof; otherwise the shanty will not be square and shipshape when put up. Allowing for waste in cutting, it takes nearly 3 yards of cloth for each side. The only labor required in making is to cut the sides to the proper shape and stitch them to the roof. No buttons, strings, or loops. The cloth does not even require hemming. It does, however, need a little waterproofing, for which the following receipt will answer very well and add little or nothing to the weight: To 10 quarts of water add 10 ounces of lime and 4 ounces of alum; let it stand until clear; fold the cloth snugly and put it in another vessel, pour the solution on it, let it soak for 12 hours; then rinse in lukewarm rainwater, stretch and dry in the sun, and the shanty-tent is ready for use.

SHANTY-TENT
SPREAD OUT

## Construction

To put it up properly, make a neat frame as follows: two strong stakes or posts for the front, driven firmly in the ground 4½ feet apart; at a distance of 6 feet 10 inches from these, drive two other posts—these to be 4 feet apart—for back end of shanty. The front posts to be 4½ feet high, the back rests only 2 feet. The former also to incline a little toward each other above, so as to measure from outside of posts, just 4 feet at top. This gives a little more width at front end of shanty, adding space and warmth. No crotches are used in putting up the shanty-tent. Each of the four posts is fitted on the top to receive a flat-ended cross-pole and admit of nailing. When the posts are squarely ranged and driven, select two straight, hardwood rods, 2 inches in diameter and 7 feet in length—or a little more. Flatten the ends carefully and truly, lay them alongside on top from post to post, and fasten them with a light nail at each end. Now, select two more straight rods of the same size but a little over 4 feet in length; flatten the ends of these as you did the others, lay them crosswise from side to side, and lap the ends of the other rods; fasten them solidly by driving a six-penny nail through the ends and into the posts, and you have a square frame 7×4 feet. But it is not yet complete. Three light rods are needed for rafters. These are to be placed lengthwise of the roof at equal distances apart and nailed or tied to keep them in place. Then take two straight poles a little over 7 feet long and some 3 inches in diameter. These are to be accurately flattened at the ends and nailed to the bottom of the posts, snug to the ground, on outside of posts. A foot-log and head-log are indispensable. These should be about 5 inches in diameter and of a length to just reach from outside to outside of posts. They should be squared at ends, and the foot-log placed against the front post, outside, and held firmly in place by two wooden pins. The head-log is fastened the same way, except that it goes against the inside of the back posts, and the frame is complete. Round off all sharp angles or corners with knife and hatchet, and proceed to spread and fasten the cloth. Lay the roof on evenly, and tack it truly to the front cross-rod, using about a dozen 6-ounce tacks. Stretch the cloth to its bearings, and tack it at the back end in the same manner. Stretch it sidewise and tack the sides to the side poles, fore and aft. Tack front and back ends of sides to the front and back posts. Bring down the 2-foot flap of roof at back end of shanty; stretch and tack it snugly to the back posts—and your sylvan house is done. It is rainproof, windproof, warm, and comfortable. The foot- and head-logs define the limits of your forest dwelling, within which you may pile fragrant hemlock browse as thick as you please and renew it from day to day. It is the perfect camp.

You may put it up with less care and labor and make it do very well. But I have tried to explain how to do it in the best manner, to make it all sufficient for an entire season. And it takes longer to tell it on paper than to do it.

When I go to the woods with a partner, and we arrive at our camping ground,

I like him to get his fishing rig together and start out for a half day's exercise with his favorite flies, leaving me to make the camp according to my own notions of woodcraft. If he will come back about dusk with a few pounds of trout, I will have a pleasant camp and a bright fire for him. And if he has enjoyed wading an icy stream more than I have making the camp—he has had a good day.

Perhaps it may not be out of place to say that the camp, made as above, calls for fifteen bits of timber, posts, rods, etc.; a few shingle nails; and some six-penny wrought nails, with a paper of six-ounce tacks. Nails and tacks will weigh about five ounces and are always useful. In tacking the cloth, turn the raw edge in until you have four thicknesses, as a single thickness is apt to tear. If you desire to strike camp, it takes about ten minutes to draw and save all the nails and tacks, fold the cloth smoothly, and deposit the whole in your knapsack. If you wish to get up a shelter tent on fifteen minutes' notice, cut and sharpen a twelve-foot pole as for the Indian camp, stick one end in the ground, the other in the rough bark of a large tree—hemlock is best—hang the cloth on the pole, fasten the sides to rods, and the rods to the ground with inverted crotches, and your shelter tent is ready for you to creep under.

The above description of the shanty-tent may seem a trifle elaborate, but I hope it is plain. The affair weighs just three pounds, and it takes a skillful woodsman about three hours of easy work to put it in the shape described.

Leaving out some of the work, and only aiming to get it up in square shape as quickly as possible, I can put it up in an hour. The shanty as it should be, is shown in the illustration very fairly. And the shape of the cloth when spread out is shown in the diagram on page 179. On the whole, it is the best form of close-side tent I have found. It admits of a bright fire in front, without which a forest camp is just no camp at all to me. I have suffered enough in close, dark, cheerless, damp tents.

More than thirty years ago I became disgusted with the clumsy, awkward, comfortless affairs that, under many different forms, went under the name of camps. Gradually I came to make a study of "camping out." It would take too much time and space, should I undertake to describe all the different styles and forms I have tried. But I will mention a few of the best and worst.

## Other Camps

The old Down East "coal cabin" embodied the principle of the Indian camp. The frame was simply two strong crotches set firmly in the ground at a distance of eight feet apart and interlocking at top. These supported a stiff ridgepole fifteen feet long, the small end sharpened and set in the ground. Refuse boards, shooks, stakes, etc., were placed thickly from the ridgepole to the ground; a thick layer of straw was laid over these, and the whole was covered a foot thick with earth and sods, well beaten down. A stone wall five feet high at back and sides made a most excellent fireplace; and these cabins were weatherproof and warm, even in zero weather. But they were too cumbersome and included too much labor for the ordinary hunter and angler. Also, they were open to the objection, that while wide enough in front, they ran down to a dismal, cold peak at the far end. Remembering, however, the many pleasant winter nights I had passed with the coal-burners, I bought a supply of oilcloth and rigged it on the same principle. It was a partial success, and I used it for one season. But that cold, peaked, dark space was always back of my head, and it seemed like an iceberg. It was in vain that I tied a handkerchief about my head or drew a stocking leg over it. That miserable, icy angle was always there. And it would only shelter one man anyhow. When winter drove me out of the woods, I gave it to an enthusiastic young friend, bought some more oilcloth, and commenced a shanty-tent that was meant to be perfect. A good many leisure hours were spent in cutting and sewing that shanty, which proved rather a success. It afforded a perfect shelter for a space 7×4 feet but was a trifle heavy to pack, and the glazing began to crack and peel off in a short time. I made another and larger one of stout drilling,[139] soaked in lime-water and alum, and this was all that could be asked when put up properly on a frame. But the sides and ends being sewed to the roof made it unhandy to use as a shelter, when shelter was needed on short notice. So I ripped the back ends of the sides loose from the flap, leaving it, when spread out, as shown in the diagram. This was better; when it was necessary to make some sort of shelter in short order, it could be

done with a single pole as used in the Indian camp, laying the tent across the pole and using a few tacks to keep it in place at sides and center. This can be done in ten minutes and makes a shelter-tent that will turn a heavy rain for hours.

On the whole, for all kinds of weather, the shanty-tent is perhaps the best style of camp to be had at equal expense and trouble.

For a summer camp, however, I have finally come to prefer the simple lean-to or shed roof. It is the lightest, simplest, and cheapest of all cloth devices for camping out, and I have found it sufficient for all weathers from June until the fall of the leaves. It is only a sheet of strong cotton cloth 9×7 feet and soaked in lime and alum-water as the other. The only labor in making it is sewing two breadths of sheeting together. It needs no hemming, binding, loops, or buttons, but is to be stretched on a frame as described for the brush shanty and held in place with tacks. The one I have used for two seasons cost sixty cents and weighs 2¼ pounds. It makes a good shelter for a party of three, and if it be

139  A sturdy cotton fabric

found a little too breezy for cool nights, a sufficient windbreak can be made by driving light stakes at the sides and weaving in a siding of hemlock boughs.

## Sparks

Lastly, whatever cloth structure you may elect to use for a camp, do not fail to cover the roof with a screen of green boughs before building your campfire. Because there will usually be one fellow in camp who has a penchant for feeding the fire with old mulchy deadwood and brush, for the fun of watching the blaze, and the sparks that are prone to fly upward, forgetting that the blazing cinders are also prone to drop downward on the roof of the tent, burning holes in it.

I have spoken of some of the best camps I know. The worst ones are the A and wall tents, with all closed camps in which one is required to seclude himself through the hours of sleep in damp and darkness, utterly cut off from the cheerful, healthful light and warmth of the campfire.

## CHAPTER IV

# CAMPFIRES AND THEIR IMPORTANCE– THE WASTEFUL, WRONG WAY THEY ARE USUALLY MADE AND THE RIGHT WAY TO MAKE THEM

HARDLY SECOND IN IMPORTANCE TO A WARM, dry camp is the campfire. In point of fact, the warmth, dryness, and healthfulness of a forest camp are mainly dependent on the way the fire is managed and kept up. No asthmatic or consumptive patient ever regained health by dwelling in a close, damp tent. I once camped for a week in a wall tent, with a Philadelphia party, and in cold weather. We had a little sheet iron fiend, called a camp-stove. When well fed with bark, knots, and chips, it would get red hot, and, heaven knows, give out heat enough. By the time we were sound asleep, it would subside, and we would presently awake with chattering teeth to kindle her up again, take a smoke and a nip, turn in for another nap—to awaken again half frozen. It was a poor substitute for the open camp and bright fire. An experience of fifty years convinces me that a large percentage of the benefit obtained by invalids from camp-life is attributable to the open camp and well-managed campfire. And the latter is usually handled in a way that is too sad, too wasteful; in short, badly botched. For instance.

# The "Guides' Camp"

It happened in the summer of '81 that I was making a canoe trip in the Northern Wilderness, and as Raquette Lake is the largest and about the most interesting lake in the North Woods, I spent about a week paddling, fishing, etc. I made my headquarters at Ed Bennett's woodland hostelry, "Under the Hemlocks." As the hotel was filled with men, women, and crying children, bitten to agony by punkies and mosquitoes, I chose to spread my blanket in a well-made bark shanty, which a signboard in black and white said was the "Guides' Camp."

And this camp was a very popular institution. Here it was that every evening, when night had settled down on forest and lake, the guests of the hotel would gather to lounge on the bed of fresh balsam browse, chat, sing, and enjoy the huge campfire.

No woodland hotel will long remain popular that does not keep up a bright, cheery, out-o'-door fire. And the fun of it—to an old woodsman—is in noting how like a lot of schoolchildren they all act about the fire. Ed Bennett had a man, a North Woods trapper, in his employ, whose chief business was to furnish plenty of wood for the guides' camp and start a good fire every evening by sundown. As it grew dark and the blaze shone high and bright, the guests would begin to straggle in, and every man, woman, and child seemed to view it as a religious duty to pause by the fire and add a stick or two before passing into camp. The wood was thrown on endwise, crosswise, or any way, so that it would burn, precisely as a crowd of boys make a bonfire on the village green. The object being, apparently, to get rid of the wood in the shortest possible time.

When the fire burnt low, toward midnight, the guests would saunter off to the hotel, and the guides, who had been waiting impatiently, would organize what was left of the fire, roll themselves in their blankets, and turn in. I suggested to the trapper that he and I make one fire as it should be, and maybe they would follow suit—which would save half the fuel, with a better fire. But he said, "No; they like to build bonfires, and 'Ed' can stand the wood, because it is best to let them have their own way. Time seems to hang heavy on their hands— and they pay well." Summer boarders, tourists and sportsmen, are not the only men who know how to build a campfire all wrong.

When I first came to northern Pennsylvania, thirty-five years ago, I found game fairly abundant, and as I wanted to learn the country where deer most abounded, I naturally cottoned to the local hunters. Good fellows enough, and conceited, as all local hunters and anglers are apt to be. Strong, good hunters and axmen, to the manner born, and prone to look on any outsider as a tenderfoot. Their mode of building campfires was a constant vexation to me. They made it a point to always have a heavy sharp axe in camp, and toward night some sturdy chopper would cut eight or ten logs as heavy as the whole party could lug to camp with handspikes. The size of the logs was proportioned to the muscular force in camp. If there was a party of six or eight, the logs would be twice as heavy as when we were three or four. Just at dark, there would be a log heap built in front of the camp, well chinked with bark, knots, and small sticks, and for the next two hours, one could hardly get at the fire to light a pipe. But the fire was sure though slow. By 10:00 or 11:00 p.m., it would work its way to the front, and the camp would be warm and light. The party would turn in, and deep sleep would fall on a lot of tired hunters—

for two or three hours. By which time some fellow near the middle was sure to throw his blanket off with a spiteful jerk and dash out of camp with, "Holy Moses! I can't stand this; it's an oven."

Another Snorer (partially waking): "N-r-r-rm, gu-r-r, ugh. Can't you—deaden—fire—a little?"

First Speaker: "Deaden h——. If you want the fire deadened, get up and help throw off some of these logs."

Another (in coldest corner of shanty): "What's 'er matter—with a-you fellows? Better dig out—an' cool off in the snow. Shanty's comfor'ble enough."

His minority report goes unheeded. The camp is roasted out. Strong hands and handspikes pry a couple of glowing logs from the front and replace them with two cold, green logs; the camp cools off, and the party takes to blankets once more—to turn out again at 5:00 a.m. and inaugurate breakfast. The fire is not in favorable shape for culinary operations, the heat is mainly on the back side, just where it isn't wanted. The few places level enough to set a pot or pan are too hot, and, in short, where there is any fire, there is too much. One man sees, with intense disgust, the nozzle of his coffeepot drop into the fire. He makes a rash grab to save his coffee, and gets away—with the handle, which hangs on just enough to upset the pot.

"Old Al," who is frying a slice of pork over a bed of coals that would melt a gun barrel, starts a horse laugh that is cut short by a blue flash and an explosion of pork fat, which nearly blinds him. And the writer, taking in these mishaps in the very spirit of fun and frolic, is suddenly sobered and silenced by seeing his venison steak drop from the end of the "frizzling[140] stick," and disappear between two glowing logs. The party manages, however, to get off on the hunt at daylight, with full stomachs, and perhaps the hearty fun and laughter more than compensate for these little mishaps.

---

140  Frying or crisping

This is a digression. But I am led to it by the recollection of many nights spent in camps and around campfires, pretty much as described above. I can smile today at the remembrance of the calm, superior way in which the old hunters of that day would look down on me, as from the upper branches of a tall hemlock, when I ventured to suggest that a better fire could be made with half the fuel and less than half the labor. They would kindly remark, "Oh, you are a Boston boy. You are used to paying $8.00 a cord for wood. We have no call to save wood here. We can afford to burn it by the acre." Which was more true than logical. Most of these men had commenced life with a stern declaration of war against the forest, and although the men usually won at last, the battle was a long and hard one. Small wonder that they came to look upon a forest tree as a natural enemy. The campfire question came to a crisis, however, with two or three of these old settlers. And, as the story well illustrates my point, I will venture to tell it.

## A Winter Camp

It was in the "dark days before Christmas" that a party of four started from W., bound for a camp on Second Fork, in the deepest part of the wilderness that lies between Wellsboro and the Block House. The party consisted of Sile J., Old Al, Eli J., and the writer. The two first were gray-haired men, the others past thirty; all the same, they called us "the boys." The weather was not inviting, and there was small danger of our camp being invaded by summer outers or tenderfeet. It cost twelve miles of hard travel to reach that camp, and though we started at daylight, it was past noon when we arrived. The first seven miles could be made on wheels, the balance by hard tramping. The road was execrable; no one cared to ride, but it was necessary to have our loads carried as far as possible. The clearings looked dreary enough, and the woods forbidding to a degree, but our old camp was the picture of desolation. There was six inches of damp snow on the leafless brush roof, the blackened brands of our last fire were sticking their charred ends out of the snow, the hemlocks were bending sadly under their loads of wet snow, and the entire surroundings had a cold, cheerless, slushy look, very little like the ideal hunter's camp. We placed our knapsacks in the shanty, Eli got out his nail hatchet, I drew my little pocket-axe, and we proceeded to start a fire, while the two older men went upstream a few rods to unearth a full-grown axe and a bottle of old rye, which they had cached under a log three months before. They never fooled with pocket-axes. They were gone so long that we sauntered up the band, thinking it might be the rye that detained them. We found them with their coats off, working like beavers, each with a stout, sharpened stick. There had been an October freshet,[141] and a flood-jam at the bend had sent the mad stream over its banks, washing the log out of position and piling a gravel bar two feet deep over the spot where the axe and flask should have been. About the only thing left to do was to cut a couple of stout sticks, organize a mining company, limited, and go in; which they did. Sile was drifting into the side of the sandbar savagely, trying to strike the axe-helve,[142] and Old Al was sinking numberless miniature shafts from the surface in a vain attempt to strike whiskey. The company failed in about half an hour. Sile resumed his coat and sat down on a log—which was one of his best holds, by the way. He looked at Al; Al looked at him; then both looked at us, and Sile remarked that if one of the boys wanted to go out to the clearings and "borry" an axe, and come back in the morning, he thought the others could pick up wood enough to tough it out one night. Of course, nobody could stay in an open winter camp without an axe.

It was my time to come to the front. I said: "You two just go at the camp; clean the snow off and slick up the inside. Put my shelter-cloth with Eli's, and cover the roof with them, and if you don't have just as good a fire tonight as you ever had, you can tie me to a beech and leave me here. Come on, Eli." And Eli did come on. And this is how we did it: We first felled a thrifty butternut tree ten inches in diameter, cut off three lengths at five feet each, and carried them to camp. These were the backlogs. Two stout stakes were driven at the back of the fire, and the logs, on top of each other, were laid firmly against the stakes. The latter were slanted a little back, and the largest log placed at bottom, the smallest on top, to prevent tipping forward. A couple of short, thick sticks were laid with the ends against the bottom log by way of fire dogs;[143] a fore stick, five

---

141  Rise of the stream due to hard rainfall or snowmelt
142  Handle
143  Andirons, which are supports for the firewood

feet long and five inches in diameter; a well-built pyramid of bark, knots, and small logs completed the campfire, which sent a pleasant glow of warmth and heat to the farthest corner of the shanty. For "night wood," we cut a dozen birch and ash poles from four to six inches across, trimmed them to the tips, and dragged them to camp. Then we denuded a dry hemlock of its bark by the aid of ten-foot poles, flattened at one end, and packed the bark to camp. We had a bright, cheery fire from the early evening until morning, and four tired hunters never slept more soundly.

We stayed in that camp a week, and though the weather was rough and cold, the little pocket-axes kept us well in firewood. We selected butternut for backlogs, because, when green, it burns very slowly and lasts a long time. And we dragged our smaller wood to camp in lengths of twenty to thirty feet, because it was easier to lay them on the fire and burn them in two than to cut them shorter with light hatchets. With a heavy axe, we should have cut them to lengths of five or six feet.

## Our Luck

Our luck, I may mention, was good—as good as we desired. Not that four smallish deer are anything to brag about for a week's hunt by four men and two dogs. I have known a pot-hunter[144] to kill nine in a single day. But we had enough.

As it was, we were obliged to "double trip it" in order to get our deer and duffel down to "Babb's." And we gave away more than half our venison. For the rest, the illustrations show the campfire—all but the fire—as it should be made.

144  One who hunts for food, not sport

## CHAPTER V

# FISHING, WITH AND WITHOUT FLIES— SOME TACKLE AND LURES—DISCURSIVE REMARKS ON THE GENTLE ART— THE HEADLIGHT— FROGGING

**T**HERE IS PROBABLY NO SUBJECT CONNECTED with outdoor sport so thoroughly and exhaustively written up as fly-fishing and all that pertains thereto. Fly-fishing for speckled trout always, and deservedly, takes the lead. Bass fishing usually comes next, though some writers accord second place to the lake trout, salmon trout, or landlocked salmon. The muskellunge,[145] as a game fish, is scarcely behind the smallmouth bass, and is certainly more gamy than the lake trout. The largemouth bass and pickerel are usually ranked about with the yellow perch. I don't know why; they are certainly gamy enough. Perhaps it is because they do not leap out of water when hooked. Both are good on the table.

---

145  A freshwater fish in the pike family

A dozen able and interesting authors have written books wherein trout, flies, and fly-fishing are treated in a manner that leaves an old backwoodsman little to say. Rods, reels, casting lines, flies, and fish are described and descanted on in a way, and in a language, the reading whereof reduces me to temporary insanity. And yet I seem to recollect some bygone incidents concerning fish and fishing. I have a well-defined notion that I once stood on Flat Rock, in Big Pine Creek, and caught over 350 fine trout in a short day's fishing. Also that many times I left home on a bright May or June morning, walked eight miles, caught a twelve-pound creel of trout, and walked home before bedtime.

I remember that once, in Michigan, on the advice of local fishermen, I dragged a spoon around Highbank Lake two days, with little result save half a dozen blisters on my hands and that on the next morning, taking a long tamarack pole and my own way of fishing, I caught, before 10:00 a.m., fifty pounds of bass and pickerel, weighing from two to ten pounds each.

Gibson, whose spoon, line, and skiff I had been using and who was the fishing oracle of that region, could hardly believe his eyes. I kept that country inn, and the neighborhood as well, supplied with fish for the next two weeks.

It is truth to say that I have never struck salt- or freshwaters, where edible fish were at all plentiful, without being able to take, in some way, all that I needed. Notably and preferably with the fly if that might be. If not, then with worms, grubs, minnows, grasshoppers, crickets, or any sort of doodle bug their highnesses might affect. When a plump, two-pound trout refuses to eat a tinseled, feathered fraud, I am not the man to refuse him something more edible.

That I may not be misunderstood, let me say that I recognized the speckled brook trout as the very emperor of all game fish, and angling for him with the fly as the neatest, most fascinating sport attainable by the angler. But there are thousands of outers who, from choice or necessity, take their summer vacations where *Salmo fontinalis* is not to be had. They would prefer him, either on the leader or the table, but he is not there; "And a man has got a stomach, and we live by what we eat."

Wherefore, they go a-fishing for other fish. So that they are successful and sufficiently fed, the difference is not so material. I have enjoyed myself hugely catching catties[146] on a dark night from a skiff with a hand-line.

I can add nothing in a scientific way to the literature of fly-fishing, but I can give a few hints that may be conducive to practical success, as well with trout as with less noble fish. In fly-fishing, one serviceable four-ounce rod is enough, and a plain click reel, of small size, is just as satisfactory as a more costly affair. Twenty yards of tapered, waterproof line, with a six-foot leader, and a cost of two flies, complete the rig and will be found sufficient. In common with most fly-fishers, I have mostly thrown a cast of three flies but have found two just as effective, and handier.

## The Best Flies

We all carry too many flies. Some of my friends have more than sixty dozen and will never use a tenth of them. In the summer of '88, finding I had more than seemed needful, I left all but four dozen behind me. I wet only fifteen of them in a seven weeks' outing. And they filled the bill. I have no time or space for a dissertation on the hundreds of different flies made and sold at the present day. Abler pens have done that. I will, however, name a few that I have found good in widely different localities (i.e., the Northern Wilderness of New York and the upper waters of northern Pennsylvania). For the Northern Wilderness: Scarlet ibis, split ibis, Romeyn, white-winged coachman, royal coachman, red hackle, red-bodied ashy, and gray-bodied ashy. The ashies were good for black bass also. For northern Pennsylvania: Queen of the waters, professor, red fox, coachman, black may, white-winged coachman, wasp, brown hackle, Seth Green. Ibis flies are worthless here. Using the dark flies in bright water and clear weather, and the brighter colors for evening, the list was long enough.

At the commencement of the open season, and until the young maple leaves are half grown, bait will be found far more successful than the fly. At this time the trout are pretty evenly distributed along lakeshores and streams, choosing to lie quietly in rather deep pools and avoiding swift water. A few may rise to

---

146 Catfish

the fly in a logy, indifferent way, but the best way to take them is bait-fishing with well-cleansed angleworms or white grubs, the latter being the best bait I have ever tried. They take the bait sluggishly at this season, but on feeling the hook, wake up to their normal activity and fight gamely to the last. When young, newborn insects begin to drop freely on the water about the 20th of May, trout leave the pools and take to the riffles. And from this time until the latter part of June the fly-fisherman is in his glory. It may be true that the skillful bait-fisherman will rather beat his creel. He cares not for that. He can take enough, and he had rather take ten trout with the fly than a score with bait. As for the man who goes a-fishing simply to catch fish, the fly-fisher does not recognize him as an angler at all.

When the sun is hot and the weather grows warm, trout leave the ripples and take to cold springs and spring holes; the largest fish, of course, monopolizing the deepest and coolest places, while the smaller ones hover around, or content themselves with shallower water. As the weather gets hotter, the fly-fishing falls off badly. A few trout of four to eight ounces in weight may still be raised, but the larger ones are lying on the bottom and are not to be fooled with feathers. They will take a tempting bait when held before their noses—sometimes; at other times, not. As to raising them with a fly—as well attempt to raise a sick Indian with the temperance pledge. And yet, they may be taken in bright daylight by a ruse that I learned long ago, of a youngster less than half my age, a little, freckled, thin-visaged young man, whose health was evidently affected by a daily struggle with a pair of tow-colored side whiskers and a light mustache. There was hardly enough of the whole affair to make a doormat for a beehive. But he seemed so proud of the plant, that I forbore to rig him. He was better than he looked—as often happens. The landlord said, "He brings in large trout every day, when our best fly-fishermen fail." One night, around an outdoor fire, we got acquainted, and I found him a witty, pleasant companion. Before turning in I ventured to ask him how he succeeded in taking large trout, while the experts only caught small ones, or failed altogether.

"Go with me tomorrow morning to a spring hole three miles up the river, and I'll show you," he said.

## At the Spring Hole

Of course, we went. He, rowing a light skiff, and I paddling a still lighter canoe. The spring hole was in a narrow bay that set back from the river, and at the mouth of a cold, clear brook; it was ten to twelve feet deep, and at the lower end a large balsam had fallen in with the top in just the right place for getting away with large fish, or tangling lines and leaders. We moored some twenty feet above the spring hole and commenced fishing, I with my favorite cast of flies, my friend with the tail of a minnow. He caught a 1½-pound trout almost at the outset, but I got no rise; did not expect it. Then I went above, where the water was shallower, and raised a couple of half-pounders, but could get no more. I thought he had better go to the hotel with what he had, but my friend said "wait"; he went ashore and picked up a long pole with a bushy tip; it had evidently been used before. Dropping down to the spring hole, he thrust the tip to the bottom and slashed it around in a way to scare and scatter every trout within a hundred feet.

"And what does all that mean?" I asked.

"Well," he said, "every trout will be back in less than an hour, and when they first come back, they take the bait greedily. Better take off your leader and try bait."

Which I did. Dropping our hooks to the bottom, we waited some twenty minutes, when he had a bite, and, having strong tackle, soon took in a trout that turned the scale at $2\frac{1}{4}$ pounds. Then my turn came and I saved one weighing $1\frac{1}{2}$ pounds. He caught another of $1\frac{1}{4}$ pounds, and I took one of 1 pound. Then they ceased biting altogether.

"And now," said my friend, "if you will work your canoe carefully around to that old balsam top and get the light where you can see the bottom, you may see some large trout."

I did as directed and, making a telescope of my hand, looked intently for the bottom of the spring hole. At first I could see nothing but water; then I made out some dead sticks, and finally began to dimly trace the outlines of large fish. There they were, more than forty of them, lying quietly on the bottom like suckers, but genuine brook trout, every one of them.

"This," said he, "makes the fifth time I have brushed them out of here, and I have never missed taking from two to five large trout. I have two other places where I always get one or two, but this is the best."

At the hotel we found two fly-fishers who had been out all the morning. They each had three or four small trout.

During the next week we worked the spring holes daily in the same way, and always with success. I have also had good success by building a bright fire on the bank and fishing a spring hole by the light—a mode of fishing especially successful with catties and perch.

A bright, bull's-eye headlight, strapped on a stiff hat, so that the light can be thrown where it is wanted, is an excellent device for night fishing. And during the heated term, when fish are slow and sluggish, I have found the following plan works well: Bake a hard, well-salted water "johnnycake,"[147] break it into

---

147 Corn bread

pieces the size of a hen's egg, and drop the pieces into a spring hole. This calls a host of minnows, and the larger fish follow the minnows. It will prove more successful on perch, catties, chubs, etc., than on trout, however. By this plan, I have kept a camp of five men well supplied with fish when their best flies failed—as they mostly do in very hot weather.

Fishing for muskellunge, pickerel, and bass is quite another thing, though by many valued as a sport scarcely inferior to fly-fishing for trout. I claim no especial skill with the fly rod. It is a good day when I get my tail fly more than fifteen yards beyond the reel, with any degree of accuracy.

My success lies mainly with the tribes of *Esox* and *Micropterus*.[148] Among these, I have seldom or never failed during the last thirty-six years, when the water was free of ice, and I have had just as good luck when largemouth bass and pickerel were in the "off season," as at any time. For in many waters there comes a time—in late August and September—when neither bass nor pickerel will notice the spoon, be it handled never so wisely. Even the muskellunge looks on the flashing cheat with indifference; though a very hungry specimen may occasionally immolate himself. It was at such a season that I fished Highbank Lake—as before mentioned—catching from forty to fifty pounds of fine fish every morning for nearly two weeks, after the best local fishermen had assured me that not a decent-sized fish could be taken at that season. Perhaps a brief description of the modes and means that have proved invariably successful for many years may afford a few useful hints, even to old anglers.

## Frog-Bait and Gangs

To begin with, I utterly discard all modern "gangs" and "trains," carrying from seven to thirteen hooks each. They are all too small, and all too many; better calculated to scratch and tear than to catch and hold. Three hooks are enough at the end of any line, and better than more. These should be fined or honed to a perfect point, and the abrupt part of the barb filed down one-half. All hooks, as usually made, have twice as much barb as they should have, and

---

148  Both genera of freshwater fish

the sharp bend of the barb prevents the entering of the hook in hard bony structures, wherefore the fish only stays hooked so long as there is a taut pull on the line. A little loosening of the line and shake of the head sets him free. But no fish can shake out a hook well sunken in mouth or gills, though two-thirds of the barb be filed away.

For muskellunge or pickerel I invariably use wire snells made as follows: Lay off four or more strands of fine brass wire 13 inches long; turn one end of the wires smoothly over a No. 1 iron wire, and work the ends in between the strands below. Now, with a pair of pincers hold the ends and, using No. 1 as a handle, twist the ends and body of the snell firmly together; this gives the loop. Next, twist the snell evenly and strongly from end to end. Wax the end of the snell thoroughly for two or three inches, and wax the tapers of two strong Sproat or O'Shaughnessy hooks, and wind the lower hook on with strong, waxed silk, to the end of the taper; then lay the second hook at right angles with the first, and one inch above it; wind this as the other, and then fasten a third and smaller hook above that for a lip hook. This gives the snell about one foot in length, with the two lower hooks standing at right angles, one above the other, and a third and smaller hook in line with the second.

The bait is the element of success; it is made as follows: Slice off a clean, white pork rind, four or five inches long by an inch and a half wide; lay it on a board, and, with a sharp knife cut it as nearly to the shape of a frog as your ingenuity permits. Prick a slight gash in the head to admit the lip hook, which should be an inch and a half above the second one, and see that the fork of the bait rests securely in the barb of the middle hook.

Use a stout bait-rod and a strong line. Fish from a boat, with a second man to handle the oars, if convenient. Let the oarsman lay the boat ten feet inside the edge of the lily pads, and make your cast, say, with thirty feet of line; land the bait neatly to the right, at the edge of the lily pads, let it sink a few inches, and then with the tip well lowered, bring the bait around on a slight curve by a quick succession of draws, with a momentary pause between each; the object being to imitate as nearly as possible a swimming frog. If this be neatly done, and if the bait be made as it should be, at every short halt the legs will spread naturally, and the imitation is perfect enough to deceive the most experienced bass or pickerel. When half a dozen casts to right and left have been made without success, it is best to move on, still keeping inside and casting outside the lily pads.

A pickerel of three pounds or more will take in all three hooks at the first snap, and as he closes his mouth tightly and starts for the bottom, strike quickly, but not too hard, and let the boatman put you out into deep water at once, where you are safe from the strong roots of the yellow lily.

It is logically certain your fish is well hooked. You cannot pull two strong, sharp hooks through that tightly closed mouth without fastening at least one of them where it will do most good. Oftener both will catch, and it frequently happens that one hook will catch each lip, holding the mouth nearly closed, and shortening the struggles of a large fish very materially. On taking off a fish, and before casting again, see that the two lower hooks stand at right angles. If they have got turned in the struggle, you can turn them at any angle you like; the twisted wire is stiff enough to hold them in place. Every angler knows the bold, determined manner in which the muskellunge strikes his prey.

He will take in bait and hooks at the first dash, and if the rod be held stiffly usually hooks himself. Barring large trout, he is the king of game fish. The largemouth bass is less savage in his attacks but is a free biter. He is apt to come up behind and seize the bait about two-thirds of its length, turn, and bore down for the bottom. He will mostly take in the lower hooks, however, and is certain to get fastened. His large mouth is excellent for retaining the hook.

As for the smallmouth (*Micropterus dolomieu*, if you want to be scientific), I have found him more capricious than any game fish on the list. One day he will take only Dobsons, or crawfish; the next, he may prefer minnows, and again, he will rise to the fly or a bucktail spinner.

On the whole, I have found the pork frog the most successful lure in his case, but the hooks and bait must be arranged differently. Three strands of fine wire will make a snell strong enough, and the hooks should be strong, sharp, and rather small, the lower hooks placed only half an inch apart, and a small lip hook two and a quarter inches above the middle one. As the fork of the bait will not reach the bend of the middle hook, it must be fastened to the snell by a few stitches taken with stout thread, and the lower end of the bait should not reach more than a quarter of an inch beyond the bottom of the hook, because the smallmouth has a villainous trick of giving his prey a stern chase, nipping constantly and viciously at the tail, and the above arrangement will be apt to hook him at the first snap. Owing to this trait, some artificial minnows with one or two hooks at the caudal[149] end are very killing—when he will take them.

## Lake Trout

Lake, or salmon trout, may be trolled for successfully with the above lure, but I do not much affect fishing for them. Excellent sport may be had with them, however, early in the season, when they are working near the shore, but they soon retire to water from fifty to seventy feet deep and can only be caught by deep trolling or buoy-fishing. I have no fancy for sitting in a slow-moving boat for hours, dragging three or four hundred feet of line in deep water, a four-pound

---

149 Tail

sinker tied by six feet of lighter line some twenty feet above the hooks. The sinker is supposed to go bumping along the bottom, while the bait follows three or four feet above it. The drag of the line and the constant joggling of the sinker on rocks and snags make it difficult to tell when one has a strike—and it is always too long between bites.

Sitting for hours at a baited buoy with a hand-line, and without taking a fish, is still worse, as more than once I have been compelled to acknowledge in very weariness of soul. There are enthusiastic anglers, however, whose specialty is trolling for lake trout. A gentleman by the name of Thatcher, who has a fine residence on Raquette Lake—which he calls a camp—makes this his leading sport, and keeps a log of his fishing, putting nothing on record of less than ten pounds weight. His largest fish was booked at twenty-eight pounds, and he added that a well-conditioned salmon trout was superior to a brook trout on the table, in which I quite agree with him. But he seemed quite disgusted when I ventured to suggest that a well-conditioned cattie or bullhead—caught in the same waters—was better than either.

"Do you call the cattie a game fish?" he asked.

Yes; I call any fish a game fish that is taken for sport with hook and line. I can no more explain the common prejudice against the catfish and eel than I can tell why an experienced angler should drag a gang of thirteen hooks through the water—ten of them being worse than superfluous. "Frank Forester" gives five hooks as the number for a trolling gang. We mostly use hooks too small and do not look after points and barbs closely enough. A pair of No. 1 O'Shaughnessy, or 1½ Sproat, or five tapered blackfish hooks, will make a killing rig for smallmouth bass using No. 4 Sproat for lip hook. Larger hooks are better for the largemouth, a four-pound specimen of which will easily take in one's fist. A pair of 5-0 O'Shaughnessy's or Sproat's will be found none too large, and as for the muskellunge and pickerel, if I must err, let it be on the side of large hooks and strong lines.

# Stout Tackle

It is idle to talk of playing the fish in water where the giving of a few yards ensures a hopeless tangle among roots, treetops, etc. I was once fishing in Western waters where the pickerel ran very large, and I used a pair of the largest salmon hooks with tackle strong enough to hold a fish of fifteen pounds, without any playing; notwithstanding which, I had five trains of three hooks each taken off in as many days by monster pickerel. An expert muskellunge fisherman—Davis by name—happened to take board at the farmhouse where I was staying, and he had a notion that he could "beat some of them big fellows," and he did it; with three large cod hooks, a bit of fine, strong chain, twelve yards of cod-line, an eighteen-foot tamarack pole, and a twelve-inch sucker for bait. I thought it the most outlandish rig I had ever seen but went with him in the early gray of the morning to see it tried, just where I had lost my hooks and fish.

Raising the heavy bait in the air, he would give it a whirl to gather headway and launch it forty feet away with a splash that might have been heard thirty rods. It looked more likely to scare than catch but was a success. At the third or fourth cast we plainly saw a huge pickerel rise, shut his immense mouth over bait, hooks, and a few inches of chain, turn lazily, and head for the bottom, where Mr. D let him rest a minute, and then struck steadily but strongly. The subsequent struggle depended largely on main strength, though there was a good deal of skill and cool judgment shown in the handling and landing of the fish. A pickerel of forty pounds or more is not to be snatched out of the water on his first mad rush; something must be yielded—and with no reel there is little chance of giving line. It struck me my friend managed his fish remarkably well, towing him back and forth with a strong pull, never giving him a rest and finally sliding him out on a low muddy bank, as though he were a smooth log. We took him up to the house and tested the size of his mouth by putting a quart cup in it, which went in easily. Then we weighed him, and he turned the scales at forty-four pounds. It was some consolation to find three of my hooks sticking in his mouth. Lastly, we had a large section of him stuffed and baked. It was good, but a ten-pound fish would have been better. The moral of all this—if it has any moral—is, use hooks according to the size of fish you expect to catch.

And, when you are in a permanent camp, and fishing is very poor, try frogging. It is not a sport of a high order, though it may be called angling—and it can be made amusing, with hook and line. I have seen educated ladies in the wilderness, fishing for frogs with an eagerness and enthusiasm not surpassed by the most devoted angler with his favorite cast of flies.

There are several modes of taking the festive batrachian. He is speared with a frog-spear; caught under the chin with snatch-hooks; taken with hook and line or picked up from a canoe with the aid of a headlight, or jack-lamp.[150] The two latter modes are best.

To take him with hook and line: a light rod, six to eight feet of line, a snell of single gut with a 1-0 Sproat or O'Shaughnessy hook, and a bit of bright scarlet flannel for bait; this is the rig. To use it, paddle up behind him silently and drop the rag just in front of his nose. He is pretty certain to take it on the instant.

---

150  A handheld lamp

Knock him on the head before cutting off his legs. It is unpleasant to see him squirm and hear him cry like a child while you are sawing at his thigh joints.

By far the most effective manner of frogging is by the headlight on dark nights. To do this most successfully, one man in a light canoe, a good headlight, and a light, one-handed paddle are the requirements. The frog is easily located, either by his croaking, or by his peculiar shape. Paddle up to him silently and throw the light in his eyes; you may then pick him up as you would a potato. I have known a North Woods guide to pick up a five-quart pail of frogs in an hour, on a dark evening. On the table, frogs' legs are usually conceded first place for delicacy and flavor. For an appetizing breakfast in camp, they have no equal, in my judgment. The high price they bring at the best hotels, and their growing scarcity, attest the value placed on them by men who know how and what to eat. And, not many years ago, an old pork-gobbling backwoodsman threw his frying pan into the river because I had cooked frogs' legs in it. While another, equally intelligent, refused to use my frying pan, because I had cooked eels in it, remarking sententiously, "Eels is snakes, an' I know it."

It may be well, just here and now, to say a word on the importance of the headlight. I know of no more pleasant and satisfactory adjunct of a camp than a good light that can be adjusted to the head, used as a jack[151] in floating, carried in the hand, or fastened up inside the shanty. Once fairly tried, it will never be ignored or forgotten. Not that it will show a deer's head seventeen rods distant with sufficient clearness for a shot—or your sights with distinctness enough to make it

A headlight that will show a deer plainly at six rods, while lighting the sights of a rifle with clearness, is an exceptionally good light. More deer are killed in floating under than over four rods. There are various styles of headlights, jack-lamps, etc., in use. They are bright, easily adjusted, and will show rifle sights, or a deer, up to 100 feet—which is enough. They are also convenient in camp and better than a lantern on a dim forest path.

---

151 Jack-lamp

Before leaving the subject of bait-fishing, I have a point or two I wish to make. I have attempted to explain the frog-bait, and the manner of using it, and I shall probably never have occasion to change my belief that it is, on the whole, the most killing lure for the entire tribes of bass and pickerel. There is, however, another, which, if properly handled, is almost as good. It is as follows:

Take a bass, pickerel, or yellow perch, of one pound or less; scrape the scales clean on the underside from the caudal fin to a point just forward of the vent.

## Swivels and Snells

Next, with a sharp knife, cut up toward the backbone, commencing just behind the vent with a slant toward the tail. Run the knife smoothly along just under the backbone and out through the caudal fin, taking about one-third of the latter and making a clean, white bait, with the anal and part of the caudal by way of fins. It looks very like a white minnow in the water but is better, in that it is more showy, and infinitely tougher. A minnow soon drags to pieces. To use it, two strong hooks are tied on a wire snell at right angles, the upper one an inch above the lower, and the upper hook is passed through the bait, leaving it to draw without turning or spinning. The casting and handling is the same as with the frog-bait and is very killing for bass, pickerel, and muskellunge. It is a good lure for salmon trout also, but for him it was found better to fasten the bait with the lower hook in a way to give it a spinning motion, and this necessitates the use of a swivel, which I do not like because "a rope is as strong as its weakest part" and I have more than once found that weakest part the swivel. If, however, a swivel has been tested by a dead lift of twenty to twenty-five pounds, it will do to trust.

I have spoken only of brass or copper wire for snells, and for pickerel or muskellunge of large size nothing else is to be depended on. But for trout and bass, strong gut[152] or gimp[153] is safe enough. The possibilities as to size of the muskellunge and northern pickerel no man knows. Frank Forester thinks it

---

152 Silk
153 Silk wrapped with wire

probable that the former attains to the weight of sixty to eighty pounds, while he only accords the pickerel a weight of seventeen to eighteen pounds. I have seen several pickerel of over forty pounds, and one that turned the scale at fifty-three. And I saw a muskellunge on Georgian Bay that was longer than the Canuck guide who was toting the fish over his shoulder by a stick thrust in the mouth and gills. The snout reached to the top of the guide's head, while the caudal fin dragged on the ground. There was no chance for weighing the fish, but I hefted him several times, carefully, and am certain he weighed more than a bushel of wheat.[154] Just what tackle would be proper for such a powerful fellow I am not prepared to say, having lost the largest specimens I ever hooked. My best muskellunge weighed less than twenty pounds. My largest pickerel still less.

I will close this discursive chapter by offering a bit of advice. Do not go into the woods on a fishing tour without a stock of well-cleansed angleworms. Keep them in a tin can partly filled with damp moss and in a cool, moist place. There is no one variety of bait that the angler finds so constantly useful as the worm. Izaak Walton[155] by no means despised worm or bait-fishing.

---

154  A bushel of wheat weighs approximately sixty pounds.

155  An English writer and the author of *The Compleat Angler*, published in 1653

## CHAPTER VI

# CAMP COOKERY–
# HOW IT IS USUALLY
# DONE, WITH A FEW
# SIMPLE HINTS
# ON PLAIN COOKING–
# COOKING FIRE AND
# OUTDOOR RANGE

THE WAY IN WHICH AN AVERAGE PARTY OF summer outers will contrive to manage—or mismanage—the camp and campfire so as to get the greatest amount of smoke and discontent at the least outlay of time and force is something past all understanding and somewhat aggravating to an old woodsman who knows some better. But it is just as good fun as the cynical O.W.[156] can ask, to see a party of three or four enthusiastic youngsters organize the camp on the first day in and proceed to cook the first meal. Of course, every man is boss, and every one is bound to build the fire, which every one proceeds to do. There are no backlogs, no fore sticks, and no arrangement for level solid bases on which to place frying pans, coffeepots, etc. But there is a sufficiency of knots, dry sticks, bark and chunks, with some kindling at the bottom, and a heavy volume of smoke working its way through the awkward-looking pile. Presently thin tongues of blue flame begin to shoot up through the interstices, and four brand-new coffeepots are wriggled into level positions at as many different points on the bonfire. Four hungry youngsters commence slicing ham and pork, four frying pans are brought out from as many hinged and lidded soap boxes[157]—when one man yells out hurriedly, "Look out, Joe, there's your coffeepot handle coming off." And he drops his frying pan to save his coffeepot, which he does, minus the spout and handle. Then it is seen that the flames have increased rapidly, and all the pots are in danger. A short, sharp skirmish rescues them, at the expense of some burned fingers, and culinary operations are the order of the hour.

Coffee and tea are brewed with the loss of a handle or two, and the frying pans succeed in scorching the pork and ham to an unwholesome black mess. The potato kettle does better. It is not easy to spoil potatoes by cooking them in plenty of boiling water, and, as there is plenty of bread with fresh butter, not to mention canned goods, the hungry party feed sufficiently but not satisfactorily. Everything seems pervaded with smoke. The meat is scorched bitter, and the tea is of the sort described by Charles Dudley Warner, in his humorous description of "Camping Out": "The sort of tea that takes hold, lifts the hair, and disposes the drinker to hilariousness. There is no deception about it, it tastes of tannin, and spruce, and creosote." Of the cooking he says: "Everything has been cooked in a tin pail and a skillet—potatoes, tea, pork, mutton, slapjacks. You wonder how everything would have been prepared in so few utensils. When you eat, the wonder ceases, everything might have been cooked in one pail. It is a noble meal…. The slapjacks are a solid job of work, made to last, and not go to pieces in a person's stomach like a trivial bun."

I have before me a copy of *Forest and Stream*, in which the canoe editor, under the heading of "The Galley Fire," has some remarks well worth quoting. He

---

157 Wooden crates

says: "The question of camp cookery is one of the greatest importance to all readers of *Forest and Stream*, but most of all to the canoeists. From ignorance of what to carry the canoeist falls back on canned goods, never healthy as a steady diet, Brunswick soup[158] and eggs.... The misery of that first campfire, who has forgotten it? Tired, hungry, perhaps cold and wet, the smoke everywhere, the coffeepot melted down, the can of soup upset in the fire, the fiendish conduct of frying pan and kettle, the final surrender of the exhausted victim, sliding off to sleep with a piece of hardtack in one hand and a slice of canned beef in the other, only to dream of mother's hot biscuits, juicy steaks, etc., etc." It is very well put, and so true to the life. And again: "Frying, baking, making coffee, stews, plain biscuits, the neat and speedy preparation of a healthy 'square meal' can be easily learned." Aye, and should be learned by every man who goes to the woods with or without a canoe.

But I was describing a first day's camping out, the party being four young men and one old woodsman, the latter going along in a double character of invited guest and amateur guide. When the boys are through with their late dinner, they hustle the greasy frying pans and demoralized tinware into a corner of the shanty and get out their rods for an evening's fishing. They do it hurriedly, almost feverishly, as youngsters are apt to do at the start. The O.W. has taken no part in the dinner and has said nothing save in response to direct questions, nor has he done anything to keep up his reputation as a woodsman, except to see that the shelter roof is properly put up and fastened. Having seen to this, he reverts to his favorite pastime, sitting on a log and smoking navy plug. Long experience has taught him that it is best to let the boys effervesce a little. They will slop[159] over a trifle at first, but twenty-four hours will settle them. When they are fairly out of hearing, he takes the old knapsack from the clipped limb where it has been hung, cuts a slice of ham, butters a slice of bread, spreads the live coals and embers, makes a pot of strong green tea, broils the ham on a three-pronged birch fork, and has a clean, well-cooked plain dinner. Then he takes the sharp three-pound camp axe, and fells a dozen small birch and

---

158  A soup made with vegetables and game meat
159  Gush

ash trees, cutting them into proper lengths and leaving them for the boys to tote into camp. Next, a bushy, heavy-topped hemlock is felled, and the O.W. proceeds leisurely to pick a heap of fine hemlock browse. A few handfuls suffice to stuff the muslin pillow bag, and the rest is carefully spread on the port side of the shanty for a bed. The pillow is placed at the head, and the old Mackinac[160] blanket-bag is spread neatly over all, as a token of ownership and possession. If the youngsters want beds of fine, elastic browse, let 'em make their own beds.

No campfire should be without poker and tongs. The poker is a beech stick four feet long by two inches thick, flattened at one end, with a notch cut in it for lifting kettles, etc. To make the tongs, take a tough beech or hickory stick, one inch thick by two feet in length, shave it down nearly one-half for a foot in the center, thrust this part into hot embers until it bends freely, bring the ends together and whittle them smoothly to a fit on the inside, cross-checking them also to give them a grip; finish off by chamfering[161] the ends neatly from the outside. They will be found exceedingly handy in rescuing a bit of tinware, a slice of steak or ham, or any small article that happens to get dropped in a hot fire.

And don't neglect the camp broom. It is made by laying bushy hemlock twigs around a light handle, winding them firmly with strong twine or moose wood bark, and chopping off the ends of the twigs evenly. It can be made in ten minutes. Use it to brush any leaves, sticks, and any litter from about the camp or fire. Neatness is quite as pleasant and wholesome around the forest camp as in the home kitchen. These little details may seem trivial to the reader. But remember, if there is a spot on earth where trifles make up the sum of human enjoyment, it is to be found in a woodland camp. All of which the O.W. fully appreciates, as he finishes the above little jobs, after which he proceeds to spread the fire to a broad level bed of glowing embers, nearly covering the same with small pieces of hemlock bark, that the boys may have a decent cooking fire on their return.

---

160 Or mackinaw; a heavy wool
161 Beveling

About sundown they come straggling in, not jubilant and hilarious, footsore rather and a little cross. The effervescence is subsiding, and the noise is pretty well knocked out of them. They have caught and dressed some three score of small brook trout, which they deposit beside the shanty, and proceed at once to move on the fire, with evident intent of raising a conflagration, but are checked by the O.W., who calls their attention to the fact that for all culinary purposes, the fire is about as near the right thing as they are likely to get it. Better defer the bonfire until after supper. Listening to the voice of enlightened woodcraft, they manage to fry trout and make tea without scorch or creosote, and the supper is a decided improvement on the dinner. But the dishes are piled away as before, without washing.

## The First Night

Then follows an hour of busy work, bringing wood to camp and packing browse. The wood is sufficient, but the browse is picked, or cut, all too coarse, and there is only enough of it to make the camp look green and pleasant—not enough to rest weary shoulders and backs. But they are sound on the bonfire. They pile on the wood in the usual way, crisscross and haphazard. It makes a grand fire, and lights up the forest for fifty yards around, and the tired youngsters turn in. Having the advantage of driving a team[162] to the camping ground, they are well supplied with blankets and robes. They ought to sleep soundly, but they don't. The usual drawbacks of a first night in camp are soon manifested in uneasy twistings and turnings, grumbling at stubs, knots, and sticks that utterly ignore conformity with the angles of the human frame. But at last, tired, nature asserts her supremacy, and they sleep. Sleep soundly, for a couple of hours; when the bonfire, having reached the point of disintegration, suddenly collapses with a sputtering and crackling that brings them to their head's antipodes,[163] and four dazed, sleepy faces look out with a bewildered air to see what has caused the rumpus. All take a hand in putting the brands[164] together and rearranging the fire, which burns better than at first; some sleepy

---

162  Traveling in a horse-drawn vehicle

163  Opposites

164  Charred wood

talk, one or two feeble attempts at a smoke, and they turn in again. But there is not an hour during the remainder of the night in which someone is not pottering about the fire.

The O.W., who has abided by his blanket-bag all night—quietly taking in the fun—rouses out the party at 4:00 a.m. For two of them are to fish Asaph Run with bait, and the other two are to try the riffles of Marsh Creek with the fly. As the wood is all burned to cinders and glowing coals, there is no chance for a smoky fire, and substituting coffee for tea, the breakfast is a repetition of the supper.

By sunrise the boys are off, and the O.W. has the camp to himself. He takes it leisurely, gets up a neat breakfast of trout, bread, butter, and coffee; cleans and puts away his dishes; has a smoke; and picks up the camp axe. Selecting a bushy hemlock fifteen inches across, he lets it down in as many minutes, trims it to the very tip, piles the limbs in a heap, and cuts three lengths of six feet each from the butt. This ensures browse and backlogs for some time ahead. Two strong stakes are cut and sharpened. Four small logs, two of eight and two of nine feet in length, are prepared; plenty of night wood is made ready; a supply of bright, dry hemlock bark is carried to camp; and the O.W. rests from his labors, resuming his favorite pastime of sitting on a log and smoking navy plug. Finally it occurs to him that he is there partly as guide and mentor to the younger men and that they need a lesson on cleanliness. He brings out the frying pans and finds a filthy-looking mess of grease in each one, wherein ants, flies, and other insects have contrived to get mixed. Does he heat some water, and clean and scour the pans? Not if he knows himself. If he did it once he might keep on doing it. He is cautious about establishing precedents, and he has a taste for entomology. He places the pans in the sun where the grease will soften and goes skirmishing for ants and doodle bugs. They are not far to seek, and he soon has a score of large black ants, with a few bugs and spiders, pretty equally distributed among the frying pans. To give the thing a plausible look, a few flies are added, and the two largest pans are finished off, one with a large earwig, the other with a thousand-legged worm. The pans are replaced in the shanty, the embers are leveled and nearly covered with bits of dry hemlock bark, and the O.W. resumes his pipe and log

*With such a face of Christian satisfaction,*
*As good men wear, who have done a virtuous action.* [165]

Before noon the boys are all in, and as the catch is twice as numerous and twice as large as on the previous evening, and as the weather is all that could be asked of the longest days in June, they are in excellent spirits. The boxes are brought out, pork is sliced, a can of Indian meal[166] comes to the front, and they go for the frying pans.

"Holy Moses! Look here. Just see the ants and bugs."

Second Man: "Well, I should say! I can see your ants and bugs, and go you an earwig better."

Third Man (inverting his pan spitefully over the fire): "D—n 'em, I'll roast the beggars."

Bush D (who is something of a cook and woodsman): "Boys, I'll take the pot. I've got a thousand-legged worm at the head of a pismire[167] flush, and it serves us right, for a lot of slovens. Dishes should be cleaned as often as they are used. Now let's scour our pans and commence right."

## Their Lesson

Hot water, ashes, and soap soon restore the pans to pristine brightness; three frying pans are filled with trout well rolled in meal; a fourth is used for cooking a can of tomatoes; the coffee is strong, and everything comes out without being smoked or scorched. The trout are browned to a turn, and even the O.W. admits that the dinner is a success. When it is over and the dishes are cleaned and put away, and the camp slicked up, there comes the usual two hours of lounging, smoking, and story-telling, so dear to the hearts of those

---

165 From Lord Byron's poem "Don Juan"; the actual quotation is "Took leave with such a face of satisfaction / As good men wear who've done a virtuous action."

166 Cornmeal

167 Ant

who love to go a-fishing and camping. At length there is a lull in the conversation, and Bush D turns to the old woodsman with, "I thought, 'Uncle Mart,' you were going to show us fellows such a lot of kinks[168] about camping out, campfires, cooking, and all that sort of thing, isn't it about time to begin? Strikes me you have spent most of the last twenty-four hours holding down that log."

"Except cutting some night wood and tending the fire," adds number two.

The old woodsman, who has been rather silent up to this time, knocks the ashes leisurely from his pipe and gets on his feet for a few remarks. He says, "Boys, a bumblebee is biggest when it's first born. You've learned more than you think in the last twenty-four hours."

"Well, as how? Explain yourself," says Bush D.

O.W.: "In the first place, you have learned better than to stick your cooking-kit into a tumbled down heap of knots, mulch, and wet bark, only to upset and melt down the pots, and scorch or smoke everything in the pans, until a starving hound wouldn't eat the mess. And you have found that it doesn't take a log heap to boil a pot of coffee or fry a pan of trout. Also, that a level bed of live coals makes an excellent cooking fire, though I will show you a better. Yesterday you cooked the worst meal I ever saw in the woods. Today you get up a really good, plain dinner; you have learned that much in one day. Oh, you improve some. And I think you have taken a lesson in cleanliness today."

"Yes, but we learned that of the ant—and bug," says number two.

O.W.: "Just so. And did you think all the ants and doodlebugs blundered into that grease in one morning? I put 'em in myself—to give you a 'kink.'"

Bush D (disgusted): "You blasted, dirty old sinner."

---

168 Ingenious, unique methods

Second Man: "Oh, you miserable old swamp savage; I shan't get over that earwig in a month."

Third Man (plaintively): "This life in the woods isn't what it's cracked up to be; I don't relish bugs and spiders. I wish I were home. I'm all bitten up with punkies, and—"

Fourth Man (savagely): "Dashed old woods-loafer; let's tie his hands and fire him in the creek."

O.W. (placidly): "Exactly, boys. Your remarks are terse, and to the point. Only, as I am going to show you a trick or two on woodcraft this afternoon, you can afford to wait a little. Now, quit smoking, and get out your hatchets; we'll go to work."

Three hatchets are brought to light; one of them a two-pound clumsy hand axe, the others of an old time, Mt. Vernon, G.W. pattern. "And now," says good-natured Bush, "you give directions and we'll do the work."

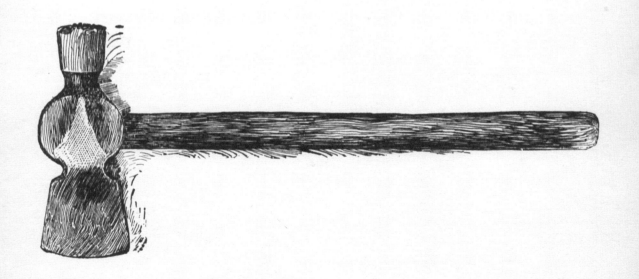

Under directions, the coarse browse of the previous night is placed outside the shanty; three active youngsters, on hands and knees, feel out and cut off every offending stub and root inside the shanty, until it is smooth as a floor. The four small logs are brought to camp; the two longest are laid at the sides and staked in place; the others are placed, one at the head, the other at the foot, also staked; and the camp has acquired definite outlines, and a measurable size of eight by nine feet. Three hemlock logs and two sharpened stakes are toted to camp, the stakes driven firmly, and the logs laid against them, one above the other. Firedogs, fore stick, etc., complete the arrangement, and the campfire is in shape for the coming night, precisely as shown in the engraving on page 187.

"And now," says the O.W., "if three of you will go down to the flat and pick the browse clean from the two hemlock tops, Bush and I will fix a cooking-range."

"A—what?" asks one.

"Going to start a boardinghouse?" says another.

"Notion of going into the hardware business?" suggests a third.

"Never mind, sonny; just tend to that browse, and when you see a smoke raising on the flat by the spring, come over and see the range." And the boys, taking a couple of blankets in which to carry the browse, saunter away to the flat below.

A very leisurely aesthetic, fragrant occupation is this picking browse. It should never be cut, but pulled, stripped, or broken. I have seen a senator, ex-governor, and a wealthy banker enjoying themselves hugely at it, varying the occupation by hacking small timber with their G.W. hatchets, like so many boys let loose from school. It may have looked a trifle undignified, but I dare say they found their account[169] in it. Newport or Long Branch would have been more expensive, and much less healthful.

---

169 Value

# The Cooking-Range

For an hour and a half tongues and fingers are busy around the hemlock tops; then a thin, long volume of blue smoke rises near the spring, and the boys walk over to inspect the range. They find it made as follows: Two logs six feet long and eight inches thick are laid parallel, but seven inches apart at one end and only four at the other. They are bedded firmly and flattened a little on the inside. On the upper sides the logs are carefully hewed and leveled until pots, pans, and kettles will sit firmly and evenly on them. A strong forked stake is driven at each end of the space, and a cross-pole, two or three inches thick, laid on, for hanging kettles. This completes the range; simple, but effective. (See illustration.) The broad end of the space is for frying pans, and the potato kettle. The narrow end, for coffeepots and utensils of lesser diameter. From six to eight dishes can be cooked at the same time. Soups, stews, and beans are to be cooked in closely covered kettles hung from the cross-pole, the bottoms of the kettles reaching within some two inches of the logs. With a moderate fire they may be left to simmer for hours without care or attention.

The fire is of the first importance. Start it with fine kindling and clean, dry hemlock bark. When you have a bright, even fire from end to end of the space, keep it up with small fagots[170] of the sweetest and most wholesome woods in the forest. These are, in the order named, black birch, hickory, sugar maple, yellow birch, and red beech. The sticks should be short, and not over two inches across. Split wood is better than round. The outdoor range can be made by one man in little more than an hour, and the camper-out, who once tries it, will never wish to see a "portable camp-stove" again.

When the sun leaves the valley in the shade of Asaph Mountain, the boys have a fragrant bed of elastic browse a foot deep in the shanty, with pillows improvised from stuffed bootlegs, cotton handkerchiefs, etc. They cook their suppers on the range, and vote it perfect, no melting or heating handles too hot for use, and no smoking of dishes, or faces.

---

170  Bundles of sticks

Just at dark—which means 9:00 p.m. in the last week of June—the fire is carefully made and chinked. An hour later it is throwing its grateful warmth and light directly into camp, and nowhere else. The camp turns in. Not to wriggle and quarrel with obdurate[171] stubs, but to sleep. And sleep they do. The sound, deep, restful sleep of healthy young manhood, inhaling pure mountain air on the healthiest bed yet known to man.

When it is past midnight, and the fire burns low, and the chill night breeze drifts into camp, they still do not rouse up, but only spoon closer, and sleep right on. Only the O.W. turns out sleepily, at two bells in the middle watch, after the manner of hunters, trappers, and sailors, the world over. He quietly rebuilds the fire, reduces a bit of navy plug to its lowest denomination, and takes a solitary smoke—still holding down his favorite log. Quizzically and quietly he regards the sleeping youngsters and wonders if among them all there is one who will do as he has done (i.e., relinquish all of what the world reckons as success, for the love of nature and a free forest life). He hopes not. And yet, as he glances at the calm yellow moon overhead and listens to the low murmur of the little waterfall below the spring, he has a faint notion that it is not all loss and dross.[172]

Knocking the ashes from his pipe, he prepares to turn in, murmuring to himself, half sadly, half humorously, "I have been young, and now I am old; yet have I never seen the true woodsman forsaken, or his seed begging bread— or anything else, so to speak—unless it might be a little tobacco or a nip of whiskey." And he creeps into his blanket-bag, backs softly out to the outside man, and joins the snorers.

## Getting Breakfast

It is broad daylight when he again turns out, leaving the rest still sleeping soundly. He starts a lively fire in the range, treats two coffeepots to a double handful of coffee and three pints of water each, sets on the potato kettle,

---

171 Unwilling to give in
172 Waste

washes the potatoes, then sticks his head into the camp, and rouses the party with a regular second mate's hail. "Star-a-ar-bo'lins[173] aho-o-o-y. Turn out, you beggars. Come on deck and see it rain." And the boys do turn out. Not with wakeful alacrity, but in a dazed, dreamy, sleepy way. They open wide eyes when they see that the sun is turning the somber tops of pines and hemlocks to a soft orange yellow.

"I'd have sworn," says one, "that I hadn't slept over fifteen minutes by the watch."

"And I," says another, "was just watching the fire, when I dropped off in a doze. In about five minutes I opened my eyes, and I'll be shot if it wasn't sunrise."

"As for me," says a third, "I don't know as I've slept at all. I remember seeing somebody poking the fire last night. Next thing I knew, some lunatic was yelling around camp about 'starbolins' and 'turning out.' Guess I'll lay down and have my nap out."

"Yes," says the O.W., "I would. If I was a healthy youngster and couldn't get along with seven hours and a half of solid sleep, I'd take the next forenoon for it. Just at present, I want to remark that I've got the coffee and potato business under way, and I'll attend to them. If you want anything else for breakfast, you'll have to cook it."

And the boys, rising to the occasion, go about the breakfast with willing hands. It is noticeable, however, that only one pan of trout is cooked, two of the youngsters preferring to fall back on broiled ham, remarking that brook trout is too rich and cloying for a steady diet. Which is true. The appetite for trout has very sensibly subsided, and the boyish eagerness for trout fishing has fallen off immensely. Only two of the party show any interest in the riffles. They stroll downstream leisurely to try their flies for an hour or two. The others

---

173 A starbolin is someone who is part of the starboard watch on board a ship.

elect to amuse themselves about the camp, cutting small timber with their little hatchets, picking fresh browse, or skirmishing the mountainside for wintergreen berries and sassafras. The fishermen return in a couple of hours, with a score of fair-sized trout. They remark apologetically that it is blazing hot—and there are plenty of trout ahead. Then they lean their rods against the shanty, and lounge on the blankets, and smoke and dose.

It is less than forty-eight hours since the cross-pole was laid, and using a little common sense woodcraft, the camp has already attained to a systematic no-system of rest, freedom, and idleness. Every man is free to "loaf, and invite his soul." There is good trouting within an hour's walk for those who choose, and there is some interest, with a little exercise, in cooking and cutting night wood, slicking up, etc. But the whole party is stricken with "camp-fever," "Indian laziness," the *dolce far niente*.[174] It is over and around every man, enveloping him as with a roseate[175] blanket from the Castle of Indolence.[176]

It is the perfect summer camp.

174  In Italian, the "sweet doing nothing"
175  Abundantly optimistic
176  *The Castle of Indolence* is a poem by Scottish poet James Thomson, published in 1748.

And it is no myth, but a literal résumé of a five days' outing at Poplar Spring, on Marsh Creek, in Pennsylvania. Alas, for the beautiful valley, that once afforded the finest camping grounds I have ever known.

*Never any more*
*Can it be*
*Unto me (or anybody else)*
*As before.*

A huge tannery, six miles above Poplar Spring, poisons and blackens the stream with chemicals, bark, and ooze. The land has been brought into market, and every acre eagerly bought up by actual settlers. The once fine covers and thickets are converted into fields thickly dotted with blackened stumps. And, to crown the desolation, heavy laden trains of "The Pine Creek and Jersey Shore R. R." go thundering almost hourly over the very spot where stood our camp by Poplar Spring.

## Progress?

Of course, this is progress, but whether backward or forward, had better be decided sixty years hence. And just what has happened to the obscure valley of Marsh Creek is happening today, on a larger scale, all over the land. It is the same old story of grab and greed. Let us go on the "make":[177] today, and "whack up"[178] tomorrow; cheating each other as villainously as we may, and posterity be d—d. "What's all the w-u-u-rld to a man when his wife is a widdy?"

This is the moral: From Maine to Montana, from the Adirondacks to Alaska, from Yosemite to Yellowstone, the trout-hog, the deer-wolf, the netter, the skin-hunter, each and all have it their own way, and the law is a farce—only to be enforced where the game has vanished forever. Perhaps the man-child is born who will live to write the moral of all this—when it is too late.

---

177  In pursuit of more money
178  Divide it up

## CHAPTER VII

# MORE HINTS ON COOKING, WITH SOME SIMPLE RECEIPTS–BREAD, COFFEE, POTATOES, SOUPS, STEWS, BEANS, FISH, MEAT, VENISON

*We may live without friends, we may live without books,*
*But civilized man cannot live without cooks.*[179]

**I**T IS PROBABLY TRUE THAT NOTHING CONNECTED with outdoor life in camp is so badly botched as the cooking. It is not through any lack of the raw material, which may be had of excellent quality in any country village. It is not from lack of intelligence or education, for the men you meet in the woods, as outers or sportsmen, are rather over

---

than under the average in these respects. Perhaps it is because it has been dinned[180] into our ears from early childhood that an appetite, a healthy longing for something good to eat, a tickling of the palate with wholesome, appetizing food, is beneath the attention of an aesthetic, intellectual man. Forgetting that the entire man, mental and physical, depends on proper aliment[181] and the healthy assimilation thereof, and that a thin, dyspeptic man can no more keep up in the struggle of life than the lightning express can make connections, drawn by a worn-out locomotive.

I have never been able to get much help from cookbooks, or the scores of recipes published in various works on outdoor sport. Take, for example, *Frank Forester's Fish and Fishing*. He has more than seventy recipes for cooking fish, over forty of which contain terms or names in French. I daresay they are good—for a first-class hotel. I neither cook nor converse in French, and I have come to know that the plainest cooking is the best, so that it be well done and wholesome. In making up the rations for camping out, the first thing usually attended to is bread. And if this be light, well-made bread, enough may be taken along to last four or five days, and this may be eked out with Boston crackers[182] or the best hardtack, for a couple or three days more, without the least hardship. Also, there are few camps in which someone is not going out to the clearings every few days for mail, small stores, etc., and a supply of bread can be arranged for, with less trouble than it can be made. There are times, however, when this is not feasible, and there are men who prefer warm bread all the time. In this case the usual resort, from Maine to Alaska, is the universal flapjack. I do not like it; I seldom make it; it is not good. But it may be eaten, with maple syrup or sugar and butter. I prefer a plain water johnnycake, made as follows (supposing your tins are something like those described in Chapter II): Put a little more than a pint of water in your kettle and bring it to a sharp boil, adding a small teaspoonful of salt and two of sugar. Stir in slowly enough good corn meal to make a rather stiff mush, let it cook a few minutes, and set

---

180  Impressed
181  Food
182  A thick unsalted cracker

it off the fire; then grease your largest tin dish and put the mush in it, smoothing it on top. Set the dish on the outdoor range described in the previous chapter, with a lively bed of coal beneath—but no blaze. Invert the second-sized tin over the cake, and cover the dish with bright live coals, that bottom and top may bake evenly, and give it from thirty-five to forty minutes for baking. It makes wholesome, palatable bread, which gains on the taste with use.

Those who prefer wheat bread can make a passable article by using the best wheat flour with baking powders, mixing three tablespoonfuls of the powders to a quart of flour. Mix and knead thoroughly with warm water to a rather thin dough, and bake as above. Use the same proportions for pancake batter. When stopping in a permanent camp with plenty of time to cook, excellent light bread may be made by using dry yeast cakes, though it is not necessary to "set" the sponge as directed on the papers. Scrape and dissolve half a cake of the yeast in a gill[183] of warm water, and mix it with the flour. Add warm water enough to make it pliable and not too stiff; set in a warm place until it rises sufficiently, and bake as directed above. It takes several hours to rise.

I am afraid I shall discount my credit on camp cooking when I admit that—if I must use fine flour—I prefer unleavened bread; what my friends irreverently call "club bread." Not that it was ever made or endorsed by any club of men that I know of, but because it is baked on a veritable club, sassafras, or black birch. This is how to make it: Cut a club two feet long and three inches thick at the broadest end; peel or shave off the bark smoothly, and sharpen the smaller end neatly. Then stick the sharpened end in the ground near the fire, leaning the broad end toward a bed of live coals, where it will get screeching hot. While it is heating, mix rather more than a half pint of best Minnesota flour with enough warm water to make a dough. Add a half teaspoonful of salt and a teaspoonful of sugar, and mold and pull the dough until it becomes lively.[184] Now, work it into a ribbon two inches wide and half an inch thick,

---

183  Four fluid ounces
184  Sears likely means lively in the sense of "springy"; the dough bounces back when poked.

wind the ribbon spirally around the broad end of the club, stick the latter in front of the fire so that the bread will bake evenly and quickly to a light brown, and turn frequently until done, which will be in about thirty minutes. When done, take it from the fire, stand the club firmly upright, and pick the bread off in pieces as you want it to eat. It will keep hot a long time, and one soon becomes fond of it.

## Coffee

To make perfect coffee, just two ingredients are necessary, and only two. These are water and coffee. It is owing to the bad management of the latter that we drink poor coffee.

Mocha[185] is generally considered to be the best type of coffee, with java[186] a close second. It is the fashion at present to mix the two in proportions to suit, some taking two parts java to one of mocha, others reversing these proportions. Either way is good, or the mocha is quite as good alone. But there is a better berry than either for the genuine coffee toper.[187] This is the small, dark green berry that comes to market under the generic name of Rio, that name covering half a dozen grades of coffee raised in different provinces of Brazil, throughout a country extending north and south for more than 1,200 miles. The berry alluded to is produced along the range of high hills to the westward of Bahia and extending north toward the Parnaíba. It has never arrested attention as a distinct grade of the article, but it contains more coffee or caffeine to the pound than any berry known to commerce. It is the smallest, heaviest, and darkest green of any coffee that comes to our market from Brazil and may be known by these traits. I have tested it in the land where it is grown, and also at home, for the past sixteen years, and I place it at the head of the list, with mocha next. Either will make perfect coffee, if treated as follows: Of the berry, browned and ground, take six heaping tablespoonfuls and add three pints of cold water; place the kettle over the fire and bring to a sharp boil; set it a little

---

185  Probably coffee from the town of Mocha in present-day Yemen
186  Probably coffee from the island of Java in Indonesia
187  Drunkard

aside where it will bubble and simmer until wanted, and just before pouring, drip in a half gill of cold water to settle it. That is all there is to it. The quantity of berry is about twice as much as usually given in recipes, but if you want coffee, you had better add two spoonfuls than cut off one.

In 1867, and again in 1870, I had occasion to visit the West India Islands[188] and Brazil. In common with most coffee topers, I had heard much of the super-excellence ascribed to "West India coffee" and "Brazilian coffee." I concluded to investigate. I had rooms at the Hotel d'Europe, Pará, North Brazil. There were six of us, English and American boarders. Every morning, before we were out of our hammocks, a barefooted, half-naked Mina negress came around and served each of us with a small cup of strong, black coffee and sugar ad libitum. There was not enough of it for a drink; it was rather in the nature of a medicine, and so intended—"To kill the biscos," they said. The coffee was above criticism.

I went, in the dark of a tropical morning with Senhor João, to the coffee factory where they browned the berry, and saw him buy a pound, smoking hot, for which he paid twenty-five cents, or quite as much as it would cost in New York. In ten minutes the coffee was at the hotel and ground. This is the way they brewed it: A round-bottomed kettle was sitting on the brick range with a half gallon of boiling water in it. Over the kettle a square piece of white flannel was suspended, caught up at the corners like a dip net. In this the coffee was placed, and a small darky put in his time steadily with a soup ladle, dipping the boiling water from the kettle and pouring it on the coffee. There was a constant stream percolating through coffee and cloth, which, in the course of half an hour, became almost black and clear as brandy. This was "Brazilian coffee." As the cups used were very small, and as none but the Northerners drank more than one cup, I found that the hotel did not use over two quarts of coffee each morning. It struck me that a pound of fresh Rio coffee berry ought to make a half gallon of rather powerful coffee.

---

188 The West Indies, in the Caribbean

On my arrival home—not having any small darky or any convenient arrangement for the dip net—I had a sack made of light, white flannel, holding about one pint. In this I put one-quarter pound of freshly ground berry, with water enough for five large cups. It was boiled thoroughly and proved just as good as the Brazilian article, but too strong for any of the family except the writer. Those who have a fancy for clear, strong "Brazilian coffee" will see how easily and simply it can be made.

But on a heavy knapsack-and-rifle tramp among the mountains, or a lone canoe cruise in a strange wilderness, I do not carry coffee. I prefer tea. Often, when too utterly tired and beaten for further travel, I have tried coffee, whiskey, or brandy, and a long experience convinces me that there is nothing so restful and refreshing to an exhausted man as a dish of strong, green tea. To make it as it should be made, bring the water to a high boil, and let it continue to boil for a full minute. Set it off the fire and it will cease boiling; put in a handful of tea, and it will instantly boil up again; then set it near the fire, where it will simmer for a few minutes, when it will be ready for use. Buy the best green tea you can find, and use it freely on a hard tramp. Black, or oolong tea, is excellent in camp. It should be put in the pot with cold water and brought to the boiling point.

## Potatoes

Almost any man can cook potatoes, but few cook them well. Most people think them best boiled in their jackets, and to cook them perfectly in this manner is so simple and easy that the wonder is how anyone can fail. A kettle of screeching hot water with a small handful of salt in it, good potatoes of nearly equal size, washed clean and clipped at the ends, these are the requisites. Put the potatoes in the boiling water, cover closely, and keep the water at high boiling pitch until you can thrust a sharp sliver through the largest potato. Then drain off the water and set the kettle in a hot place with the lid partly off. Take them out only as they are wanted; lukewarm potatoes are not good. They will be found about as good as potatoes can be, when cooked in their jackets. But there is a better way, as thus: Select enough for a mess,[189] of smooth, sound tubers; pare[190] them carefully, taking off as little as possible, because the best of the potato lies nearest the skin, and cook as above. When done, pour the water off to the last drop; sprinkle a spoonful of salt and fine cracker crumbs over them; then shake, roll, and rattle them in the kettle until the outsides are white and floury. Keep them piping hot until wanted. It is the way to have perfect boiled potatoes.

Many outers are fond of roast potatoes in camp, and they mostly spoil them in the roasting, although there is no better place than the campfire in which to do it. To cook them aright,[191] scoop out a basinlike depression under the fore-stick, three or four inches deep, and large enough to hold the tubers when laid side by side; fill it with bright, hardwood coals, and keep up a strong heat for half an hour or more. Next, clean out the hollow, place the potatoes in it, and cover them with hot sand or ashes, topped with a heap of glowing coals, and keep up all the heat you like. In about forty minutes commence to try them with a sharpened hardwood sliver; when this will pass through them, they are done and should be raked out at once. Run the sliver through them from end to end, to let the steam escape, and use immediately, as a roast potato quickly becomes soggy and bitter. I will add that, in selecting a supply of potatoes for camp, only the finest and smoothest should be taken.

A man may be a trout-crank, he may have been looking forward for ten weary months to the time when he is to strike the much dreamed of mountain stream, where trout may be taken and eaten without stint.[192] Occasionally—not often—his dream is realized. For two or three days he revels in fly-fishing and eating brook trout. Then his enthusiasm begins to subside. He talks less of his favorite flies and hints that wading hour after hour in ice water gives him cramps in the calves of his legs. Also, he finds that brook trout, eaten for days

---

189  An amount of food for a meal
190  Peel
191  Correctly
192  Limit

in succession, pall[193] on the appetite. He hankers for the fleshpots of the restaurant, and his soul yearns for the bean-pot of home.

Luckily, someone has brought a sack of white beans, and the expert—there is always an expert in camp—is deputed[194] to cook them. He accepts the trust[195] and proceeds to do it. He puts a quart of dry beans and a liberal chunk of pork in a two-quart kettle, covers the mess with water, and brings it to a rapid boil. Presently the beans begin to swell and lift the lid of the kettle; their conduct is simply demoniacal. They lift up the lid of the kettle, they tumble out over the rim in a way to provoke a saint, and they have scarcely begun to cook. The expert is not to be beaten. As they rise, he spoons them out and throws them away, until half of the best beans being wasted, the rest settle to business. He fills the kettle with water and watches it for an hour. When bean-skins and scum arise, he uses the spoon, and when a ring of greasy salt forms around the rim of the kettle, he carefully scrapes it off, but most of it drops back into the pot. When the beans seem cooked to the point of disintegration, he lifts off the kettle and announces dinner. It is not a success. The largest beans are granulated rather than cooked, while the mealy portion of them has fallen to the bottom of the kettle and become scorched thereon, and the smaller beans are too hard to be eatable. The liquid, that should be palatable bean soup, is greasy salt water, and the pork is half raw. The party falls back, hungry and disgusted. Even if the mess were well cooked, it is too salty for eating. And why should this be so? Why should any sensible man spend years in acquiring an education that shall fit him for the struggle of life, yet refuse to spend a single day in learning how to cook the food that must sustain the life? It is one of the conundrums no one will ever find out.

## Beans

There is no article of food more easily carried, and none that contains more nourishment to the pound, than the bean. Limas are usually preferred, but the

---

193  Ceases to incite interest
194  Assigned
195  Duty

large white marrow is just as good. It will pay to select them carefully. Keep an eye on grocery stocks, and when you strike a lot of extra-large, clean beans, buy twice as many as you need for camp use. Spread them on a table, a quart at a time, and separate the largest and best from the others. Fully one-half will go to the side of the largest and finest, and these may be put in a muslin bag and kept till wanted. Select the expeditionary pork with equal care, buying nothing but thick, solid, "clear,"[196] with a pink tinge. Reject that which is white and lardy. With such material, if you cannot lay over Boston baked beans, you had better sweep the cook out of camp.

This is how to cook them: Put a pound or a little more of clean pork in the kettle, with water enough to cover it. Let it boil slowly half an hour. In the meantime, wash and parboil one pint of beans. Drain the water from the pork and place the beans around it; add two quarts of water and hang the kettle where it will boil steadily, but not rapidly, for two hours. Pare neatly and thinly five or six medium-sized potatoes and allow them from thirty to forty minutes (according to size and variety) in which to cook. They must be pressed down among the beans so as to be entirely covered. If the beans be fresh and fine, they will probably fall to pieces before time is up. This, if they are not allowed to scorch, makes them all the better. If a portion of pork be left over, it is excellent sliced very thin when cold and eaten with bread. The above is a dinner for three or four hungry men.

It is usually the case that some of the party prefer baked beans. To have these in perfection, add one gill of raw beans and a piece of pork three inches square to the foregoing proportions. Boil as above, until the beans begin to crack open; then fork out the smaller piece of pork, place it in the center of your largest cooking tin, take beans enough from the kettle to nearly fill the tin, set it over a bright fire on the range, invert the second-sized tin for a cover, place live hardwood coals on top, and bake precisely as directed for bread— only, when the coals on top become dull and black, brush them off, raise the cover, and take a look. If the beans are getting too dry, add three or four

---

196  Salted pork belly taken from fatted pigs, with the backbone and half the ribs taken out

spoonfuls of liquor from the kettle, replace cover and coals, and let them bake until they are of a rich light brown on top. Then serve. It is a good dish. If Boston can beat it, I don't want to lay up anything for old age.

Brown bread and baked beans have a natural connection in the average American mind, and rightly. They supplement each other, even as spring lamb and green peas with our transatlantic cousins. But there is a better recipe for brown bread than is known to the dwellers of the Hub—one that has captured first prizes at country fairs and won the approval of epicures from Maine to Minnesota; the one that brought honest old Greeley down, on his strictures anent[197] "country bread." And here is the recipe; take it for what it is worth, and try it fairly before condemning it. It is for home use: One quart of sweet milk, one quart of sour, two quarts of Indian meal and one quart of flour, and a cupful of dark, thin Porto Rico molasses. Use one teaspoonful of soda only. Bake in a steady, moderate oven, for four hours. Knead thoroughly before baking.

Soup is, or should be, a leading food element in every woodland camp. I am sorry to say that nothing is, as a rule, more badly botched, while nothing is more easily or simply cooked as it should be. Soup requires time, and a solid basis of the right material. Venison is the basis, and the best material is the bloody part of the deer, where the bullet went through. We used to throw this away; we have learned better. Cut about four pounds of the bloody meat into convenient pieces and wipe them as clean as possible with leaves or a damp cloth, but don't wash them. Put the meat into a five-quart kettle nearly filled with water and raise it to a lively boiling pitch. Let it boil for two hours. Have ready a three-tined fork made from a branch of birch or beech, and with this test the meat from time to time; when it parts readily from the bones, slice in a large onion. Pare six large, smooth potatoes, cut five of them into quarters, and drop them into the kettle; scrape the sixth one into the soup for thickening. Season with salt and white pepper to taste.

When, by skirmishing with the wooden fork, you can fish up bones with no

197 About

meat on them, the soup is cooked, and the kettle may be set aside to cool. Any hungry sportsman can order the next motion. Squirrels—red, black, gray, or fox—make nearly as good a soup as venison, and better stew. Hares, rabbits, grouse, quail, or any of the smaller game birds, may be used in making soup; but all small game is better in a stew.

## Stews and Fries

To make a stew, proceed for the first two hours precisely as directed for soup; then slice in a couple of good-sized onions and six medium potatoes. When the meat begins to fall from the bones, make a thickening by rubbing three tablespoonfuls of flour and two spoonfuls of melted butter together; thin to the consistency of cream with liquor from the kettle, and drip slowly into the stew, stirring briskly meanwhile. Allow all soups and stews to boil two hours before seasoning, and use only the best table salt and white (or black) pepper. Season sparingly; it is easier to put salt in than to get it out. Cayenne pepper adds zest to a soup or stew, but as some dislike it, let each man season his plate to his own cheek.

Fried squirrels are excellent for a change but are mostly spoiled by poor cooks, who put tough old and tender young squirrels together, treating all alike. To dress and cook them properly, chop off heads, tails, and feet with the hatchet; cut the skin on the back crosswise, and, inserting the two middle fingers, pull the skin off in two parts (head and tail). Clean and cut them in halves, leaving two ribs on the hindquarters. Put hind- and forequarters into the kettle, and parboil until tender. This will take about twenty minutes for young ones, and twice as long for the old.

When a sharpened sliver will pass easily through the flesh, take the hindquarters from the kettle, drain, and place them in the frying pan with pork fat hissing hot. Fry to a light, rich brown. It is the only proper way to cook squirrels. The forequarters are to be left in the kettle for a stew.

It sometimes happens that pigeons are very plentiful, and the camp is tempted into overshooting and overcooking, until everyone is thoroughly sick of pigeons. This is all wrong. No party is, or can be, justified in wanton slaughter, just because birds happen to be plentiful; they will soon be scarce enough. Pigeons are hardly game, and they are not a first-class bird, but a good deal may be got out of them by the following method: Dress them, at the rate of two birds to one man; save the giblets; place in the kettle, and boil until the sliver will easily pierce the breast; fork them out, cut the thick meat from each side of the breast bone, roll slightly in flour, and put the pieces in the pan, frying them in the same way as directed for squirrels. Put the remainder of the birds in the kettle for a stew.

Quail are good cooked in the same manner but are better roasted or broiled. To roast them, parboil for fifteen minutes, and in the meantime cut a thin hardwood stick, eighteen inches long for each bird. Sharpen the sticks neatly at both ends; impale the birds on one end and thrust the sticks into the ground near the fire, leaning them so that the heat will strike strongly and evenly. Hang a strip of pork between the legs of each bird and turn frequently until they are a rich brown. When the sharpened sliver will pass easily through the breast, they are done.

Woodcock are to be plucked but not drawn.[198] Suspend the bird in a bright, clear heat, hang a ribbon of fat pork between the legs, and roast until well done; do not parboil him.

Ruffed grouse are excellent roasted in the same manner but should first be parboiled. Mallards, teal, butterballs, all edible ducks, are to be treated the same as grouse. If you are ever lucky enough to feast on a canvasback roasted as above, you will be apt to borrow a leaf from Oliver Twist.[199]

Venison steak should be pounded to tenderness, pressed, and worked into shape with the hunting knife, and broiled over a bed of clean hardwood coals.

---

198 Eviscerated

199 Oliver, in Charles Dickens's classic, said to the master when he wanted more gruel, "Please, sir, I want some more."

A three-pronged birch fork makes the best broiler. For roast venison, the best portion is the forward part of the saddle.[200] Trim off the flanky parts and ends of the ribs; split the backbone lengthwise, that the inner surface may be well exposed; hang it by a strong cord or bark string in a powerful, even heat; lay thin strips of pork along the upper edge, and turn from time to time until done. It had better be left a little rare than overdone. Next to the saddle for roasting comes the shoulder. Peel this smoothly from the side, using the hunting knife; trim neatly, and cut off the leg at the knee; gash the thickest part of the flesh, and press shreds of pork into the gashes, with two or three thin slices skewered to the upper part. Treat it in the roasting as described above. It is not equal to the saddle when warm, but sliced and eaten cold, is quite as good.

And do not despise the fretful porcupine; he is better than he looks. If you happen on a healthy young specimen when you are needing meat, give him a show before condemning him. Shoot him humanely in the head and dress him. It is easily done; there are no quills on the belly, and the skin peels as freely as a rabbit's. Take him to camp, parboil him for thirty minutes, and roast or broil him to a rich brown over a bed of glowing coals. He will need no pork to make him juicy, and you will find him very like spring lamb, only better.

I do not accept the decision that ranks the little gray rabbit as a hare, simply because he has a slit in his lip; at all events I shall call him a rabbit for convenience, to distinguish him from his long-legged cousin, who turns white in winter, never takes to a hole, and can keep ahead of hounds nearly all day, affording a game, musical chase that is seldom out of hearing. He never by any chance has an ounce of fat on him and is not very good eating. He can, however, be worked into a good stew or a passable soup—provided he has not been feeding on laurel. The rabbit is an animal of different habits and different attributes. When jumped from his form, he is apt to "dig out"[201] for a hole or the nearest stone heap. Sometimes an old one will potter around a thicket,

---

200  The middle of the back
201  Take off

ahead of a slow dog, but his tendency is always to hole. But he affords some sport, and as an article of food, beats the long-legged hare out of sight. He is excellent in stews or soups, while the after half of him, flattened down with the hatchet, parboiled and fried brown in butter or pork fat, is equal to spring chicken.

# Fish

In the cooking of fish, as of flesh and fowl, the plainest and simplest methods are best, and for anything under two pounds, it is not necessary to go beyond the frying pan. Trout of over a pound should be split down the back that they may lie well in the pan and cook evenly. Roll well in meal, or a mixture of meal and flour, and fry to a rich brown in pork fat, piping hot. Larger fish may just as well be fried but are also adapted to other methods, and there are people who like fish broiled and buttered, or boiled. To broil a fish, split him on the back and broil him four minutes, flesh side down, turn and broil the other side an equal time. Butter and season to taste. To boil, the fish should weigh three pounds or more. Clean and crimp him by gashing the sides deeply with a sharp knife. Put him in a kettle of boiling water strongly salted, and boil twenty-five minutes. For each additional pound above three, add five minutes. For gravy, rub together two tablespoonfuls of flour and one of melted butter, add one heaping teaspoonful of evaporated milk, and thin with liquor from the kettle. When done, it should have the consistency of cream. Take the fish from the kettle, drain, pour the gravy over it, and eat only with wheat bread or hardtack, with butter. The simplest is best, healthiest, and most appetizing.

As a rule, on a mountain tramp or a canoe cruise, I do not tote canned goods. I carry my duffel in a light, pliable knapsack, and there is an aggravating antagonism between the uncompromising rims of a fruit can and the knobs of my vertebrae that twenty years of practice have utterly failed to reconcile. And yet, I have found my account in a can of condensed milk, not for tea or coffee, but on bread as a substitute for butter. And I have found a small can of Boston baked beans a most helpful lunch, with a nine-mile carry ahead. It was not epicurean but had staying qualities.

I often have a call to pilot some muscular young friend into the deep forest, and he usually carries a large packbasket, with a full supply of quart cans of salmon, tomatoes, peaches, etc. As in duty bound, I admonish him kindly, but firmly, on the folly of loading his young shoulders with such effeminate luxuries; often, I fear, hurting his young feelings by brusque advice. But at night, when the campfire burns brightly, and he begins to fish out his tins, the heart of the Old Woodsman relents, and I make amends by allowing him to divide the groceries.

There is a method of cooking usually called "mudding up," which I have found to preserve the flavor and juiciness of ducks, grouse, etc., better than any other method. I described the method in *Forest and Stream* more than a year ago, but a brief repetition may not be out of place here. Suppose the bird to be cooked is a mallard, or better still, a canvasback. Cut off the head and most part of the neck; cut off the pinions and pull out the tail feathers, make a plastic cake of clay or tenacious earth an inch thick and large enough to envelop the bird, and cover him with it snugly. Dig an oval pit under the fore stick, large enough to hold him, and fill it with hot coals, keeping up a strong heat. Just before turning in for the night, clean out the pit, put in the bird, cover with hot embers and coals, keeping up a brisk fire over it all night. When taken out in the morning, you will have an oval, oblong mass of baked clay, with a well-roasted bird inside. Let the mass cool until it can be handled, break off the clay, and feathers and skin will come with it, leaving the bird clean and skinless. Season it as you eat, with salt, pepper, and a squeeze of lemon if you like, nothing else.

## Condiments

In selecting salt, choose that which has a gritty feel when rubbed between the thumb and finger, and use white pepper rather than black, grinding the berry yourself. Procure a common tin pepperbox, and fill it with a mixture of fine salt and cayenne pepper—ten spoonsful of the former and one of the latter. Have it always where you can lay your hand on it; you will come to use it daily in camp, and if you ever get lost, you will find it of value. Fish and game have a flat, flashy[202] taste eaten without salt and are also unwholesome.

Do not carry any of the one hundred and one condiments, sauces, garnishes, etc., laid down in the books. Salt, pepper, and lemons fill the bill in that line. Lobster sauce, shrimp sauce, marjoram, celery, parsley, thyme, anchovies, etc., may be left at the hotels.

It may be expected that a pocket volume on woodcraft should contain a liberal chapter of instruction on hunting. It would be quite useless. Hunters, like poets, are born, not made. The art cannot be taught on paper. A few simple hints, however, may not be misplaced. To start aright, have your clothes fitted for hunting. Select good cassimere of a sort of dull, no-colored, neutral tint, like a decayed stump, and have coat, pants, and cap made of it. For footgear, two pairs of heavy yarn socks with rubber shoes or buckskin moccasins. In hunting, "silence is gold." Go quietly, slowly, and silently. Remember that the bright-eyed, sharp-eared woodfolk can see, hear, and smell, with a keenness

202 Flavorless

that throws your dull faculties quite in the shade. As you go lumbering and stick-breaking through the woods, you will never know how many of these quietly leave your path to right and left, allowing you to pass, while they glide away, unseen, unknown. It is easily seen that a sharp-sensed, light-bodied denizen of the woods can detect the approach of a heavy, bifurcated, booted animal, a long way ahead, and avoid him accordingly.

But there is an art, little known and practiced, that invariably succeeds in outflanking most wild animals, an art, simple in conception and execution, but requiring patience; a species, so to speak, of high art in forestry—the art of "sitting on a log." I could enlarge on this. I might say that the only writer of any note who has mentioned this phase of woodcraft is Mr. Charles D. Warner; and he only speaks of it in painting the character of that lazy guide "Old Phelps."

Sitting on a log includes a deal of patience, with oftentimes cold feet and chattering teeth but, attended to faithfully and patiently, is quite as successful as chasing a deer all day on tracking snow, while it can be practiced when the leaves are dry, and no other mode of still-hunting offers the ghost of a chance. When a man is moving through the woods, wary, watchful animals are pretty certain to catch sight of him. But let him keep perfectly quiet and the conditions are reversed. I have had my best luck, and killed my best deer, by practically waiting hour after hour on runways. But the time when a hunter could get four or five fair shots in a day by watching a runway has passed away forever. Never anymore will buffalo be seen in solid masses covering square miles in one pack. The immense bands of elk and droves of deer are things of the past, and "the game must go."

## CHAPTER VIII

# A TEN DAYS' TRIP IN THE WILDERNESS— GOING IT ALONE

BOUT THE ONLY INDUCEMENTS I CAN THINK of for making a ten days' journey through a strong wilderness, solitary and alone, were a liking for adventure, intense love of nature in her wildest dress, and a strange fondness for being in deep forests by myself. The choice of route was determined by the fact that two old friends and schoolmates had chosen to cast their lots in Michigan, one near Saginaw Bay, the other among the pines of the Muskegon. And both were a little homesick, and both wrote frequent letters, in which, knowing my weak point, they exhausted their adjectives and adverbs in describing the abundance of game and the marvelous fishing. Now, the Muskegon friend— Davis—was pretty well out of reach. But Pete Williams, only a few miles out of Saginaw, was easily accessible. And so it happened, on a bright October morning, when there came a frost that cut from Maine to Missouri, that a sudden fancy took me to use my new Billinghurst[203] on something larger than squirrels. It took about one minute to decide and an hour to pack such duffel as I needed for a few weeks in the woods.

---

203  A rifle; William Billinghurst was a well-known gunsmith and a contemporary of Sears.

Remembering Pete's two brown-eyed "kids" and knowing that they were ague-stricken[204] and homesick, I made place for a few apples and peaches, with a ripe melon. For Pete and I had been chums in Rochester, and I had bunked in his attic on Galusha Street, for two years. Also, his babies thought as much of me as of their father. The trip to Saginaw was easy and pleasant. A "Redbird" packet[205] to Buffalo, the old propeller *Globe*[206] to Lower Saginaw, and a ride of half a day on a buckboard, brought me to Pete Williams's clearing. Were they glad to see me? Well, I think so. Pete and his wife cried like children, while the two little homesick "kids" laid their silken heads on my knees and sobbed for very joy. When I brought out the apples and peaches, assuring them that these came from the little garden of their old home—liar that I was—their delight was boundless. And the fact that their favorite tree was a "sour bough," while these were sweet, did not shake their faith in the least.

## At Pete Williams's

I stayed ten days or more with the Williams family, and the fishing and hunting were all that he had said—all that could be asked. The woods swarmed with pigeons and squirrels; grouse, quail, ducks, and wild turkeys were too plentiful, while a good hunter could scarcely fail of getting a standing shot at a deer in a morning's hunt. But, *cui bono*?[207] What use could be made of fish or game in such a place? They were all half sick and had little appetite. Mrs. Williams could not endure the smell of fish; they had been cloyed on small game and were surfeited on[208] venison.

My sporting ardor sank to zero. I had the decency not to slaughter game for the love of killing and leave it to rot, or hook large fish that could not be used. I soon grew restless and began to think often about the lumber camp on the Muskegon. By surveyors' lines it was hardly more than sixty miles from Pete Williams's clearing to the Joe Davis camp on the Muskegon. "But practically,"

---

204  Fever-stricken
205  The Red Bird Line took passengers up and down the Erie Canal in packet boats.
206  The *Globe* was a steamboat.
207  In Latin, "for whose benefit?"
208  Had an excess of

said Pete, "Joe and I are a thousand miles apart. White men, as a rule, don't undertake to cross this wilderness. The only one I know who has tried it is old Bill Hance; he can tell you all about it."

Hance was the hunting and trapping genius of Saginaw Bay—a man who dwelt in the woods summer and winter and never trimmed his hair or wore any other covering on his head. Not a misanthrope, or taciturn, but friendly and talkative rather; liking best to live alone, but fond of tramping across the woods to gossip with neighbors; a very tall man withal, and so thin that, as he went rapidly winding and turning among fallen logs, you looked to see him tangle up and tumble in a loose coil, like a wet rope, but he was better than he looked. He had a high reputation as trailer, guide, or trapper, and was mentioned as a "bad man in a racket." I had met him several times, and as he was decidedly a character, had rather laid myself out to cultivate him. And now that I began to have a strong notion of crossing the woods alone, I took counsel of Bill Hance. Unlike Williams, he thought it perfectly feasible, and rather a neat, gamy thing for a youngster to do. He had crossed the woods several times with surveying parties, and once alone. He knew an Indian trail that led to an old camp within ten miles of the Muskegon and thought the trail could be followed. It took him a little less than three days to go through; "but," he added, "I nat'rally travel a little faster in the woods than most men. If you can follow the trail, you ought to get through in a little more'n three days—if you keep moggin'."[209]

One afternoon I carefully packed the knapsack and organized for a long woods tramp. I took little stock in that trail, or the three days' notion as to time. I made calculations on losing the trail the first day and being out a full week. The outfit consisted of rifle, hatchet, compass, blanket-bag, knapsack, and knife. For rations, one loaf of bread, two quarts of meal, two pounds of pork, one pound of sugar, with tea, salt, etc., and a supply of jerked venison. One tin dish, twelve rounds of ammunition, and the bullet-molds filled the list and did not make a heavy load.

---

209  Moving at a consistent pace

Early on a crisp, bright October morning I kissed the little fellows good-bye and started out with Hance, who was to put me on the trail. I left the children with sorrow and pity at heart. I am glad now that my visit was a golden hiatus in the sick monotony of their young lives and that I was able to brighten a few days of their dreary existence. They had begged for the privilege of sleeping with me on a shakedown[210] from the first; and when, as often happened, a pair of little feverish lips would murmur timidly and pleadingly, "I'm so dry; can I have er drink?" I am thankful that I did not put the pleader off with a sip of tepid water but always brought it from the spring, sparkling and cold. For, a twelvemonth later, there were two little graves in a corner of the stump-blackened garden and two sore hearts in Pete Williams's cabin.

Hance found the trail easily, but the Indians had been gone a long time, and it was filled with leaves, dim, and not easy to follow. It ended as nearly all trails do; it branched off to right and left, grew dimmer and slimmer, degenerated to a deer path, petered out to a squirrel track, ran up a tree, and ended in a knot hole. I was not sorry. It left me free to follow my nose, my inclination, and—the compass.

There are men who, on finding themselves alone in a pathless forest, become appalled, almost panic stricken. The vastness of an unbroken wilderness subdues them, and they quail before the relentless, untamed forces of nature. These are the men who grow enthusiastic—at home—about sylvan life, outdoor sports, but always strike camp and come home rather sooner than they intended. And there be some who plunge into an unbroken forest with a feeling of fresh, free, invigorating delight, as they might dash into a crisp ocean surf on a hot day. These know that nature is stern, hard, immovable, and terrible in unrelenting cruelty. When wintry winds are out and the mercury far below zero, she will allow her most ardent lover to freeze on her snowy breast without waving a leaf in pity or offering him a match, and scores of her devotees may starve to death in as many different languages before she will offer a loaf of bread. She does not deal in matches and loaves; rather in thunderbolts and granite mountains. And the ashes of her campfires bury

---

210 A makeshift bed

proud cities. But like all tyrants, she yields to force and gives the more, the more she is beaten. She may starve or freeze the poet, the scholar, the scientist; all the same, she has in store food, fuel, and shelter, which the skillful, self-reliant woodsman can wring from her savage hand with axe and rifle.

> Only to him whose coat of rags
> Has pressed at night her regal feet,
> Shall come the secrets, strange and sweet,
> Of century pines and beetling crags.
> For him the goddess shall unlock
> The golden secrets which have lain
> Ten thousand years, through frost and rain,
> Deep in the bosom of the rock.

The trip was a long and tiresome one, considering the distance. There were no hairbreadth escapes; I was not tackled by bears, treed by wolves, or nearly killed by a hand-to-claw "racket" with a panther, and there were no Indians to come sneak-hunting around after hair. Animal life was abundant, exuberant, even. But the bright-eyed woodfolk seemed tame, nay, almost friendly, and quite intent on minding their own business. It was a "pigeon year," a "squirrel year," and also a marvelous year for shack, or mast.[211] Every nut-bearing tree was loaded with sweet well-filled nuts, and this, coupled with the fact that the Indians had left and the whites had not yet got in, probably accounted for the plentitude of game.

## Wood Life

I do not think there was an hour of daylight on the trip when squirrels were not too numerous to be counted, while pigeons were a constant quantity from start to finish. Grouse in the thickets and quail in the high oak openings, or small prairies, with droves of wild turkeys among heavy timber, were met with almost hourly, and there was scarcely a day on which I could not have had a standing shot at a bear. But the most interesting point about the game was—to

---

211  Fallen nuts on the ground

me, at least—the marvelous abundance of deer. They were everywhere, on all sorts of ground and among all varieties of timber; very tame they were, too, often stopping to look at the stranger, offering easy shots at short range, and finally going off quite leisurely.

No ardent lover of forest life could be lonely in such company, and in such weather. The only drawback was the harassing and vexatious manner in which lakes, streams, swamps, and marshes constantly persisted in getting across the way, compelling long detours to the north or south, when the true course was nearly due west. I think there were days on which ten hours of pretty faithful tramping did not result in more than three or four miles of direct headway. The headwaters of the Salt and Chippewa Rivers were especially obstructive, and when more than half the distance was covered, I ran into a tangle of small lakes, marshes, and swamps, not marked on the map, which cost a hard day's work to leave behind.

While there were no startling adventures and no danger connected with the trip, there was a constant succession of incidents that made the lonely tramp far from monotonous. Some of these occurrences were intensely interesting and a little exciting. Perhaps the brief recital of a few may not be uninteresting at the present day, when game is so rapidly disappearing.

My rifle was a neat, hair-triggered Billinghurst, carrying sixty round balls to the pound, a muzzle-loader, of course, and a nail-driver. I made just three shots in ten days, and each shot stood for a plump young deer in the "short blue." It seemed wicked to murder such a bright, graceful animal, when no more than the loins and a couple of slices from the ham could be used, leaving the balance to the wolves, who never failed to take possession before I was out of earshot. But I condoned the excess, if excess it were, by the many chances I allowed to pass, not only on deer but bear, and once on a big brute of a wild hog, the wickedest and most formidable-looking animal I ever met in the woods. The meeting happened in this wise.[212] I had been bothered and wearied for half a day by a bad piece of low, marshy ground and had at length struck a dry, rolling oak opening where I sat down at the foot of a small oak to rest. I had scarcely been resting ten minutes when I caught sight of a large, dirty-white animal, slowly working its way in my direction through the low bushes, evidently nosing around for acorns. I was puzzled to say what it was. It looked like a hog but stood too high on its legs, and how would such a beast get there anyhow? Nearer and nearer he came and at last walked out into an open spot less than twenty yards distant. It was a wild hog of the ugliest and largest description; tall as a yearling, with an unnaturally large head and dangerous-looking tusks that curved above his savage snout like small horns. There was promise of magnificent power in his immense shoulders, while flanks and hams were disproportionately light. He came out to the open leisurely munching his acorns or amusing himself by ploughing deep furrows with his nose, and not until within ten yards did he appear to note the presence of a stranger. Suddenly he raised his head and became rigid as though frozen to stone; he was taking an observation. For a few seconds he remained immovable; then his bristles became erect, and with a deep guttural, grunting noise, he commenced hitching himself along in my direction, sidewise. My hair raised,

212 Way

and in an instant I was on my feet with the cocked rifle to my shoulder—meaning to shoot before his charge, and then make good time up the tree. But there was no need. As I sprang to my feet, he sprang for the hazel bushes and went tearing through them with the speed of a deer, keeping up a succession of snorts and grunts that could be heard long after he had passed out of sight. I am not subject to buck fever and was disgusted to find myself so badly "rattled" that I could scarcely handle the rifle. At first I was provoked at myself for not getting a good ready and shooting him in the head as he came out of the bushes, but it was better to let him live. He was not carnivorous, or a beast of prey, and ugly as he was, certainly looked better alive than he would as a porcine corpse. No doubt he relished his acorns as well as though he had been less ugly, and he was a savage power in the forest. Bears love pork, and the fact that the hog was picking up a comfortable living in that wilderness is presumptive evidence that he was a match for the largest bear, or he would have been eaten long before.

## Incidents

Another little incident, in which Bruin played a leading part, rises vividly to memory. It was hardly an adventure, only the meeting of man and bear, and they parted on good terms, with no hardness on either side.

The meeting occurred, as usually was the case with large game, on dry, oak lands, where the undergrowth was hazel, sassafras, and wild grapevine. As before, I had paused for a rest, when I began to catch glimpses of a very black animal working its way among the hazel bushes, under the scattering oaks, and toward me. With no definite intention of shooting, but just to see how easy it might be to kill him, I got a good ready and waited. Slowly and lazily he nuzzled his way among the trees, sitting up occasionally to crunch acorns, until he was within twenty-five yards of me, with the bright bead neatly showing at the butt of his ear, and he sitting on his haunches, calmly chewing his acorns, oblivious of danger. He was the shortest-legged, blackest, and glossiest bear I had ever seen, and such a fair shot. But I could not use either skin or meat, and he was a splendid picture just as he sat. Shot down and left to taint the blessed air, he would not look as wholesome, let alone that it would be unwarrantable murder. And so, when he came nosing under the very tree where I was sitting, I suddenly jumped up, threw my hat at him and gave a Comanche[213] yell. He tumbled over in a limp heap, grunting and whining for very terror, gathered himself up, got up headway, and disappeared with wonderful speed—considering the length of his legs.

On another occasion—and this was in heavy timber—I was resting on a log, partially concealed by spice bushes, when I noticed a large flock of turkeys coming in my direction. As they rapidly advanced with their quick, gliding walk, the flock grew to a drove, the drove became a swarm—an army. To right and on the left, as far as I could see in front, a legion of turkeys was marching, steadily marching to the eastward. Among them were some of the grandest gobblers I had ever seen, and one magnificent fellow came straight toward me. Never before or since have I seen such a splendid wild bird. His thick, glossy black beard nearly reached the ground, his bronze uniform was of the richest, and he was decidedly the largest I have ever seen. When within fifty feet of the

213 A Native American tribe that used to live throughout the Southwest

spot where I was nearly hidden, his wary eye caught something suspicious and he raised his superb head for an instant in an attitude of motionless attention. Then, with lowered head and drooping tail, he turned right about, gave the note of alarm, put the trunk of a large tree quickly between himself and the enemy, and went away like the wind. With the speed of thought the warning note was sounded along the whole line, and in a moment the woods seemed alive with turkeys, running for dear life. In less time than it takes to tell it, that gallinaceous[214] army had passed out of sight, forever. And the like of it will never again be possible on this continent.

## Turkeys and Deer

And again, on the morning of the sixth day out, I blundered on to such an aggregation of deer as a man sees but once in a lifetime. I had camped overnight on low land, among heavy timber, but soon after striking camp, came to a place where the timber was scattering and the land had a gentle rise to the westward. Scarcely had I left the low land behind when a few deer got out of their beds and commenced lazily bounding away. They were soon joined by others; on the right flank, on the left, and ahead, they continued to rise and canter off leisurely, stopping at a distance of one or two hundred yards to look back. It struck me finally that I had started something rather unusual, and I began counting the deer in sight. It was useless to attempt it; their white flags were flying in front and on both flanks, as far as one could see, and new ones seemed constantly joining the procession. Among them were several very large bucks with superb antlers, and these seemed very little afraid of the small, quiet biped in leaf-colored rig. They often paused to gaze back with bold, fearless front, as though inclined to call a halt and face the music, but when within a hundred yards would turn and canter leisurely away. As the herd neared the summit of the low-lying ridge, I tried to make a reasonable guess at their numbers, by counting a part and estimating the rest, but could come to no satisfactory conclusion. As they passed the summit and loped down the gentle decline toward heavy timber, they began to scatter, and soon not a flag was in sight. It was a magnificent cervine army with white banners, and I

---

214  Part of the order of birds known as *Galliformes*.

shall never look upon its like again. The largest drove of deer I have seen in twenty years consisted of seven only.

And with much of interest, much of tramping, and not a little vexatious delay, I came at length to a stream that I knew must be the south branch of the Muskegon. The main river could scarcely be more than ten miles to the west and might be easily reached in one day.

It was time. The meal and pork were nearly gone, sugar and tea were at low ebb, and I was tired of venison; tired anyhow; ready for human speech and human companionship.

It was in the afternoon of the ninth day that I crossed the South Muskegon and laid a course west by north. The traveling was not bad, and in less than an hour I ran on to the ruins of a camp that I knew to be the work of Indians. It had evidently been a permanent winter camp and was almost certainly the Indian camp spoken of by Bill Hance. Pausing a short time to look over the ruins, with the lonely feeling always induced by a decayed, rotting camp, I struck due west and made several miles before sundown.

I camped on a little rill, near a huge dry stub that would peel, made the last of the meal into a johnnycake, broiled the last slice of pork, and lay down with the notion that a ten days' tramp, where it took an average of fifteen miles to make six, ought to end on the morrow. At sunrise I was again on foot, and after three hours of steady tramping, saw a smoky opening ahead. In five minutes I was standing on the left bank of the Muskegon.

And the Joe Davis camp—was it upstream or down? I decided on the latter and started slowly downstream, keeping an eye out for signs. In less than an hour I struck a dim log road that led to the river, and there was a "landing," with the usual debris of skids, loose bark, chocks, and some pieces of broken boards. It did not take long to construct an efficient log raft from the dry skids, and as I drifted placidly down the deep, wild river, munching the last bit of johnnycake, I inwardly swore that my next wilderness cruise should be by water.

It was in late afternoon that I heard—blessed sound—the eager clank, clank, clank of the old-fashioned sawmill. It grew nearer and more distinct; presently I could distinguish the rumble of machinery as the carriage[215] gigged[216] back; then the raft rounded a gentle bend, and a mill, with its long, log boardinghouse, came full in sight.

As the raft swung into the landing, the mill became silent; a brown-bearded, red-shirted fellow came down to welcome me, a pair of strong hands grasped both my own, and the voice of Joe Davis said earnestly, "Why, George! I never was so d—d glad to see a man in my life!"

The ten days' tramp was ended. It had been wearisome to a degree, but interesting and instructive. I had seen more game birds and animals in the time than I ever saw before or since in a whole season, and though I came out with clothes pretty well worn and torn off my back and legs, I was a little disposed to plume myself on the achievement. Even at this day I am a little proud of the fact that, with so many temptations to slaughter, I only fired three shots on the route. Nothing but the exceptionally fine, dry weather rendered such a trip possible in a wilderness so cut up with swamps, lakes, marshes, and streams. A week of steady rain or a premature snowstorm—either likely enough at that season—would have been most disastrous; while a forest fire like that of '56, and later ones, would simply have proved fatal.

Reader, if ever you are tempted to make a similar thoughtless, reckless trip— don't do it.

215  The carriage holds the logs as they are being sawed.
216  Whirled

# CANOEING– THE LIGHT CANOE AND DOUBLE BLADE– VARIOUS CANOES FOR VARIOUS CANOEISTS– REASONS FOR PREFERRING THE CLINKER-BUILT CEDAR

THE CANOE IS COMING TO THE FRONT, AND canoeing is gaining rapidly in popular favor, in spite of the disparaging remark that "a canoe is a poor man's yacht." The canoe editor of *Forest and Stream* pertinently says, "We may as properly call a bicycle 'the poor man's express train.'" But suppose it is the poor man's yacht? Are we to be debarred from aquatic sports because we are not rich? And are we such weak flunkies as to be ashamed of poverty? Or to attempt shams and subterfuges to hide it? For myself, I freely accept the imputation. In common with nine-tenths of my fellow citizens I am poor—and the canoe is my yacht, as it would be were I a millionaire. We are a nation of many millions, and comparatively few of us are rich enough to support a yacht, let alone the fact that not one man in fifty lives near enough to yachting waters to make such an acquisition desirable—or feasible, even. It is different with the canoe. A man like myself may live in the backwoods, a hundred miles from a decent-sized inland lake, and much farther from the sea coast, and yet be an enthusiastic canoeist. For instance.

Last July I made my preparations for a canoe cruise and spun out with as little delay as possible. I had pitched on the Adirondacks as cruising ground and had more than 250 miles of railroads and buckboards to take before launching the canoe on Moose River. She was carried thirteen miles over the Browns Tract road on the head of her skipper, cruised from the western side of the Wilderness to the Lower St. Regis on the east side, cruised back again by a somewhat different route, was taken home to Pennsylvania on the cars, 250 miles, sent back to her builder, St. Lawrence County, NY, over 300 miles, thence by rail to New York City, where, the last I heard of her, she was on exhibition at the *Forest and Stream* office. She took her chances in the baggage car, with no special care, and is today, so far as I know, staunch and tight, with not a check in her frail siding.

Such cruising can only be made in a very light canoe and with a very light outfit. It was sometimes necessary to make several carries in one day, aggregating as much as ten miles, besides from fifteen to twenty miles under paddle. No heavy, decked, paddling, or sailing canoe would have been available for such a trip with a man of ordinary muscle.

The difference between a lone, independent cruise through an almost unbroken wilderness and cruising along civilized routes, where the canoeist can interview farmhouses and village groceries for supplies, getting gratuitous stonings from the small boy, and much reviling from ye ancient mariner of the towpath—I say, the difference is just immense. Whence it comes that I always prefer a very light, open canoe, one that I can carry almost as easily as my hat, and yet that will float me easily, buoyantly, and safely. And such a canoe was my last cruiser. She only weighed ten and one-half pounds when first launched, and after an all-summer rattling by land and water had only gained half a pound. I do not therefore advise any one to buy a ten-and-a-half-pound canoe; although she would prove competent for a skillful lightweight. She was built to order, as a test of lightness and was the third experiment in that line.

I have nothing to say against the really fine canoes that are in highest favor today. Were I fond of sailing and satisfied to cruise on routes where clearings are more plentiful than carries, I daresay I should run a Shadow, or Stella Maris, at a cost of considerably more than $100—though I should hardly call it a "poor man's yacht." Much is being said and written at the present day as to the "perfect canoe." One writer decides in favor of a Pearl 15×31½ inches. In the same column another says, "The perfect canoe does not exist." I should rather say there are several types of the modern canoe, each nearly perfect in its way and for the use to which it is best adapted. The perfect paddling canoe is by no means perfect under canvas, and vice versa. The best cruiser is not a perfect racer, while neither of them is at all perfect as a paddling cruiser where much carrying is to be done. And the most perfect canoe for fishing and gunning around shallow, marshy waters, would be a very imperfect canoe for a rough and ready cruise of one hundred miles through a strange wilderness, where a day's cruise will sometimes include a dozen miles of carrying.

## A Light Canoe

Believing, as I do, that the light, single canoe with double-bladed paddle is bound to soon become a leading—if not the leading—feature in summer recreation, and having been a light canoeist for nearly fifty years, during the last twenty of which I experimented much with the view of reducing weight, perhaps I can give some hints that may help a younger man in the selection of a canoe that shall be safe, pleasant to ride, and not burdensome to carry.

Let me promise that, up to four years ago, I was never able to get a canoe that entirely satisfied me as to weight and model. I bought the smallest birches I could find, procured a tiny Chippewa[217] dugout from North Michigan, and once owned a kayak. They were all too heavy, and they were cranky to a degree.

About twenty years ago I commenced making my own canoes. The construction was of the simplest; a 22-inch pine board for the bottom, planed to ¾ of an inch thickness; two wide ½-inch boards for the sides, and two light oak stems; five pieces of wood in all. I found that the bend of the siding gave too much shear; for instance, if the siding was 12 inches wide, she would have a rise of 12 inches at stems and less than 5 inches at center. But the flat bottom made her very stiff, and for river work she was better than anything I had yet tried. She was too heavy, however, always weighing from 45 to 50 pounds, and awkward to carry.

My last canoe of this style went down the Susquehanna with an ice jam in the spring of '79, and in the meantime canoeing began to loom up. The best paper in the country that makes outdoor sport a specialty, devoted liberal space to canoeing, and skilled boatbuilders were advertising canoes of various models and widely different material. I commenced interviewing the builders by letter and studying catalogues carefully. There was a wide margin of choice. You could have lapstreak, smooth skin, paper, veneer, or canvas. What I wanted was lightweight, and good model. I liked the Peterborough canoes; they were decidedly canoey. Also, the veneered Racines, but neither of them talked of a 20-pound canoe. The "Osgood folding canvas" did. But I had some knowledge of canvas boats. I knew they could make her down to 20 pounds. How much would she weigh after being in the water a week, and how would she behave when swamped in the middle of a lake, were questions to be asked, for I always get swamped. One builder of cedar canoes thought he could make me the boat I wanted, inside of 20 pounds, clinker-built, and at my own risk, as he hardly believed in so light a boat. I sent him the order, and he turned out what is pretty well known in Browns Tract as the "Nessmuk canoe." She weighed just 17 pounds 13¾ ounces, and was thought to be the lightest working canoe in existence. Her builder gave me some advice about

---

217  A tribe of Native Americans that lived primarily in what is now the northern United States.

stiffening her with braces, etc., if I found her too frail, "and he never expected another like her."

"He builded better than he knew." She needed no bracing, and she was, and is, a staunch, seaworthy little model. I fell in love with her from the start. I had at last found the canoe that I could ride in rough water, sleep in afloat, and carry with ease for miles. I paddled her early and late, mainly on the Fulton Chain, but I also cruised her on Raquette Lake, Eagle, Utowana, Blue Mountain, and Forked Lakes. I paddled her until there were black and blue streaks along the muscles from wrist to elbow. Thank heaven, I had found something that made me a boy again. Her log shows a cruise for 1880 of over 550 miles.

As regards her capacity (she is now on Third Lake, Browns Tract), James P. Fifield, a muscular young Forge House guide of 6 feet 2 inches and 185 pounds weight, took her through the Fulton Chain to Raquette Lake last summer, and happening on his camp, Seventh Lake, last July, I asked him how she performed under his weight. He said, "I never made the trip to Raquette so lightly and easily in my life." And as to the opinion of her builder, he wrote me, under date of November 18, '83: "I thought when I built the *Nessmuk*, no one else would ever want one. But I now build about a dozen of them a year. Great big men, ladies, and two, aye, three schoolboys ride in them. It is wonderful how few pounds of cedar, rightly modeled and properly put together, it takes to float a man." Just so, Mr. Builder. That's what I said when I ordered her. But few seemed to see it then.

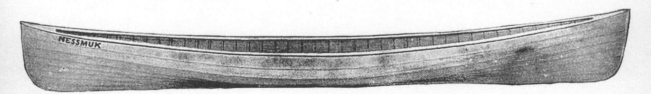

## Experiments

The *Nessmuk* was by no means the ultimatum of lightness, and I ordered another six inches longer, two inches wider, and to weigh about fifteen pounds. When she came to hand, she was a beauty, finished in oil and shellac. But she weighed sixteen pounds and would not only carry me and my duffel, but I could easily carry a passenger of my weight. I cruised her in the summer of '81 over the Fulton Chain, Raquette Lake, Forked Lake, down the Raquette River, and on Long Lake. But her log only showed a record of 206 miles. The cruise that had been mapped for 600 miles was cut short by sickness, and I went into quarantine at the hostelry of Mitchell Sabattis. Slowly and feebly I crept back to the Fulton Chain, hung up at the Forge House, and the cruise of the *Susan Nipper* was ended. Later in the season, I sent for her, and she was forwarded by express, coming out over the fearful Browns Tract road to Boonville (twenty-five and a half miles) by buckboard. From Boonville home, she took her chances in the baggage car without protection and reached her destination without a check or scratch. She hangs in her slings under the porch, a thing of beauty—and, like many beauties, a trifle frail—but staunch as the day I took her. Her proper lading[218] is about 200 pounds. She can float 300 pounds.

Of my last and lightest venture, the *Sairy Gamp*, little more need be said. I will only add that a Mr. Dutton, of Philadelphia, got into her at the Forge House and paddled her like an old canoeist, though it was his first experience with the double blade. He gave his age as sixty-four years, and weight, 140 pounds. Billy Cornell, a bright young guide, cruised her on Raquette Lake quite as well as her owner could do it, and I thought she trimmed better with him. He paddled at 141½ pounds, which is just about her right lading. And she was only an experiment, anyhow. I wanted to find out how light a canoe it took to drown her skipper, and I do not yet know. I never shall. But, most of all, I desired to settle the question—approximately at least, of weight, as regards canoe and canoeist.

Many years ago, I became convinced that we were all, as canoeists, carrying and paddling just twice as much wood as was at all needful, and something more than a year since, I advanced the opinion in *Forest and Stream* that ten pounds of well-made cedar ought to carry one hundred pounds of man. The

218 Weight of the load

past season has more than proved it, but, as I may be a little exceptional, I leave myself out of the question and have ordered my next canoe on lines and dimensions that, in my judgment, will be found nearly perfect for the average canoeist of 150 to 160 pounds. She will be much stronger than either of my other canoes, because few men would like a canoe so frail and limber that she can be sprung inward by hand pressure on the gunwales, as easily as a hatbox. And many men are clumsy or careless with a boat, while others are lubberly[219] by nature. Her dimensions are: length, 10½ feet; beam, 26 inches; rise at center, 9 inches; at seams, 15 inches; oval red elm ribs, 1 inch apart; an inch home tumble;[220] stems, plumb and sharp; oak keel and keelson; clinker-built, of white cedar.

Such a canoe will weigh about 22 pounds and will do just as well for the man of 140 or 170 pounds, while even a lightweight of 110 pounds ought to take her over a portage with a light, elastic carrying frame, without distress. She will trim best, however, at about 160 pounds. For a welter, say of some 200 pounds, add 6 inches to her length, 2 inches to her beam, and 1-inch rise at center. The lightweight canoeist will find that either of these two canoes will prove satisfactory, that is 10 feet in length, weight 16 pounds, or 10½ feet length, weight 18 pounds. Either is capable of 160 pounds, and they are very steady and buoyant, as I happen to know. I daresay any first-class manufacturers will build canoes of these dimensions.

Provide your canoe with a flooring of oilcloth 3½ feet long by 15 inches wide; punch holes in it and tie it neatly to the ribbing, just where it will best protect the bottom from wear and danger. Use only a cushion for a seat, and do not buy a fancy one with permanent stuffing, but get sixpence worth of good, unbleached cotton cloth and have it sewed into bag shape. Stuff the bag with fine browse, dry grass, or leaves; settle it well together; and fasten the open end by turning it flatly back and using two or three pins. You can empty it if you like when going over a carry, and it makes a good pillow at night.

---

219 Clumsy

220 Tumble home is the inward curve of a boat's upper sides above the waterline.

# The Proper Craft

Select a canoe that fits you, just as you would a coat or hat. A 16-pound canoe may fit me exactly but would be a bad misfit for a man of 180 pounds. And don't neglect the auxiliary paddle, or "pudding stick," as my friends call it. The notion may be new to most canoeists but will be found exceedingly handy and useful. It is simply a little one-handed paddle weighing 5 to 7 ounces, 20 to 22 inches long, with a blade 3½ inches wide. Work it out of half-inch cherry or maple, and fine the blade down thin. Tie it to a rib with a slipknot, having the handle in easy reach, and when you come to a narrow, tortuous channel, where shrubs and weeds crowd you on both sides, take the double blade inboard, use the pudding stick, and you can go almost anywhere that a muskrat can.

In fishing for trout or floating deer, remember you are dealing with the wary and that the broad blades are very showy in motion. Therefore, on approaching a spring hole, lay the double blade on the lily pads, where you can pick it up when wanted and handle your canoe with the auxiliary. On hooking a large fish, handle the rod with one hand and with the other lay the canoe out into deep water, away from all entangling alliances. You may be surprised to find how easily, with a little practice, you can make a two-pound trout or bass tow the canoe the way you want it to go.

In floating for deer, use the double blade only in making the passage to the ground; then take it apart and lay it inboard, using only the little paddle to float with, tying it to a rib with a yard and a half of linen line. On approaching a deer near enough to shoot, let go the paddle, leaving it to drift alongside while you attend to venison.

## CHAPTER X

# ODDS AND ENDS– WHERE TO GO FOR AN OUTING– WHY A CLINKER?– BOUGHS AND BROWSE

THE OFT-RECURRING QUESTION AS TO WHERE to go for the outing can hardly be answered at all satisfactorily. In a general way, any place may, and ought to be, satisfactory, where there are fresh green woods, pleasant scenery, and fish and game plenty enough to supply the camp abundantly, with boating facilities and pure water.

"It's more in the man than it is in the land,"[221] and there are thousands of such places on the waters of the Susquehanna, the Delaware, the rivers and lakes of Maine, Michigan, Wisconsin, and Canada.

Among the lakes of Central New York, one may easily select a camping ground, healthy, pleasant, easily reached, and with the advantage of cheapness. A little too much civilization, perhaps, but the farmers are friendly and kindly disposed to all summer outers who behave like gentlemen.

For fine forest scenery and unequaled canoeing facilities, it must be admitted that the Adirondack region stands at the head. There is also fine fishing and good hunting, for those who know the right places to go for deer and trout. But it is a tedious, expensive job getting into the heart of the wilderness, and it is the most costly woodland resort I know of when you are there. You can keep expenses down (and also have a much better sport) by avoiding the hotels and going into camp at once, and staying there. The best way is for two men to hire a guide, live in camp altogether, and divide the expense.

All along the Allegheny range, from Maine to Michigan, and from Pennsylvania to the Provinces, numberless resorts exist as pleasant, as healthy, as prolific of sport, as the famed Adirondacks, and at half the cost. But for an all-summer canoe cruise, with more than 600 accessible lakes and ponds, the Northern Wilderness stands alone. And as a wealthy cockney once remarked to me in Browns Tract, "It's no place for a poor man."

And now I will give my reasons for preferring the clinker-built cedar boat, or canoe, to any other. First, as to material. Cedar is stronger, more elastic, more enduring, and shrinks less than pine or any other light wood used as boat siding. As one of the best builders in the country says, "It has been thoroughly demonstrated that a cedar canoe will stand more hard knocks than an oak one; for where it only receives bruises, the oak streaks[222] will split." And he

---

221 The poem "Thar's More in the Man Than Thar Is in the Land" was written in 1869 by the American poet Sidney Lanier.

222 Strakes

268

might add, the pine will break. But I suppose it is settled beyond dispute that white cedar stands at the head for boat streaks. I prefer it, then, because it is the best. And I prefer the clinker, because it is the strongest, simplest, most enduring, and most easily repaired in case of accident. To prove the strength theory, take a cedar (or pine) strip eight feet long and six inches wide. Bend it to a certain point by an equal strain on each end, and carefully note the result. Next, strip it lengthwise with the rip saw, lap the two halves an inch, and nail the lap as in boat building. Test it again, and you will find it has gained in strength about twenty percent. That is the clinker of it.

Now work the laps down until the strip is of uniform thickness its entire length, and test it once more; you will find it much weaker than on first trial. That is the smooth skin, sometimes called *lapstrake*. They, the clinker canoes, are easily tightened when they spring a leak through being rattled over stones in rapids. It is only to hunt a smooth pebble for a clinch[223] head and settle the nails that have started with the hatchet, putting in a few new ones if needed. And they are put together, at least by the best builders, without any cement or white lead, naked wood to wood, and depending only on close work for waterproofing. And each pair of strips is cut to fit and lie in its proper place without strain, no two pairs being alike, but each pair, from garboards to upper streak, having easy, natural form for its destined position.

## Various Craft

The veneered canoes are very fine for deep water, but a few cuts on sharp stones will be found ruinous, and if exposed much to weather they are liable to warp. The builders understand this, and plainly say that they prefer not to build fine boats for those who will neglect the proper care of them.

The paper boat, also, will not stand much cutting on sharp stones, and it is not buoyant when swamped, unless fitted with watertight compartments, which I abhor.

---

223  A nail with its end bent over

The canvas is rather a logy, limp sort of craft, to my thinking, and liable to drown her crew if swamped.

But each and all have their admirers, and purchasers as well, while each is good in its way, and I only mention a few reasons for my preference of the cedar.

When running an ugly rapid or crossing a stormy lake, I like to feel that I have enough light, seasoned wood under me to keep my mouth and nose above water all day, besides saving the rifle and knapsack, which, when running into danger, I always tie to the ribbing with strong linen line, as I do the paddle also, giving it about line enough to just allow free play.

## Overboard

I am not—to use a little modern slang—going to "give myself away" on canoeing or talk of startling adventure. But for the possible advantage of some future canoeist, I will briefly relate what happened to me on a certain windy morning one summer. It was on one of the larger lakes—no matter which—between Paul Smith's and the Fulton Chain. I had camped overnight in a spot that did not suit me in the least, but it seemed the best I could do then and there. The night was rough, and the early morning threatening. However, I managed a cup of coffee, "tied in," and made a slippery carry of two miles a little after sunrise. Arrived on the shore of the lake, and things did not look promising. The whirling, twirling clouds were black and dangerous looking, the crisp, dark waves were crested with spume, and I had a notion of just making a comfortable camp and waiting for better weather. But the commissary department was reduced to six Boston crackers, with a single slice of pork, and it was twelve miles of wilderness to the nearest point of supplies, four miles of it carries, included. Such weather might last a week, and I decided to go. For half an hour I sat on the beach, taking weather notes. The wind was northeast; my course was due west, giving me four points free. Taking five feet of strong line, I tied one end under a rib next the keelson, and the other around the paddle. Stripping to shirt and drawers, I stowed everything in the knapsack and tied that safely in the forepeak.[224]

---

224  A hold in the bow of the boat

Then I swung out. Before I was a half mile out, I fervently wished myself back. But it was too late. How that little, corky, light canoe did bound and snap, with a constant tendency to come up in the wind's eye, that kept me on the qui vive[225] every instant. She shipped no water; she was too buoyant for that. But she was all the time in danger of pitching her crew overboard. It soon came to a crisis. About the middle of the lake, on the north side, there is a sharp, low gulch that runs away back through the hills, looking like a level cut through a railroad embankment. And down this gulch came a fierce thunder gust that was like a small cyclone. It knocked down trees, swept over the lake, and—caught the little canoe on the crest of a wave, right under the garboard streak. I went overboard like a shot, but I kept my grip on the paddle. That grip was worth a thousand dollars to the "Travelers' Accidental" and another thousand to the "Equitable Company," because the paddle, with its line, enabled me to keep the canoe in hand and prevent her from going away to leeward like a dry leaf. When I once got my nose above water, and my hand on her after-stem, I knew I had the whole business under control. Pressing the stem down, I took a look inboard. The little jilt![226] She had not shipped a quart of water. And there was the knapsack, the rod, the little auxiliary paddle, all just as I had tied them in; only the crew and the double blade had gone overboard. As I am elderly and out of practice in the swimming line, and it was nearly half a mile to a lee shore, and, as I was out of breath and waterlogged, it is quite possible that a little forethought and four cents' worth of fish line saved the insurance companies $2,000.

How I slowly kicked that canoe ashore; how the sun came out bright and hot; how, instead of making the remaining eleven miles, I raised a conflagration and a comfortable camp, dried out, and had a pleasant night of it; all this is neither here nor there. The point I wish to make is, keep your duffel safe to float and your paddle and canoe sufficiently in hand to always hold your breathing works above water level. So shall your children look confidently for your safe return, while the "Accidentals" arise and call you a good investment.

---

225  On the alert
226 One who rejects a lover

There is only one objection to the clinker-built canoe that occurs to me as at all plausible. This is that the ridge-like projections of her clinker laps offer resistance to the water and retard her speed. Theoretically, this is correct. Practically, it is not proven. Her streaks are so nearly on her water line that the resistance, if any, must be infinitesimal. It is possible, however, that this element might lessen her speed one or two minutes in a mile race. I am not racing but taking leisurely recreation. I can wait two or three minutes as well as not. Three or four knots an hour will take me through to the last carry quite as soon as I care to make the landing.

A few words of explanation and advice may not be out of place. I have used the words *boughs* and *browse* quite frequently. I am sorry they are not more in use. The first settlers in the unbroken forest knew how to diagnose a tree. They came to the "Holland Purchase"[227] from the eastern states, with their families, in a covered wagon, drawn by a yoke of oxen, and the favorite cow patiently leading behind. They could not start until the ground was settled, sometime in May, and nothing could be done in late summer, save to erect a log cabin and clear a few acres for the next season. To this end, the oxen were indispensable and a cow was of first necessity, where there were children. And cows and oxen must have hay. But there was not a ton of hay in the country. A few hundred pounds of coarse wild grass was gleaned from the margins of streams and small marshes, but the main reliance was "browse." Through the warm months the cattle could take care of themselves, but when winter settled down in earnest, a large part of the settler's work consisted in providing browse for his cattle. First and best was the basswood (linden); then came maple, beech, birch, and hemlock. Some of the trees would be nearly three feet in diameter, and when felled, much of the browse would be twenty feet above the reach of cattle, on the ends of huge limbs. Then the boughs were lopped off, and the cattle could get at the browse. The settlers divided the tree into log, limbs, boughs, and browse. Anything small enough for a cow or deer to masticate was browse. And that is just what you want for a camp in the forest. Not twigs, that may come from a thorn, or boughs, that may be as thick as your wrist, but browse, which may be used for a mattress, the healthiest in the world.

---

227  Land in what is now western New York State

And now for a little useless advice. In going into the woods, don't take a medicine chest or a set of surgical instruments with you. A bit of sticking salve, a wooden vial of anti-pain tablets and another of rhubarb regulars, your fly medicine, and a pair of tweezers will be enough. Of course you have needles and thread.

If you go before the open season for shooting, take no gun. It will simply be a useless encumbrance and a nuisance.

If you go to hunt, take a solemn oath never to point the shooting end of your gun toward yourself or any other human being.

In still-hunting, swear yourself black in the face never to shoot at a dim, moving object in the woods for a deer, unless you have seen that it is a deer. In these days there are quite as many hunters as deer in the woods, and it is a heavy, wearisome job to pack a dead or wounded man ten or twelve miles out to a clearing, let alone that it spoils all the pleasure of the hunt and is apt to raise hard feelings among his relations.

In a word, act coolly and rationally. So shall your outing be a delight in conception and the fulfillment thereof; while the memory of it shall come back to you in pleasant dreams, when legs and shoulders are too stiff and old for knapsack and rifle.

That is me. That is why I sit here tonight—with the north wind and sleet rattling the one window of my little den-writing what I hope younger and stronger men will like to take into the woods with them and read. Not that I am so very old. The youngsters are still not anxious to buck against the muzzle-loader in offhand shooting. But in common with a thousand other old graybeards, I feel that the fire, the fervor, the steel that once carried me over the trail from dawn until dark is dulled and deadened within me.

*We had our day of youth and May;*
*We may have grown a trifle sober;*
*But life may reach a wintry way,*
*And we are only in October.*

## Final Advice

Wherefore, let us be thankful that there are still thousands of cool, green nooks beside crystal springs, where the weary soul may hide for a time, away from debts, duns,[228] and deviltries, and a while commune with nature in her undress.

And with kindness to all true woodsmen and with malice toward none, save the trout-hog, the netter, the cruster,[229] and skin-butcher, let us

PREPARE TO TURN IN.

---

228  Someone who urgently demands payment
229  Crust hunter

# INDEX

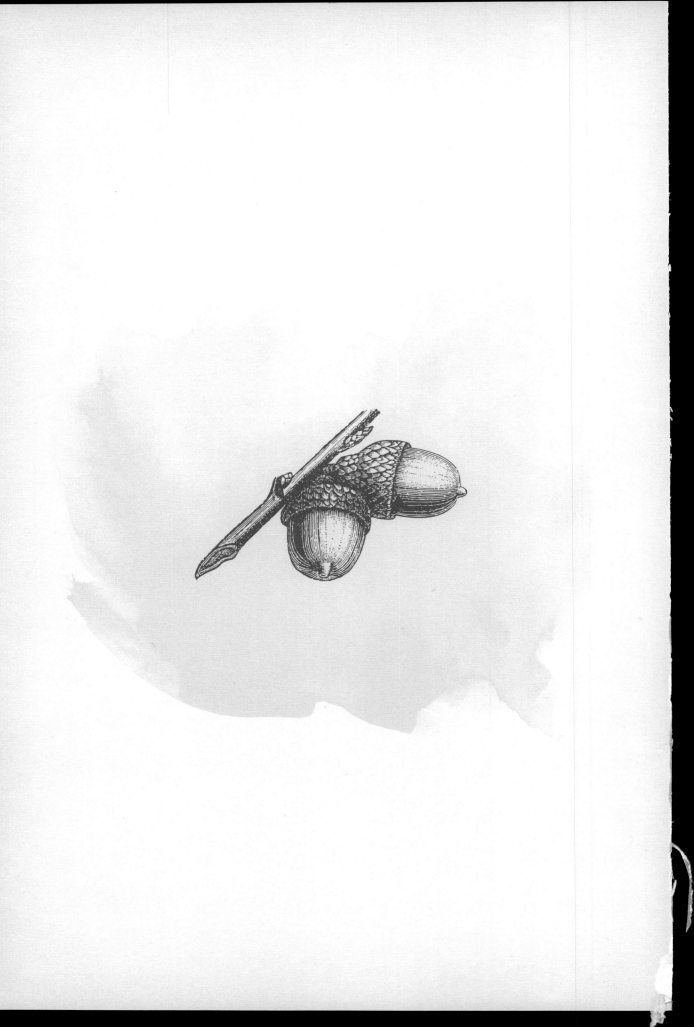